The Problem of the Fetish

The Problem of
the Fetish

William Pietz

Edited by Francesco Pellizzi,
Stefanos Geroulanos, and Ben Kafka

The University of Chicago Press   Chicago and London

The University of Chicago Press, Chicago 60637
The University of Chicago Press, Ltd., London
© 2022 by The University of Chicago
Published 2022
Printed in the United States of America

31 30 29 28 27 26 25 24 23 22   1 2 3 4 5

ISBN-13: 978-0-226-82179-5 (cloth)
ISBN-13: 978-0-226-82181-8 (paper)
ISBN-13: 978-0-226-82180-1 (e-book)
DOI: https://doi.org/10.7208/chicago/9780226821801.001.0001

Library of Congress Cataloging-in-Publication Data

Names: Pietz, William, author. | Pellizzi, Francesco, 1940– editor, writer of foreword. |
    Geroulanos, Stefanos, 1979– editor. | Kafka, Ben, editor.
Title: The problem of the fetish / William Pietz ; edited by Francesco Pellizzi,
    Stefanos Geroulanos, and Ben Kafka.
Description: Chicago : University of Chicago Press, 2022. | Includes bibliographical
    references and index.
Identifiers: LCCN 2022014555 | ISBN 9780226821795 (cloth) | ISBN 9780226821818
    (paperback) | ISBN 9780226821801 (ebook)
Subjects: LCSH: Fetishism—History. | Fetishism—Philosophy.
Classification: LCC GN472 .P54 2022 | DDC 202/.1—dc23/eng/20220404
LC record available at https://lccn.loc.gov/2022014555

Contents

Foreword:
William Pietz in the 1980s

Francesco Pellizzi

In the mid-1980s, I had hoped to interest James Clifford—already known for his innovative approaches to a critical study of the history and practice of anthropology—in collaborating in some substantial way with the project of the journal *RES: Anthropology and Aesthetics*, a publication dedicated to the multidisciplinary study of "cult" and "art" objects that Remo Guidieri and I had founded a few years prior at Harvard's Peabody Museum of Archaeology and Ethnology and at the University of Paris X, Nanterre. It was during my only and fortunate meeting with Clifford that he strongly recommended to me a young American scholar and thinker, William Pietz, who had been working in the orbit of Clifford and Hayden White within the famed (though in some conservative quarters still notorious) History of Consciousness Program at the University of California, Santa Cruz. The general theme of Pietz's research was a critical history of the origins and development of the notion of the fetish, between West Africa and Europe, from the late Middle Ages onward. Needless to say, I jumped at the opportunity to connect with someone who sounded like a most original and promising prospect for our journal, even though it appeared that Pietz's underlying ideological perspective on his subject was not (at least on the face of it) particularly attuned to ours, which could be said to have been at the time prevalently phenomenological, while Pietz's was Marxian. Still, if almost everything studied in *RES* could be viewed, in some modern metaphorical sense at least, as fetishes of sorts (notably in post-Marxian and post-Freudian perspectives), how not to encourage, through dialogue and publication, a rigorous dialectical-materialist exploration of the genesis and development of the fetish object and of its definitions and derivations?

From the start, the plan was to publish a series of essays in *RES* that followed the origins and development of the notion of fetish from its inception and throughout the modern era all the way to Marx and Freud (and, possibly, to Kafka and the Surrealists). Not all that we had hoped for could be accomplished (and not all of what was accomplished found its way into the pages of the journal), but our receptivity to Pietz's approach to metahistorical issues touching on the ramifications of Enlightenment and post-Enlightenment dialectics opened the pages of the journal, beyond the seminal ones, to further Pietz essays not directly focused on, but certainly related to, the transformative dynamics of the fetish notion, touching on issues of monetary value, sacrifice, debt, and even information; in all these, the original heuristic device of the fetish notion lives on, if implicitly, as an idea construct acquiring ever new relevance, as novel *figurations* of the powerful (and of the beautiful) gradually take hold.

For my part, an early familiarity with aspects of the thought of T. W. Adorno, particularly in his *Minima Moralia: Reflections from Damaged Life* (1951)—his critical-dialectical ethnography of the consumer world—made me well disposed to new strains of Marxian thinking that would call into question reductive (i.e., positivistic and scientistic) trends that from our beginnings at *RES* we had considered of limited value in much social-anthropological literature of the previous half century (especially in the Anglo-Saxon milieu) to an understanding of cult and aesthetic objects. The fact that Pietz was both outlining and exploring a vast (if precisely defined) ethnohistorical and theoretical canvas while attempting to define the contours of an issue as elusive as the diachronic definition of the fetish presented itself to me as an irresistible opportunity that could not be missed. In fact, our journal (as the artist Dan Flavin, who I had asked from the start to give it a visual form, imaginatively understood) had itself been originally conceived as a metafetish of sorts, a printed object with the vocation to become, over time, the transcultural receptacle for diverse, even heterogeneous, items of scholarship in conjunction with equally disparate art documents that could all be brought together into a series of distinctive collections. It was as if our open-ended aim in conflating anthropology and aesthetics (a project ostensibly deemed not perspicuous, and even disconcerting, to many in academic circles at the time) had been one of shaping paper fetishes that could generate renewed interest in the unspoken wonders at the roots of the fashioning of human artifacts and of the will of which they may be the embodiment. Because for us, insofar as any made thing could be said to be the product of an objectifying intention whose source, in the end, would remain unrevealed as to its essence, even possibly in the very process of becoming visible, to that same extent every cult or aesthetic artifact could also be viewed as a fetish of sorts—that is, a multipurpose interactive device capable of both shielding and hurting, attracting and repulsing, adding and subtracting, or even healing and killing. Now, William Pietz, for his part, had chosen to focus on the one category of objects that had actually given its name to a varied and yet also specific array of artifacts (and discourse about them), a category of objects whose destiny, through the rise of Western modernity, was to be, as he revealed, fundamentally intercultural, and hence irreducibly opaque in terms of any one given civilizational perspective (including, ultimately, the emerging and objectifying one of anthropology).

Despite the cordiality over the years of our sustained editorial dialogue across the American continent, Bill (as he liked to be called) remained throughout a somewhat enigmatic figure. It was as if his sharp, brilliant intelligence (ever in evidence) could also function as a luminous protective shield around a biographical persona that he in no way denied or rejected but seemed to accept as a sort of incidental circumstance of his role in the world of ideas. Several years after his three epochal fetish essays in *RES*, he came to New York City in October 1995 to deliver a forward-looking essay "The Future of Treason: Political Boundaries in the Information Age" at a conference gathered at the Italian Academy for the Advancement of Art and Science at Columbia University titled "Tradition—Translation—Treason" to celebrate the journal's fifteenth anniversary. On that occasion, in an uncharacteristically freewheeling personal conversation, he alluded to his alienation from his own "redneck" origins in the American South, but in a way that also hinted that these still indelibly constituted—in an almost physical way—the very substance of which he was made. And then he also stunned me by revealing that he made ends meet, at the time (when not teaching), by playing "professional" poker. I could never get a full sense of what was truly factual about these candid disclosures, but I must confess that I did not really try, as I found irresistible the improbability, the scandal almost, of the convergence of these sparse revelations that he so jovially threw my way. What I am trying to evoke, now—through the fog of time and the present distancing and isolation beyond which we seek to keep our spirit attuned to the uniqueness, even the magic, of old and significant close encounters—is the distinctiveness (and distinction) of a spirit possibly given to contradictions that seemed to permeate his worldly circumstances, yet in some way accidentally, as if he had been the reincarnation of a carefree medieval monk (this, counterintuitively, is the image that comes to me in retrospect), but one for whom the rules and constrictions of *any* vocational order remained wholly incidental.

In general terms akin to those explored by William Pietz, the fetish, this mental-physical construct that at one and the same time displays and conceals the intentions from which it originated, can also be seen, tran-shistorically, as perched between the active potentialities of its material substance and the (also potential) inertias of its *destinataires*—in other words, between physical performance and visual spectacle. That may be why many fetishes are kept invisible to the uninitiated, in some ritual settings, but then also unveiled in others. A tension between seeing and not being seen is invariably attached to them, so that their very power tends to be ensconced in what one could almost refer to, metaphori-cally, as a quantum-like fog of unknowing. Because any action associ-ated with the fetish could also be viewed as a spooky one at a distance, or a time-deferred one, whereby space and time might be conceived as entropically fading into each other or as made of one substance (or of no substance?), in both objective and relational terms.

The philosopher Emanuele Severino has called attention to the West-ern pursuit of dominance—through logic and science—in the work of rational "pre-diction," notably in statistical thinking, beyond the apo-dictic fixity of ancient Greek episteme. Such a striving for objectual control may in some ways have been foreshadowed or paralleled by the apotropaic workings of the fetish, where replacement, substitution, and, more generally, the manipulation of components all seek to coun-ter the randomness of events in order to *pre-dictate* their effects—or at least to defuse them by fragmentation and dispersion or some form of anesthetization, or confinement, through their eminently material and sensory qualities. And it may be in this compounding of disparate elements—another characteristic feature of most fetishes—that beauty and ugliness, attraction and repulsion, desire and fear, are joined, in an object that poses itself (or is posited) as that which cannot be avoided (or ignored), the ultimate (or at least transitional) guarantor of an order at one and the same time invoked and feared but that in any event can-not (or should not) be eluded.

Once again, such a transactionally (and trans-*actively*) fetishistic landscape is also implicitly evoked in Pietz's later (and ever-original) es-says, such as those on blood sacrifice, monetary debt, deodand, and even death (as a boundary state): they all deal with physical objects standing before and on the side of the metaphysics of episteme, that is, on the confines between potentially or actually incompatible entities and con-ditions, and they can in the end all be reduced, in one form or another, to the unfathomed that precedes life and the corresponding obscurity of that which follows death. Like the fetish, these object concepts are as if suspended neither here nor there, poisonous and thaumaturgic, patent and hidden, positing the unknown as knowable, but also the (suppos-edly) known—in many of its forms—as ultimately unspeakable and mysterious. And that is also how the fetish becomes a cult object, first when it is removed and excluded from public display and interaction—through a disappearing act (because it is this seclusion, or taboo, that sanctions its capacity to negotiate the tensions between irreducibly alien forces)—but then also, possibly, in its eventual commodification (even in museographic enshrinement, because it is in such indiscriminate and exoteric sharing that the sacred becomes fetishistic, purporting to make us all initiates).

It is customary these days to speak of power, in all contexts and occur-rences. The power of images, the power of and in relations, the power of intentions, the power of objects, etc. This is for the most part viewed as the differential grading and structuring of hierarchies within a sociologi-cal setting. And the fetish is considered a power object par excellence—both explicitly (and ideologically) and implicitly (i.e., paradoxically, by the explicit concealment of its makeup, and, at least possibly, of its aims). What Pietz may have been the first to see—both anthropologi-cally and historically, as in his configuration of thought the two modes converged most originally and fruitfully—was that the phantasmatic power of the fetish was actually consubstantial with its materiality and that it was this fusion that determined dialectically its uniqueness. This, once more, made the young thinker's enterprise especially well suited to the novelty of the *RES* project, which rested in a reevaluation of the role and significance of "cult" and "aesthetic" objects, not just in "archaic" cultures (according to Marcel Mauss's antiprimitivistic definition) but also in so-called high civilizations (those, that is, that have adopted a written record of their own identity). Because in his intrinsically prob-lematic, diachronic, and dialectical definition, the fetish object, as well as the fetish concept—Severino, following Carnap, would argue for the "coincidence" of the two—merged into the distillation of an ideological product in which and through which *both* the West and the societies it encountered in its expansion could see themselves as if reflected in their dominance relation (and related fears). And from whatever angle one may choose to consider it (as a thing or as a notion), one overriding quality of the fetish is that of being at one and the same time both a virtual and an actual entity, yet one whose physicality is as inescapable as the dominance relation itself in all its ebbs and flows. But the fetish is also a *thing* that oscillates, as it were, between the imaginary and the objective, without ever escaping either dimension, at least for as long as it can be deemed to maintain what is considered its efficacy. That is to say that, as already mentioned, the agency of which this entity is invested is in some way both active (as a *projection* of intention) and passive (as the *recipient*, or reflection, of that very intention); in other words, the fetish, in order to stay such, can never be reduced to being just a mental object or just a physical one.

All this may also mean that in fact, since the protocolonial inception of the modern era, anything at all could be posited as fetish—that is, as something that might be able to trigger (or at least imply) a potential for shocking visual impact, thereby also promoting a suspension of critical discrimination. In this perspective, the fetish object, by being removed from its material source, while staying rooted in the *factura* that indelibly links it to that source, may also be seen as a forerunner of the modern art object. This, once again, is part and parcel of its substantially inter-active nature, of course. But what the dialectical historical explorations of its appearances and reappearances by William Pietz have brought into evidence is that this identification and disidentification of the fetish with both its makers and its public calls for meta-ideological readings of its modes of operation that can take into account both its ever-present ma-teriality (there is no fetish, once again, without a body) *and* its equally irreducible ideality (its residual imaginal quality). That conjunction, in the end, is what gives the fetish object its aura, which tends to coincide with its power. The fact that this is a power given to the thing, an artifi-cial one (i.e., not one actually intrinsic to it ab principio), is what alerts us to its essentially contextual nature. Anything and everything can be fetishized, given the opportune circumstances, and yet—there lies its intrinsically dialectical core—anything and everything, once conferred such condition, may be seen as clinging to it through circumstantial changes and transformations. We are forever grateful to William Pietz for choosing to make *RES* the vehicle of his groundbreaking discover-ies in diachronic fetish-dialectics—a journal in which, over forty years, manifestations of the fetishistic qualities of artifacts (and objects *taken as artifacts*) would appear and reappear through historical anthropologi-cal studies of their making, use, and reception.

An Introduction to the Sheer Incommensurable Togetherness of the Living Existence of the Personal Self and the Living Otherness of the Material World

Stefanos Geroulanos and Ben Kafka

Sometimes concepts excite us. This is a bodily sensation as much as a mental one. We lean forward in our chairs, trying to hear a bit better. Our eyes linger on the page to prolong the experience, or they skip to the next paragraph, trying to take it all in as fast as possible. Our brows furrow, or we find ourselves nodding as things fall into place. Many of the people reading this book will remember that moment in college when this first happened. Many of the people reading this book will spend their careers trying to provide similar experiences to their own students.

This excitement need not only be pleasurable. Concepts also irritate or enrage. While there may also be some pleasure in this experience (the quiet sadism of smugness), it is often accompanied by a distinctly unpleasurable sensation of urgency. This sense, which also has a corporeal correlate, manifests itself as an overwhelming need to make sure the other knows how wrong they are—or, more precisely, to make sure everyone knows. From one perspective it is odd that we would have such an intense reaction to an article, a conference paper, a tweet. But from another perspective, how could it be otherwise?

One way to approach the history of concepts would be to take this excitement, which no doubt has its origins in our infantile sexual researches, seriously. What makes a concept exciting to a given individual? What makes a concept exciting at a given historical moment? How does this excitement link up to other historical processes, including forms of identification, influence anxiety, and group dynamics more generally? And what happens when we tire of concepts, even ones—especially ones—that we have long been wedded to? What happens when the excitement subsides, when the restlessness sets back in, when our eyes begin to wander—when the thrill is gone?

One place to begin such an investigation would be the shotgun wedding that gave birth to theory as we know it: the coupling of Marx and Freud in the 1930s. It was an anxious and awkward hookup, embarked upon under the immense pressure of social upheaval, political catastrophe, and metaphysical collapse. In some ways these circumstances only added to the excitement, which we can still feel in so many of the texts nearly a century later. "Repression posits its own destruction, since as a result of repression, instinctual energy is powerfully dammed up until it finally breaks through the repression," wrote Wilhelm Reich in 1929 in "Dialectical Materialism and Psychoanalysis," arguably the founding text of the Freudo-Marxist tradition. "The new process of breaking through the repression is a result of the contradiction between suppression and the increased strength of the dammed-up instinct; just as repression itself was the result of a contradiction between the instinctual wish and its denial by the outside world."[1] The metapsychology is imprecise, the dialectics mechanistic—*Minima Moralia* this isn't—but nearly a century later the excitement is still palpable, and, in some ways, enviable.

A number of concepts were born, or born again, from this coupling: repression, alienation, interpellation, overdetermination, the subject, the apparatus, and so on. That the concept of fetishism should have found such a prominent place among these, and within twentieth-century intellectual history more broadly, was not, on the surface of it, self-evident. We can imagine that neither Marx nor Freud themselves would have listed the concept among their top ten, or even top twenty. Twenty, in fact, is the sum you get if you add Marx's pages on fetishism (in the Penguin edition) to Freud's (in the Standard Edition)—out of the thousands of pages constituting their combined oeuvre. Twenty pages that have since multiplied many times over as the concept caught the eye of one scholar after another.

The excitement seems to have peaked in the final decades of the twentieth century. Indeed, from the 1970s to the 1990s the concept of fetishism focused the energies of some of the most creative and rigorous minds in the human sciences, not to mention art, film, and literature. To return to these texts now is to encounter remarkable moments of insight and creativity. "The mother's memorabilia—the way she saves the lock of hair, the tooth, or school reports—signals a disavowal of the lack inscribed by separation from the child," the artist Mary Kelly tells Emily Apter in an interview for the landmark volume Apter coedited with William Pietz, *Fetishism as Cultural Discourse*.[2] It is the kind of observation that sneaks up on us and takes us by surprise. Suddenly our family collections, albums, rituals—or lack thereof—seem a bit more fraught, which is also to say, a bit more interesting.

Marx's dancing tables, Freud's gleaming noses—surely part of the excitement was that this concept was all about excitement. Indeed, of all the concepts of the Freudo-Marxist synthesis, it was the one that seemed to know how we felt, to tap into the structure of feeling accompanying sex, capital, and colonialism alike. No disrespect to overdetermination, but it only titillates the hardest-core among us. Fetishism, on the other hand, describes an experience, or set of experiences, pulling us back from abstractions toward sensations—sensations, we would add, that people tend to find easier to attribute to others than themselves. So much surreptitious peeping and purchasing. So many instances, still and maybe always, of people taking pleasure in what Kobena Mercer called the "ontological reduction" implicit in fetishism—indigenous cultures reduced to artifacts, workers to units of labor power, women to bits of their bodies, Black men to bits of theirs.[3] So much disavowal of this excitement, too—in some ways, these days, more than ever. This was the point being made by both Marx and Freud, and it is just as radical now as it was in their respective thens. Every document of civilization is also a document of fetishization.

To write the history of concepts as a history of excitement, libidinal *and* destructive, would require us to take these unacknowledged and unwanted aspects of ourselves seriously. And it would require us to look at all the ways we defend against our urges, or even the knowledge of our urges, through forms of *knowingness* that simultaneously know and do not know. Perhaps this explains what Rosalind Morris, in her recent essay on fetishism—which we consider essential, and to which readers of this volume are enthusiastically referred for a comprehensive understanding of the concept's history—has called the "tyranny of detail" that always threatens to overwhelm discussions of the concept.[4] This need for distantiation would explain, too, the ironic stance that, a generation earlier, the theorist Naomi Schor identified in the discourse on fetishism, and from which she hoped to extricate it for a feminist politics.[5] The comforts of knowing defend against the discomforts of encountering, by which we do not only mean the encounter with the exciting, fetishized object—human, dehumanized, or nonhuman—but also with the fetishizing, excited self. Or to put it another way, the comforts of knowing defend against the anxiety and aggression of being, particularly when we are the subjects supposed to know *better*.

The Missing Piece

Our shared interest in William Pietz's series of articles tracing the history of the concept of the fetish began long before we knew each other and remained with us as we followed our respective paths into (and, in one of our cases, out of) the historical profession. We are hardly alone in our fascination. The essays were, and still are, outstanding works of intellectual history—sophisticated, erudite, provocative, and a bit sly. Their impact was felt, and is still felt, across disciplines and fields. And while their account of the concept's emergence out of the violent world of the West African coast in the sixteenth and seventeenth centuries has since been supplemented, it remains unsurpassed, a remarkable achievement given how much scholarship has evolved over these past few decades.

But these qualities, remarkable as they are, do not fully account for the aura surrounding these articles—for us, or for others. There were other forces at work. Foremost among these was the peculiar feature of their publication history. Three essays appeared in the journal *RES: Anthropology and Aesthetics*, edited by Francesco Pellizzi. The first article in the series, "The Problem of the Fetish, I," appeared in 1985; the second, "The Problem of the Fetish, II: The Origin of the Fetish," in 1987; and the third, "The Problem of the Fetish, IIIa: Bosman's Guinea and the Enlightenment Theory of Fetishism," in 1988. Articulating the stakes of the fetish as it spread across modern thought, its conceptual and etymological development, and its difference from the idol, these essays culminated in an account of the entry of the fetish into mercantile and Enlightenment discourse.

The "IIIa" in the title of the final *RES* essay implied that there would be more, at minimum a "IIIb," but no sequels appeared. Moreover, Pietz himself was an enigmatic, almost Pynchonesque figure. Who was he? Where was he? It can be hard to remember, now, that in the days before Google these sorts of questions often remained unanswered. But even once the search engines were chugging along, information about Pietz's whereabouts remained scarce. We find traces of him teaching at the Claremont Colleges; taking on committee work for the National Writers Union; organizing for the Los Angeles County chapter of the Green Party and other environmental causes. Speaking to those who knew him in the eighties and nineties suggests he cultivated an air of mystery, sharing stories of gun collections and professional poker. The last published trace of him that we have been able to find is in the volume *Critical Terms in the Study of Buddhism* (2005), for which he authored the entry on "Person." The contributor note identifies him as director of the Hypnosis Center in Ojai, a spa town northwest of Los Angeles. It is tempting, reading this, to imagine Dr. Krokowski tending to a tanned Hans Castorp stretched out on a pool chair—checking, not a thermometer, but a flip phone.

Fantasy, as we know, follows the program of the pleasure principle. Reality, on the other hand, has no principles at all. We went to meet with Pellizzi to discuss our curiosity about Pietz's missing fetishism essay. Pellizzi recalled that his final communication with Pietz had been an email from Pietz in 2007 informing him that he had been diagnosed with multiple sclerosis, and would no longer be able to write. Pietz had attached to this email his fetishism typescript—including the mysterious IIIb—for safekeeping and eventual publication. The contributor note in *Critical Terms in the Study of Buddhism*, which predated the email, mentioned that in addition to his responsibilities as the director of the Hypnosis Center, he was married to its principal hypnotist, Vickie McDonald. Though they are no longer at the center, we were able to make contact with Vickie, and through her, William Pietz expressed his enthusiasm about the publication of this book. At his request, royalties from this volume will support multiple sclerosis research.

The Shadow of the Object

An anthropologist, historian of empire, and conceptual historian, Pietz once described his task as follows:

> There must be a set of concepts able to describe and explain radically different cultures (including the ethnographer's own culture) and also the forms of interaction between these different cultures. In my own work I have attempted to develop two such concepts: debts, conceived as temporally specific social obligations established through materially mediated transfers of substantive value, and fetishes, conceived as the power objects that embody the general value substance of a society and that function as the material mediations for the establishment and settlement of debts.[6]

The book you now hold in your hands brings together seven of Pietz's essays. Collectively titled "The Problem of the Fetish," the first four essays track the origins of discourse on the fetish to their early Christian, Latin, and medieval Portuguese origins, and especially to the conquest of West Africa by the Portuguese. It was European reports of the encounter between Portugal and West Africa, Pietz argues, that established fetishism as a pliable, plastic, handy, eventually inescapable concept. This text includes IIIb, which we restore here as chapter 4, where Pietz details his argument on de Brosses, the eighteenth-century French *philosophe* who coined the word "fetishism" in 1757 and formulated, in his eccentric way, its first general theory.[7] In the three published texts, I, II, IIIa, Pietz had written little and hinted much about de Brosses, the rationale of the invention of fetishism, and the entry of that term into Enlightenment discourse and into the human sciences.

To these four essays, we add three closely related works. Chapter 5, Pietz's 1993 essay "Fetishism and Materialism: On the Limits of Theory in Marx," originally appeared in the aforementioned volume that Pietz edited with Emily Apter, *Fetishism as Cultural Discourse*. Here Pietz tackles Marx head-on in a bravura performance that criticizes then-current approaches and reconceptualizes materialism. Although not included in the typescript of "The Problem of the Fetish," this essay directly extends the argument found there to the point of satisfying some of the promises made by Pietz at the end of chapter 4. Pietz recognized as much, citing it repeatedly in "The Problem of the Fetish."

The twinned essays that make up chapters 6 and 7—"The Spirit of Civilization: Blood Sacrifice and Monetary Debt" and "Death of the Deodand: Accursed Objects and the Money Value of Human Life" (originally published in RES in 1995 and 1997)—take off from the discussion of the fetish to consider discursive and juridico-economic problems linked to the valuation of things and human life in the British empire during the later nineteenth century. Chapter 6, "The Spirit of Civilization," considers the later-nineteenth-century development of theories of human sacrifice in the context of the abolition of slavery, the transformation of the British colonies into "a civil society suited to British capitalism," and the development of modern tort law and new institutions for organizing monetary debt. Blood sacrifice was the doppelgänger of debt. Chapter 7, "Death of the Deodand," examines the assignation of pious value to accursed objects, from the time when objects that have caused death were legally forfeited to the state to the disenchantment of such "deodand" and the conclusion of the practice of its passing to the sovereign in the 1850s.

How do we understand the inception and publication of this project in the 1980s and 1990s, a period that was drowning in revaluation—from the post–oil shock transformation of the western European welfare states to the full-scale introduction of neoliberal political economy; the collapse of the Soviet Union; the dramatic privatization of the Eastern Bloc, including with new forms of vulture capitalism; and the transformation of China under Deng Xiaoping?

"Fetish" was a common term in the 1980s—certainly more so than today. Its uses, and there were several, were transitioning and not altogether commensurable. In psychoanalysis and literary theory, for one example, its value was not in doubt. But where fetish had signaled pathology, after the sexual revolution it connoted arousal, danger, and persistence and dispersal of classical norms.[8] In the particular guise of "commodity fetishism," it was a staple of post-'68 Marxism and critical theory, despite the latter's marginalization as a viable political discourse. Meanwhile, in anthropology, a discipline ever more aware of its colonial genealogy, the very term "fetish" exemplified Western violence, whether in the guise of ethnographers' bias or as what Edward Said most famously identified as Orientalism in 1979.[9] Everyday politics in the 1980s added to this array of shifting meanings. In his dissertation, "The Origin of Fetishism,"[10] Pietz reported a series of quotidian uses—for example by Ronald Reagan's budget director, who stated that the Reagan administration would not "make a fetish of the balanced budget," and by an ex-CIA official who objected to a "fetishistic obsession with openness" during the Iran-Contra hearings.[11] The use of "fetishism" as a term of abuse reflected a newly problematic status.

So when Pietz wrote the first drafts of "The Problem of the Fetish," the term was a privileged yet highly ambiguous operator in a significant number of fields. It opened up problems of universalism, materialism, history and theory, engagement with the other, nonreciprocity, figuration.

Remarkably—almost unbelievably—Pietz was still a graduate student when he published his fetishism essays. The essays *became* his dissertation in the Program in the History of Consciousness at University of California, Santa Cruz. In many ways the work bears the traces of this intellectual microclimate. Production in those years tended to be deeply concentrated, well structured, and high yield. Donna Haraway, Pietz's professor and interlocutor, published her influential "A Manifesto for Cyborgs" in 1985; another faculty member, Angela Davis, was about to publish *Women, Culture, and Politics* when Pietz defended his dissertation in 1988.

His committee, meanwhile, was made up of Hayden White, who was his adviser, and James Clifford and Robert Meister. White was both star and enfant terrible among historians and literary theorists for his *Metahistory: The Historical Imagination in Nineteenth-Century Europe* (1973). In 1976, White had published an important essay on "The Noble Savage Theme as Fetish," where he defined fetishism as follows:

A fetish is any natural object believed to possess magical or spiritual power. This is the traditional ethnological meaning of the term, and from it derive the conventional figurative use of it to designate any material object regarded with superstitious or extravagant trust or reverence. From this figurative usage, in turn, derives the psychological sense, as indicating any object or part of the body obsessively seized upon (cathected) as an exclusive source of libidinal gratification. From these three usages we derive the three senses of the term fetishism which I use here belief in magical fetishes, extravagant or irrational devotion, and pathological displacement of libidinal interest and satisfaction to a fetish. As thus envisaged, fetishism is, at one and the same time, a kind of belief, a kind of devotion, and a kind of psychological set or posture.[12]

White was extrapolating toward a new concept of the fetish, for the purpose of advancing a critical take on another concept, this time one rather more housebound in Western thought: the noble savage. For him, too, the fetish concept had weakened and faded away from its earlier reference frames, but it had not necessarily lost its meaning. If in 1973 the figurative use White referred to was intimately linked to the conventional one, by 1985 when he republished that essay in *Tropics of Discourse* while supervising Pietz's work, the anthropological, psychoanalytic, political, and theoretical debates were doubling the fetish into a fetish for theory—in White's figurative and psychological senses. At the time of Pietz's defense, White had also just published *The Content of the Form: Narrative Discourse and Historical Representation*.

For his part, Clifford, publishing at roughly the same time as Pietz was writing his dissertation, was steering the 1980s rethinking of anthropology and its history—especially in *The Predicament of Culture* (1988) and, with George E. Marcus, in *Writing Culture: The Poetics and Politics of Ethnography* (1986). *Writing Culture* influentially established why ethnographers could no longer pretend to be faithful interpreters of other peoples. The ethnographic ideology "claiming transparency of representation and immediacy of experience . . . has crumbled," Clifford wrote.[13] Other key interlocutors at the UCSC History of Consciousness Program played just as important roles in Pietz's intellectual world. Meister was writing *Political Identity: Thinking through Marx* (1991), which Pietz cites repeatedly.

But it is probably Fredric Jameson, whose time in the History of Consciousness Program overlapped with Pietz's, who looms largest and figures most ambivalently. Pietz's early essays are deeply attached to Jameson's theoretical apparatus. "My basic understanding of ideology," explains Pietz, citing *The Political Unconscious*, "is that it involves the formation of a discourse that imposes a simple semiotic (Greimasian) structure on a complex historical situation representing a problem that

resists solution in reality."[14] By the time we reach the end of the fetishism writings, however, Jameson has come to stand in for everything that
Pietz finds wrong with the poststructuralist current of the 1990s. It's
subtle, but not too subtle, as when he denounces those theorists who
developed "a conception of general 'cultural logics' whose rules were
held to structure both social institutions and a collective ('political')
unconscious." These theorists, Pietz writes, promote "an enormously
flattering conception of the critical activity of intellectuals" at the ex-
pense of radical politics.[15]

Several other debates defined Pietz's moment and influenced his
approach to the fetish. One debate—perhaps even a set of debates—
concerned the materiality of the signifier. It expanded out of the tensions caused by the explosion of structuralism in an intellectual domain
marked by the question of where to go after the sixties, how to criticize
dominant ideologies, how to pursue political projects. This was a domain where Freudo-Marxism played a leading role and where the import of French thinkers like Lacan, Foucault, and Derrida amounted to
a threat. How could Marxism outlive the turn to a political semiotics?
From a localized debate over Lacan's formulations of the split between
signifier and signified, the point on the materiality of the signifier bal-
looned to a much broader one concerning the politics of structuralist
and deconstructive logics when these appeared to extract the text from
social practices and to privilege it.[16] Several authors had contributed
to this: Pietz cites Jean Baudrillard's 1970 essay "Fetishism and Ideology: The Semiological Reduction" and of course Jameson.[17] Historians
and anthropologists—anthropologists especially, as most historians
scattered and fled this scene—had to negotiate this contrast between
ostensibly real and material practices and their linguistic and theoretical systematization. (This was not only an academic matter. For Juliet
Mitchell and Jacqueline Rose, for example, the fetish was essential to
the reabsorption of psychoanalysis into feminism precisely because of
how it participated in the construction of fantasy and femininity: "To
assume that the woman herself takes on the role of fetish only raises the
question of the difference of her position in relation to desire and to
the object."[18] For poststructuralist feminists, the status of women and
of woman in fantasy hinged on the materiality of the signifier.) Pietz
signaled his interest in the subject in an early, programmatic essay where
he proposed to bridge the history of empire with "poststructuralist"
concerns:

> I would like to examine the case for a *nondeconstructive* post-
> structuralism for historiography particularly interested in the prob-

lem of modern history and capitalism. Specifically, I wish to consider the argument of Deleuze and Guattari in their two-volume work on *Capitalism and Schizophrenia* that the social and linguistic order of capitalism is not an order of the signifier and that, therefore, the general deconstructionist critique of the phonocentrism of "western" society is particularly inapplicable to modern, capitalist society.[19]

Some of the key problems invoked by Pietz in "The Problem of the Fetish" concern that same discussion, notably the irreducible materiality that Pietz assigned to the fetish in order to distinguish it. As he writes: "The truth of the fetish resides in its status as a material embodiment. Its truth is not that of the idol, for the idol's truth lies in its relation of iconic resemblance to some immaterial model or entity."[20] Committing the fetish to the sphere of materialism was a manner of asking about the commitments to materialism replicated over and over across different social, scientific, Marxist, and other positions in the nineteenth and twentieth centuries. Here, the fetish was especially apropos.

A further relevant debate in the 1980s concerned the possibility of universalist analyses: if these were insufficient or potentially imperial, was scholarship always going to be defeated by particularism and irreducible otherness? The problem was especially pressing given the fetish concept's racist connotations. Pietz made his approach explicit in the opening essay. Both universalism and particularism missed the point, because the reality of the fetish—not as an actual object but as a concept reflecting value differentials—elided them. Particularism missed that while the concept of the fetish was heavily reductive of cultural differences, even self-consciously so, it nonetheless created and structured, even diffused into, a broad literature. Beginning with the argument that the fetish has been a factitious universal and yet a component of a Foucauldian "discursive formation," Pietz captured brilliantly its status as a hinge between worlds, as well as the polyvalence, mixture, and ambiguity of meaning that accordingly ensued.

Readers of this volume will probably find many of these methodological concerns dated, even as the social and political problems they were meant to comprehend—the rapaciousness of capital, the violence of colonialism in all its forms, the convergence of racial and sexual domination, the complicity but also critical potential of art and its institutions—remain as current as ever. Nevertheless, we imagine that most readers who come to these chapters now, either again or for the first time, will do so because the problem of *objects* has reemerged in recent years as a central one in the human sciences. On this matter, Pietz remains not only our contemporary but in the vanguard.

How to Write a History of Value

"Beginning in 1985," Pietz wrote a decade later, in an essay titled "Capitalism and Perversion: Reflections on the Fetishism of Excess in the 1980s," "I published a series of essays which traced the theoretical discourse about 'fetishes' from its origin in sixteenth-century, Afro-European cross-cultural trade on the coast of West Africa, to its elaboration as a general theory of the 'primitive' mentality by Enlightenment intellectuals in mid-eighteenth-century Europe and its subsequent appropriations by founding thinkers of the nineteenth-century human sciences." The historical research, he tells us, raised a series of theoretical questions pertaining to capitalist and noncapitalist societies alike.[21] The fundamental question across all his *RES* essays, still very much on his mind in the mid-1990s, was "how any social value could become fixed in material objects which in themselves lacked any inherent intentional meaning or orientation toward the fulfillment of human purposes."[22]

Pietz planted his flag at the juncture of three main disciplines— imperial history (which was then still in its infancy), cultural anthropology, and the history of political economy. He did so to clasp two subjects tight: (1) the legal and cultural investment of objects with meaning and agency and (2) the role of value (both material and quasi-abstract) in the making of social order. This weird incandescence of value was his business. With an eye to the way value differentials are imbued into material objects, his essays spanned the long rise of industrial and imperial capitalism. On both subjects covered here—the fetish and debt—they hopped between important moments in the development of economic and legal infrastructures for its material and intellectual organization.

The Problem of the Fetish developed its primary concept as an amalgam, a "device to enable cross-cultural commercial transactions," a "middleman's term, a pidgin word."[23] It was characterized by "irreducible materiality; event-originated singular synthesis with the power to repeat itself; culturally constructed consciousness of value; power of external objects over the desires, actions, health, and self-identity of individuals whose selfhood is conceived as inseparable from their bodies."[24] In this definition, Pietz was at once expansive vis-à-vis the domains in which the term did its work, and careful toward the frustrating elasticity of the concept. It originated, he continued, "in the cross-cultural spaces of the coast of West Africa," "triangulated between Christian feudal, African lineage, and merchant capitalist social systems."[25] In these spaces, the fetish was "a novel word, responsive to an unprecedented type of situation," an epistemological something that emerged specifically in a context where several social systems found themselves in asymmetric contrast. In that sense, the concept was itself something of an event: the descriptions of the coast of Guinea that reported "fetishes" back to Europe quickly morphed into standards for evaluating African religion and, along with it, for generating a hierarchy of civilizations.

No understanding of the fetish could ignore this moment in the later sixteenth and the seventeenth century, when Europeans experienced the coast of Guinea especially and West Africa more broadly. Yet there would have been no "fetish" without the long linguistic and religious history into which this moment was inscribed. First, a sense of "manufactured object" emerged in medieval Latin; then, over the early modern period, a protoconcept of the fetish staggered slowly out from the concept of the idol. These earlier developments allowed for "fetishes" in West Africa to be understood in terms of magical practices—that is, as objects into which magic was imbued. That identification (and misrepresentation), and the subsequent construction of the fetish as a European idea, relied on the long etymology.

Valuation and transvaluation beguiled Europe in the early eighteenth century. Paper money was first issued sporadically in the 1670s and 1690s. Government banks expanded its scale dramatically and promoted "the magic of credit" in the first decade of the new century. As modern economic schemas developed, they expressed and fed off theological and political anxieties. Then paper money collapsed due to imperial financial speculation and the bursting of the Mississippi and South Sea bubbles.[26] Think of a situation equivalent to the perplexing, fluctuating value of cryptocurrency today. The fetish concept acquired value in English and French precisely in such a context: Pietz touches repeatedly on the stages of European colonization of West Africa, the bubbles, the loss of French colonies, the domestic shifts in land values. The key elements of the fetish had all coalesced, he concludes, at "a mercantile cross-cultural space defined by the transvaluation of material objects moving across radically different social orders."[27] Against this background, Pietz concentrates the steps by which transvaluation became key to the concept as the Portuguese concept of *fetisso* launched the concepts of fetish and *fétiche* in English and French. It is here that theory becomes essential to the meaning of "fetish"—to the layers of meaning that would be jerry-rigged together in Charles de Brosses's coinage of *fétichisme*, or fetishism. That same fetish became a key term in the Enlightenment and then entered the human sciences from their foundation in the nineteenth century. De Brosses, Pietz writes, "established a problem-idea that became a sort of boundary stone for the human sciences of the nineteenth century."[28]

It is not hard to see why de Brosses's was an auspicious moment for a concept like fetishism, just as the work of Willem Bosman and others had been nearly two generations earlier (and just like Pietz's would be). He published *Du culte des dieux fétiches* in 1760, two years after the massive controversies caused by the condemnation of the *Encyclopédie* and the burning of Helvétius's *De l'esprit*. In its broad outlines, the book offered a theory of the material basis of religion but, by extrapolating the problem to Africa, avoided such public fights. The 1750s also constituted a key moment in the development of a protoanthropology both by the continued spread of travel writing and by its incorporation into a broader thinking on human nature. *On the Spirit of the Laws* had been published in 1748, the Comte de Buffon's *Histoire naturelle de l'homme* in 1749; Turgot, Mirabeau, and other physiocrats began using the word *civilisation* in the 1750s; while in 1755 Rousseau published the *Discourse on the Origin of Inequality* and Voltaire his *Essai sur les moeurs*.[29] De Brosses himself was particularly impressed by the work of Pierre Louis Maupertuis on distances and by his friend Buffon; and to develop the concept, de Brosses practiced some revaluing himself, especially when he inflected and redirected David Hume's *Natural History of Religion*, a key point in Pietz's analysis. He did so to the benefit of a "moderns'" position in the *Querelle*, the debate of the ancients and the moderns, aiming at a politically radical hermeneutics specifically concerned with world history, the inclusion of peoples not found in classical history, and political radicalism.[30]

> For the general project of the human sciences, the discourse about fetishism marked a nexus of problems at the limits of the thinkable: interconnected problems relating to the purposive causality of material life, the libidinal grounding of social obligation, the external formation of personal identity, and the indeterminate singularity of historical time. These obscure but fundamental issues, thematized in controversies about fetishism, consistently troubled nineteenth-century theorists who sought a science of society proper to an age without illusions.[31]

In the first half of the nineteenth century, Auguste Comte, the students of Henri de Saint-Simon, and Karl Marx enshrined *fetishism* in their philosophical works. For the Saint-Simonians and Comte, fetishism would become the name for the historical launch of progress—the beginning of the first of three stages of history (polytheism followed by monotheism and science).[32] From them would derive in part the schema utilized by British anthropologists in the nineteenth century, notably E. B. Tylor and James Frazer, who bubbled it over into "animism."[33] Other authors—from Wilhelm Wundt to Lewis H. Morgan and Aby Warburg—would use the same structure to administer geographical space in terms of temporal distance and backwardness from the present time. The geographic cruelty of the concept's detached vision of indigenous peoples only doubled with its role in a historicist organization of knowledge. In Marx, Pietz meanwhile writes in "Fetishism and Materialism" (chapter 5), "the capitalist social economy is understood as a repeating process of fetishization (that is, of cycles of labor valorization, monetary realization, and capital accumulation). The very legal and financial categories that establish capital's social reality bring about the fetishized consciousness appropriate to it through what Marx describes as a three-level chiasmus between people and things."[34] This reading of Marx around the fetishism problem would serve Pietz well— both as a way back to thinking of transvaluation in Christianity and capitalism and as a scalpel for slicing through then-contemporary theory with its debates on signifiers and materiality. Against structuralist post-Marxism, Pietz concludes his reading of Marx with the following: "The Marxian theory of fetishism may be described as a critical, materialist theory of social desire. It presents modern political economy as a real social metaphysics (an institutional objectification of human temporality in the form of labor power, surplus value, and credit-money) and, at the same time, as a fantastically alien misrepresentation (an inhuman, doubly inverted vision of the collective life of individuals as 'civil society')."[35] Pietz's reading of Marx reflected his own concerns, of course. The last chapters of this book follow versions of this playbook—they look at once for a "real social metaphysics" and a "fantastically alien misrepresentation" arising in what he saw as the transformation of the private sphere, its representation in social reality, and the monetary and legal institutions of nineteenth-century capitalism. At stake, once more, were new structures that shimmered with value, specifically the emergence of tort law (in chapter 6) and of the capitalism of heavy industry (in chapter 7).

The last two chapters of this volume, "The Spirit of Civilization" and "Death of the Deodand," are thus involved in the continuations of the logic of re- and transvaluation in capitalist economies.[36] Pietz's critique of civil society continues in chapter 6 specifically through the intermediary of tort law,[37] and he turns to the tales of blood sacrifice because the latter required and enforced kinship relations fundamentally different from those found in British Africa and hence intrusive upon the latter. For Pietz, debts had to be "conceived as temporally specific social obligations established through materially mediated transfers of substantive value."[38] Tort took over from blood sacrifice—and re-created it as particular hideousness elsewhere. In this same context, moreover, the deodand could not survive—either as social metaphysic or as alien misrepresentation. It stood as a reminder of precapitalist social structures and a dynamic of ownership that threatened the possibility of limited liability, private corporate entities, insurance, and credit/debt stability. For civil society to become properly capitalist, Pietz concludes in chapter 7, the monetary value of human life had to be rethought in much the same gesture as civilization had to move into private law. Here too, debt and the value of human life had to be spared of its old meanings and granted new meanings, which at the social level Pietz identified with capitalist civil society after the Fatal Accidents Act of 1846.

A Concept and Its Material Phenomenology

Concepts do not emerge thanks to some easy unfolding process. They are not invented or discovered. Nor are they built like walls, brick by brick, or layer by layer of wattle and daub. In Pietz's approach, we find concepts assembled out of very different materials then stretched, pressed, smelted. Until this last moment, very different meanings—linguistic, theological, mercantile—compete and skirmish. Each of these meanings relies on a different development, and their amalgamation can suddenly turn very creative, systematic, and also violent.

To read Pietz is to watch him pluck arrows from his methodological quiver. Each arrow gives a direction to advance in on a conceptual battlefield. This was as true of Pietz's approach to the fetish as it was to that of debt. By blending social, economic, and cross-cultural discursive problems, Pietz attached these two concepts to both the real and the phantasmatic crossing of social priorities, to the generation of asymmetry, to the disparagement of others' values. The fetish involved the production of social value and became linked, as a concept, with the contestation of that value. Pietz offered long genealogies of Latinate terms from Roman through late medieval and onto Portuguese colonial times; studied a colonial discourse in which the fetish developed in an intentional abstraction of the colonial encounter; tracked the fusion of these pasts into a new discourse for the human sciences; and offered a story of its valuation and interpretation. The fetish articulated a portion of the world, and it did so by calibrating at once values in transformation and the urgency of changing those values and modulating that transformation. The modern concept of debt became legitimized because of lopsided values, discursive inventiveness (the imagination of an unusually violent "other"), the stumbling forward of capitalism's juridical needs. At stake in it are transvaluation, the untranslatability of social practices, and the dual function thanks to which concepts leaned awkwardly on observations and powering social practices.

In teasing these concepts apart without rigidly separating them, in his practicing conceptual history as at once anthropology, imperial history, political economy, and theory, Pietz did not prioritize concepts over practices or commit to their supposed autonomy. Instead he treated concepts as elaborately intertwined with practices, lying at the interstices of very different social systems.[39] Only from this intertwining could the fetish arise out of a fundamental misrepresentation and become so effective and polyvalent—a concept with great socio-economic, secularizing, and also political range. In the 1970s and 1980s, it was possible for feminists, postcolonial intellectuals, structuralists, psychoanalysts, and anthropologists to take advantage of the concept; Pietz's method—his quiver—helped reconstruct a history and repurpose it as highly original theory.

Pietz was writing what is often called a history of the present, and he was inserting himself into it. In one key passage, he raised the question of what the fetish is, and he did so quite bluntly. "In what sense, then, is there such a thing as a fetish? If 'fetish' does name some specific 'problem-idea,' what is the truth it names?"[40] Any reader who thought that Pietz's was an exercise without current investment—or that he was a historian gazing through binoculars at some distant past without present ramifications—would be brought up short. Because Pietz offers instead a historical ontology in which concept and thing chase one another, are made all the more real and urgent by this history. This was not a history of colonial encounters and European power in which the object of study, however malicious and generative, had been simply overcome. The fetish spoke of the raw intimacies we write into our relations with objects, the way we ensconce ourselves and our worlds into them.

Pietz called this a *materialist phenomenology*. "If the notion of fetishism is to have any useful specificity, it must refer to objective phenomena that are valued with an exceptional intensity by individuals or by a society in general," he writes. "The history of the discourse about fetishism suggests that fetishes may be conceived as excessively valued material objects upon which the very existence and identity of an individual, cultural group, or society is experienced as depending." To understand this phenomenon, Pietz argues, requires a return not only to Marx but also to Merleau-Ponty. The latter, who had played a supporting role in the *RES* essays—and a slightly larger one in "Fetishism and Materialism," chapter 5—was now ready for his close-up. This new approach to fetish objects would be *materialist* insofar as it located "excessive valuation in the conflicts and contradictions between the structures of social power reified in the multiplicity of institutions that compose a given social formation." Still, and even though both Marxists and phenomenologists might find this paradoxical, this approach would remain *phenomenological* insofar as it related the "personal investment of individual identities in such objects . . . to those arguments and those dramatized scenarios of the libidinal imagination wherein people express their own understanding of the ground of their own self-worth (or lack of it)."[41]

We may notice that the person Pietz is calling "Merleau-Ponty" in this text sounds an awful lot like Freud, complete with object cathexes ("personal investments of individual identities"); unconscious phantasy ("dramatized scenarios of the libidinal imagination"); and secondary narcissism ("self-worth"). Perhaps this reflects the influence of yet another History of Consciousness faculty member, Norman O. Brown, to whom this essay is dedicated. Perhaps, too, this is what it took, circa 1995, to think psychoanalytically without the Lacanian pyrotechnics. In any case, what is most important, it seems to us, is that Pietz arrives at a critique of fetishism that remains resolutely committed to exploring unconscious dynamics, whether in the present or in the past, whether psychoanalytically or phenomenologically. This was the conclusion he reached after a decade of work on the fetish: No theory of the object without a theory of the subject.

What kind of subject? An excitable subject. In a moment in the first chapter of this book that feels ever so slightly unguarded, Pietz asks if there really is such a thing as "true fetishism." The phrase is not his, exactly, but belongs to Michel Leiris, from a very early essay on Giacometti (written, in fact, when Leiris was about the same age as Pietz was at the time). Pietz proceeds to cite Leiris telling us that true fetishism consists of the power of certain art objects to "resonate just a bit" with something inside of us. Leiris calls this something "love," but it is not a love for others, or even from others. It is a love of ourselves. Leiris is almost certainly alluding to Rousseau's *amour de soi* here, the better kind of self-love, but Pietz translates it as our "true infatuation with ourselves," emphasizing the excitement. The fetish emerges, Leiris writes, when this self-love is "projected from inside to outside and clothed in a carapace that traps it within the limits of a particular thing." The fetish *also* materializes an intimate truth. It gives a name, however difficult, to a certain desire. Leiris offered the right test case for blaring out that value is internalized to the point of turning the self inside out; and that the problem with the fetish is, so to speak, that it represents both a mirror and a foil to capitalism which asserts a certain persistent value that cannot be dematerialized, removed, undone. Thus constituted, the true fetish exists—and this is Pietz, now—as a monument to "the sheer incommensurable togetherness of the living existence of the personal self and the living otherness of the material world."[42]

To turn or return to this text now is to be startled by its historical and theoretical insight. It is to admire, even envy its intensity and creativity. It is to experience how thrilling the concept of fetishism was for intellectuals and artists across the twentieth century as they searched for a theory linking the personal to the political. And it is to join Pietz in his exploration of this incommensurable togetherness of the internal and external worlds.

Editorial Note

As indicated above, this book relies on the complete typescript sent by William Pietz to Francesco Pellizzi for safekeeping and in hope of eventual publication on September 6, 2007. This typescript accounts for chapters 1–4 of the present book, which are followed by the three previously published essays, here included as chapters 5–7. Chapter titles for chapters 1–4 are from Pietz's typescript.

Pietz's typescript updates his PhD dissertation and, on occasion, the three essays published in *RES*. Though two of the *RES* essays ostensibly predate the dissertation, they at times seem to update it and are closer to the text of the typescript. As Pietz made changes to both of these earlier versions as he worked on the typescript, we decided not to treat either the *RES* essays or the dissertation as definitive earlier versions.

The changes Pietz made resulted in a series of complications (and errata), which required us to use our editorial judgment to come to a final version, usually accepting his solutions but at times modifying for readability. In the typescript, Pietz routinely transplanted long passages containing examples or references from footnotes into the main body of the text. In both the dissertation and the articles in *RES*, these exact passages can be found in the footnotes, so Pietz's choice to move them is clearly intentional. This practice occasionally thins out the argument into a plethora of examples, but we have followed the author's decision to move the notes into the main body of the text. (For comparison, see the essays published in *RES*.) What complicates things, however, is that Pietz made some mistakes in this process, on occasion double-pasting the footnoted passages or pasting the text at a spot that breaks the continuity of his argument. Sometimes he pasted the footnoted text not only twice but in quite different parts of his text. In these cases, we have generally reverted to placing the pasted text at the site where it was footnoted in the published version. We have also removed the duplicates generally to the benefit of the order used in the articles and the dissertation. As Pietz did not "add" to his text, and as they often read awkwardly, we have treated these occasions as errors or incomplete alterations that did not work out. On a couple of occasions we also made small changes to the location of the added example in order not to break up the argument—the quote, once inserted, would otherwise harm the continuity of the sentences. At times Pietz also removed some citations while inserting these passages into the main text; we have restored these citations.

Pietz also moved some passages around, particularly in the last chapter. Some do not make sense in the place where they ended up in his typescript. We have decided how to proceed by comparing those passages with their place in the dissertation, seeing how they affect the progression of the text and in what way they might work best. While we have treated the typescript as the closest available version to the finalized text, we had to restore two passages to more or less their original position.

On one occasion, Pietz removed a passage from the dissertation when he published his essays in *RES*, but then he restored it into his typescript and placed it in a clearly unsuitable spot (two chapters, several dozen pages, even a couple of centuries too late). Thanks to the anonymous reviewer who caught the confusion, we revised this placement by re-engaging the dissertation's text, and deciding accordingly. This is the passage that begins with "The final stage in the articulation of the idea of the fetish" on page 59 and ends with "according to the Fancy of every Man" on page 62, which Pietz had placed in the typescript at the end of the section "Anti-universalist Hermeneutics" in chapter 4. We have restored this passage to almost its original place, making small changes to allow for continuity with other passages he added at that spot. We note this all because, should any reader find the decision problematic, we can only concur by noting our tentativeness on the matter and our ultimate choice to retain the passage at the best location possible.

We have also restored the discussion of Hobbes, to be found between brackets on pages 108–10. Besides being relevant and interesting, the passage extends the interpretation of de Brosses's argument on figuration and materiality which precedes it. Readers should note that this passage is not to be found in the typescript, but only in the dissertation, and that it should therefore be considered as ultimately expunged by Pietz.

Regarding translations: Pietz sometimes includes the original-language text, sometimes a translation, and sometimes both. We have retained his use of both Latin and English in chapter 2, where the practice is somewhat systematic, but we have otherwise opted to cite English translations (removing the original where both are included) because these inclusions and exclusions are too unruly in his typescript. On the few occasions where passages were left untranslated, we have translated them using either the translation to be found in *RES* or else the context. Notably, Pietz translated de Brosses in chapter 4. Despite our regard for the translation of de Brosses in Rosalind C. Morris and Daniel H. Leonard, *The Returns of Fetishism: Charles de Brosses and the Afterlives of an Idea* (University of Chicago Press, 2017), we thought it appropriate to leave Pietz's translation as it stood, citing the relevant page numbers for readers interested in comparing.

Though the text involves some repetitions (particularly between the four original chapters and the three we have added), we have not altered these passages. Significant editorial amendments are indicated with brackets.

CHAPTER 1

The Problem of the Fetish

But there is one term the indiscriminate use of which, I believe, has done infinite harm, the word "fetish." The story of its origin and introduction into West Africa is so well known that I need not here repeat it.

R. S. RATTRAY, *Ashanti* (1923)

(every historical object is a fetish)

MAURICE MERLEAU-PONTY,
The Visible and the Invisible (1964)

"Fetish" has ever been a word of sinister pedigree. Discursively promiscuous and theoretically suggestive, it has always been a word with a past, forever becoming "an embarrassment" to disciplines in the human sciences that seek to contain and control its sense.[1] Yet anthropologists of primitive religion, critics of political economy, psychiatrists of sexual deviance, philosophers of modernist aesthetics have never ceased using the term, even as they testify to its conceptual doubtfulness and referential uncertainty. It seems this word's usage is always somewhat "indiscriminate," always threatening to slide, as in Merleau-Ponty's tentative proposition, into an intolerably general theory. Yet it is precisely in the surprising history of this word as a comprehensive theoretical term indispensable to such crucial social thinkers as Comte, Marx, and Freud that the real interdisciplinary interest of "fetish" lies.

This chapter provides the introductory discussion for a more extensive exploration of this history, an exploration that must begin with a study of the origin of the fetish as a word and as a historically significant object. My thesis is that the fetish, as an idea, a problem, and as a novel object not proper to any prior discrete society, originated in the cross-cultural spaces of the coast of West Africa during the sixteenth and seventeenth centuries. Of course, origins are never absolute. While I argue that the fetish originated within a novel social formation during this period through the development of the pidgin word *fetisso*, this word in turn has a linguistic and conceptual history that may be traced. *Fetisso* derives from the Portuguese *feitiço*, which in the late Middle Ages meant "magical practice" or "witchcraft" performed by persons of humble status—men as well as women, urban as well as rural. In chapter 2, I discuss further conceptual and evaluative implications of this term as it was used by churchmen in late medieval Portugal.

Feitiço in turn derives from the Latin adjective *facticius*, which originally meant "manufactured." The historical study of the fetish must begin by considering these words in some detail in both their practical and theoretical contexts, only then going on to examine the initial application of *feitiço* on the African coast, its subsequent development into *fetisso*, and finally that word's dissemination into the languages of northern Europe, where national versions of the word developed during the seventeenth century. The study of the origin of the fetish concludes at the beginning of the eighteenth century with the text of Willem Bosman, whose *Accurate Description of the Coast of Guinea* provided the image and conception of fetishes that Enlightenment intellectuals drew on to elaborate a novel theory of primitive religion. The articulation of this general Enlightenment theory, as developed from Bayle to de Brosses and further refined by philosophers of the late eighteenth century, constitutes a second period in the history of the fetish. Its dissemination into a host of popular and scientific discourses in the nineteenth century marks a third large period, and one could view twentieth-century theoretical discourses that seek to make a unity out of the diversity of earlier fetish discourses as the last historical development of this idea.

The essentially theoretical nature of the interest in the history of the term, as well as the need for an initial schematism to establish criteria of relevance for the subsequent historical discussion, call for a preliminary consideration of the problem named by the word "fetish."

The Problem of the Fetish

By taking a historical approach that stresses the importance of the word itself, I am opposing universalist and particularist arguments that dismiss the fetish as a proper object with its own singular significance. By particularist arguments, I am referring primarily to those of ethnographers who would dismiss "fetish" as a corrupt genus that obscures the true meaning of the socioreligious practices and artifacts of various non-

Western societies. For instance, this was R. S. Rattray's position when he discussed "what the Akan-speaking African calls a *suman*—a word which I would like to see substituted altogether for 'fetish.'"[2] Such arguments are used to justify a method for reclaiming stigmatized colonial-era ethnographic texts by translating terms such as "fetish" back into the native terminology of the particular society being described.[3] This method ignores the historical and cross-cultural status of these texts in order to reconstruct the unique cultures of primitive societies in their self-contained purity. But it is equally possible to study these colonial texts, and earlier voyage accounts, as novel productions resulting from the encounter of radically heterogeneous worlds. As descriptive records they are often phantasmal, but just because of this it is possible to view them as remnants of the creative enactment of new forms of social consciousness. Similarly, the pidgin word *fetisso* as it developed in the cross-cultural spaces of the West African coast may be viewed either as the failed translation of various African terms or as something in itself, a novel word responsive to an unprecedented type of situation.

Universalist dismissals of the specificity of the fetish tend either to be empiricist and psychological or philosophical and analytic. Psychological universalists subsume fetishism to an allegedly universal human tendency toward phallic symbolism. (Lacanian psychoanalysis may be the most extreme expression of such a view). An ironic instance of this, applying the notion to the observers rather than the observed, informs a remark by Edmund Leach that, Lévi-Strauss and the structuralists aside, "everything that the anthropologists have ever had to say about 'fetishism' and 'magic' and the meaning of religious symbolism has its roots in an interest in the 'phallic' components of Hindu iconography."[4] The analytic philosopher subsumes the concept of fetishization to the general category of hypostatization and errors of logical type. This is the neo-Kantian usage of the term "fetish."[5] The logical positivist Ernst Mach had occasion to denounce the notion of physical causality as a "fetish."

While there was indeed a marked sexual dimension to the discourse about fetishes "from the beginning," the conception that the fetish's ultimate referent is the phallus was articulated only in the late nineteenth century. The earliest fetish discourse concerned witchcraft and the control of female sexuality. As for philosophy's dismissal of the fetish as the logical mistake of hypostasis—the "fallacy of misplaced concreteness" to use Whitehead's popular phrase—I would argue that the discourse of fetishism represents the emerging theoretical articulation of a materialism quite incompatible and in conflict with the philosophical tradition. When, in *Difference and Repetition*, the philosopher Gilles Deleuze writes, "The fetish is the natural object of social consciousness as common sense or recognition of value," his use of "fetish" as an affirmative term of fundamental theoretical significance is congenial to that book's Nietzschean project of radically revaluing and "reversing" the tradition of Western philosophical thought.[6] This is not at all accidental but the result of the historical origin and development of the word, a development I trace in this book.

Finally, there is the dismissal, both universalist and historical, that the discourse about fetishes is nothing but a continuation of the traditional Christian discourse concerning idolatry. The relation of the fetish to the idol, and of the notion of fetishism to Christianity's conception of its false other (idolatry), is a complex and essential question which a historical study must discuss in some detail. As I discuss in the next chapter, far from representing a continuation of the idea of idolatry, the emergence of the distinct notion of the fetish marks a breakdown of the earlier discourse under quite specific historical conditions and social forces.

This novel situation began with the formation of intercultural spaces along the West African coast whose function was to translate and transvalue objects between radically different social systems. Specifically, as I will discuss in chapter 2, these spaces, which endured for several centuries, were triangulated between Christian feudal, African lineage, and merchant capitalist social systems.[7] It was within this situation that there emerged a new problematic concerning the capacity of material objects to embody—simultaneously and sequentially—religious, sexual, aesthetic, and commercial values. My argument, then, is that the fetish originated only with the emerging articulation of the ideology of the commodity form, as it developed and defined itself within and against the social values and religious ideologies of two radically different types of noncapitalist society, as they encountered each other in an ongoing cross-cultural situation. This process is indicated in the history of the word itself as it developed from the late medieval Portuguese *feitiço* to the sixteenth-century pidgin *fetisso* on the African coast to various northern European versions of the word via the 1602 text of the Dutchman Pieter de Marees.

The fetish, then, not only originated from but remains specific to the problematic of the social value of material objects as revealed in situations formed by the encounter of radically heterogeneous social systems. A study of the history of the idea of the fetish may thus be guided by identifying those themes that persist throughout the various discourses and disciplines that have appropriated the term. This method studies the history of the usage of "fetish" as a field of exemplary instances that exemplify no model or truth prior to or outside this very "archive" itself. The fetish is viewed here as a radically historical object that is nothing other than the totalized series of its particular usages. Nevertheless, these usages, like all language, are embedded and function within a total historical reality, and the historical specificity of the fetish's problematic can provide criteria for the construction of a preliminary theoretical model of the fetish from the recurrent themes of fetish discourse.

The first characteristic essential to the notion of the fetish is that of the fetish object's irreducible materiality. The truth of the fetish resides in its status as a material embodiment. Its truth is not that of the idol, for the idol's truth lies in its relation of iconic resemblance to some immaterial model or entity. This was one basis for the distinction between the *feitiço* and the *idolo* in medieval Portuguese. For Charles de Brosses, who coined the word *fétichisme* in 1757, the fetish was essentially a terrestrial material entity; fetishism was thus to be distinguished from cults of celestial bodies (whose truth might be a sort of protodeist intimation of the rational order of nature rather than direct worship of the natural bodies themselves). For Hegel, the African culture of the fetish represented a moment just prior to History, since the fetish was precisely that object of the Spirit that failed to participate in the Idea, which never experienced a negation and *Aufhebung* to a truth beyond its natural materiality. Africa "is no historical part of the World," writes Hegel, "it has no movement or development to exhibit.... What we properly understand by Africa, is the Unhistorical, Undeveloped Spirit, still involved in the conditions of mere nature, and which has to be presented here as on the threshold of the World's History."[8] Hegel's characterization of Africans and of the religion of fetishes that actualizes "the African Spirit" typifies the accepted European understanding of African fetishism in the early nineteenth century. "The peculiarity of the African character,"[9] according to Hegel, is that it lacks

the principle which naturally accompanies all *our* ideas—the category of Universality. [Africans worship] the first thing that comes their way. This, taken quite indiscriminately, they exalt to the dignity of a "Genius"; it may be an animal, a tree, a stone, or a wooden figure.... In the Fetich, a kind of objective independence as contrasted with the arbitrary fancy [*Willkür*] of the individual seems to manifest itself; but as the objectivity that is nothing other than the fancy of the individual [*individuelle Willkür*] projecting itself into space, the human individual remains the master of the image it has adopted. If any mischance occurs which the Fetich has not averted, if the rain is suspended, if there is a failure of the crops, they bind and beat or destroy the Fetich and so get rid of it, making another immediately and thus holding it in their power. Such a Fetich has no independence as an object of religious worship; still less has it aesthetic independence as a work of art; it is merely a creation that expresses the arbitrary choice of its maker, and which always remains in his hands. Hence there is no relation of dependence in this religion.[10]

Paradoxically, this implies the second characteristic of African religion for Hegel: *absolute dependence* on the kings and priests who act as human intermediaries with the transcendent power. That is, the "natural man" can only slavishly worship the abstract power of command endowed in those who control the chaotic power of nature. The function of this view of Africans, which was far from peculiar to Hegel, as an ideology justifying the slave trade by explaining Africans as slavish by nature is obvious enough. Marxism's commodity (and capital) as fetish,[11] psychoanalysis's sexual fetish,[12] and modernism's fetish as art object all in an essential way involve the object's untranscended materiality.[13]

Second, and equally important, is the theme of singularity and repetition. The fetish has an ordering power derived from its status as the fixation or inscription of a unique originating event that has brought together previously heterogeneous elements into a novel identity. As MacGaffey stresses, "a 'fetish' is always a composite fabrication."[14] But the heterogeneous components appropriated into an identity by a fetish are not only material elements. Desires, beliefs, and narrative structures establishing a practice are also fixed (or fixated) by the fetish, whose power is precisely the power to repeat its originating act of forging an identity of articulated relations among certain otherwise heterogeneous things.

One of the most common statements about the nature of the primitive's fetish in texts from the fifteenth to the nineteenth century is what may be called the "first-encounter" theory. Bosman's principal informant at Ouidah, when asked how many gods his people worshipped,[15] replied

> that the number of their Gods was endless and innumerable: For (said he) any of us being resolved to undertake anything of importance, we first of all search out a God to prosper our designed Undertaking; and going out of doors with this Design, take the first creature that presents itself to our Eyes, whether Dog, Cat, or the most contemptible Animal in the World, for our God; or perhaps instead of that any inanimate that falls in our way, whether a stone, a piece of Wood, or any thing else of the same Nature.[16]

This fantastic explanation of African religious behavior according to the notion of a first encounter between a new purposive desire and a material object, whereby the thing becomes the divinized emblem of the project, was a commonplace among Muslims and Christians even prior to the development of the idea of the fetish. As I shall discuss in the next chapter, it became an essential component of the fetish idea as that notion came to be defined in opposition to idolatry. Unlike idolatry, which medieval Europe understood as a faith and a law—that is, as a principle of social order comparable to Christianity, Judaism, and Islam—the fetish idea as elaborated in the fifteenth and sixteenth centuries expressed the perception of a social order generated, paradoxically, by a purely natural and lawless process.

This paradoxical idea of Africans generating a social order out of a chaotic principle of contingency is evident both in sixteenth- and seventeenth-century voyage accounts and in eighteenth-century theoretical statements, such as Linnaeus's characterization of the social principle of Africans as "caprice." The social principle of American Indians was "custom" and that of Orientals "opinion." The social principle of Europeans was, of course, "law."[17] The characterization of African society and mentality as based on caprice was reinterpreted during the eighteenth century to mean something more on the order of the Lockean category of the "arbitrary." That is, as Foucault discussed in *Madness and Civilization*, the Renaissance notion of caprice as evidenced in Cervantes's *Don Quixote* or Shakespeare's *King Lear* or in the figures in Bosch presented reason's other as a fanciful madness that through its extremity revealed the depths and essence of the human condition.[18] With Locke and the thinkers of the Enlightenment, irrational mental activity was conceived merely negatively as "arbitrary" and unmotivated by external reality or any essential truth. The notion of the arbitrary as unmotivated random association had, of course, not only psychological but also linguistic and political implications. The Saussurean conception of the arbitrary sign derives from Locke,[19] while the liberal theory of politics was articulated in denouncing the "arbitrary" power of the absolute monarch.[20]

Such an explanation of the origin of irrational social beliefs in the "mechanisms" of the natural primitive mentality was basic to de Brosses's elaboration of a general theory of fetishism (and distinguished it from the fear theory of the origin of "natural religion" propounded by Hume and others). De Brosses argued that Africans' fetishes could be "the first object that strikes their fancy" and hence that the "manner of thinking" involved is not "figurism" or allegory or even euhemeristic distortion but something more arbitrary because based on contingency (chance encounters).[21]

It was the notion of a historically singular social construct able to create the illusion of natural unity among heterogeneous things that, in part, attracted Marx to the idea of the fetish.[22] For Marx the term was useful as a name for the power of a singular historical institution to fix personal consciousness in an objective illusion. For Auguste Comte and late nineteenth-century psychologists such as Alfred Binet—who first gave the word currency to denote sexual fetishes—the origin of the fetishistic fixation was in the power of a singular personal event to structure desire.[23] The idea of traumatic fixation upon a specific intense experience as the source of a repetition compulsion is, of course, fundamental to the psychoanalytic notion of the sexual fetish. Similarly, the idea of an enduring effect of aesthetic unity produced by a singular chance encounter of heterogeneous elements (the umbrella and the sewing machine) was fundamental to modernist art.

The final two themes basic to the fetish problem have already been introduced in discussing the materiality and repetitive power of a singular fixation of heterogeneous elements: these are themes of social value and individual personhood. The problem of the nonuniversality and constructedness of social value emerged in an intense form from the beginning of the European voyages to Black Africa. Thus, one of the earliest voyagers to West Africa, the Venetian Alvise Cadamosto, who sailed to Senegal under Portuguese charter in the late 1450s, was moved to write of the West Africans of Gambia, "Gold is much prized among them, in my opinion, more than by us, for they regard it as very precious; nevertheless they trade it cheaply, taking in exchange articles of little value in our eyes."[24]

The mystery of value—the dependence of social value on specific institutional systems for marking the value of material things—was a constant theme in transactions on the Guinea coast during this period. The problem was especially expressed in the category of the trifle: European traders frequently remarked on the trinkets and trifles they traded for objects of real value—just as the socioreligious order of African societies seemed to them founded on the overvaluing of "trifles" and "trash." When he tried to formulate an aesthetic explanation of African fetish worship in 1764, Immanuel Kant decided that such practices were founded on the principle of the "trifling" (*läppisch*), the ultimate degeneration of the principle of the beautiful because it lacked all sense of the sublime.[25] Nineteenth-century economic, sociological, anthropological, and psychological discourses about the fetish constantly stress the idea of certain material objects as the loci of fixed structures of the inscription, displacement, reversal, and overestimation of value.

Marxist and structuralist writers have done little to develop the notion of the fetish as a genuine problem of general theoretical significance.

At most they tend to stress the institutional structuring, and hence the objectivity, of constructed value consciousness. Marxist fetish theory explains this as false consciousness based upon an objective illusion (hence alterable only by institutional transformation, not mere subjective "consciousness raising"); material objects turned into commodities conceal exploitive social relations, displacing value consciousness from the true productive movement of social labor to the apparent movement of market prices and forces.[26]

Structuralism either dismisses the fetish as a significant problem or reduces it semiologically. For example, Lévi-Strauss enables his structuralist reinterpretation of "totemism" precisely by dividing off overly particularistic or singular religious objects from the "true" class of totems: these are the fetishes that, unconnected with clan identity or whole species, are uninteresting because less socially significant—at least according to the structuralist.[27] Alternatively, structuralists view the fetish as nothing but a nonverbal material signifier, sometimes "animated" with the pure status of sign-vehicle for a process of signification.[28] In stressing the social objectivity of the fetish, however, these theories tend to obscure the problem of the relation of the fetish to the individual person (just as psychological and psychoanalytic theories ignore the social dimension of the fetish). Both Marxist and structuralist theory view the fetish as situated at the point at which objective institutional systems are "personified" by individuals, and this in two senses. First, an order of material entities (the market, natural species) is understood to constitute the order of personal relations (social production, culture), thereby establishing a determinate consciousness of the "natural value" of social objects; second, personal activity comes to be directed by the impersonal logic of such abstract relations, as guided by the institutionalized systems of material signifiers of value arranged according to this logic.

Fetish discourse about the relations of the individual person to the material fetish object is characterized by an even more basic theme, however—that of the embodied status of the individual. The labor theory of value is only one example of this theme of the fetish as relating the activity of the embodied individual to the value of material objects. One way in which the medieval Portuguese *feitiço* was distinguished from the *idolo* was that, whereas the idol was conceived as a freestanding statue, the fetish was typically some fabricated object worn about the body. Moreover, the idea of the idol emphasized the worship of a false god or demonic spirit, whereas *feitiços* were practiced to achieve certain tangible effects (such as healing) upon or in service of the user. The fourth theme found in the idea of the fetish is, then, that of the subjection of the human body (as the material locus of action and desire) to the influence of certain material objects which, although cut off from the body, function as its controlling organs at certain moments. It was, of course, psychoanalysis which most fully developed this theme of the effective symbolization of the sexual human body "fixated" in relation to certain material things. In modernist art, the surrealistic object was often constructed to be a material thing that resonated throughout the (ethnographic, Marxist, psychoanalytic, and modernist) registers of fetish discourse by appearing as a perversely anthropomorphized or sexualized thing. The appeal by social scientists to surrealist theory to explain the efficacy of traditional African healing practices might be viewed as a nice closure of the historical circle developing this theme.[29]

The Truth of the Fetish

In this discussion I have tried only to delineate the most basic themes that recur throughout the history of fetish discourse: irreducible materiality; event-originated singular synthesis with the power to repeat itself; culturally constructed consciousness of value; power of external objects over the desires, actions, health, and self-identity of individuals whose selfhood is conceived as inseparable from their bodies. These themes will now guide an investigation of the history of fetish theory that tries to understand in what way these ideas form a unity and why this unique "problem-idea" emerged out of a particular historical situation: a mercantile cross-cultural space defined by the transvaluation of material objects moving across radically different social orders. Since my interest in studying this history lies in its theoretical implications, it seems appropriate to attempt a preliminary sketch of the theory of the fetish that may be derived from the history of fetish theory.

First, from the standpoints of particularist ethnography, structural sociology, and institutional history, "fetish" must be considered a factitious universal. The term "fetish" has, however, been a component in a "discursive formation" in Foucault's sense, in *Archaeology of Knowledge*, of a restricted and varied set. Instances are the crime of engaging in "fetish practices" in colonial West Africa (a legal category),[30] the sexual perversion termed fetishism as defined by twentieth-century medical-psychiatric discourse,[31] and the sacred fetish objects of Zuni and other Native American cultures of the American Southwest.[32] Unlike, say, the *suman* in Ashanti society or the *nkisi* in Kongo society (or, for that matter, the Eucharist in Christian culture), the fetish, with certain exceptions, has not enjoyed the social actuality of being an institutionally defined object within a particular culture or social order. (I would, however, argue that *fetisso* was a central term in routinized practices and discourse on the West African coast from the sixteenth century on—but these cross-cultural spaces were not "societies" or "cultures" in any conventional sense). From this standpoint, the fetish must be viewed as proper to no historical field other than that of the history of the term itself, and to a cross-cultural situation formed by the ongoing encounter of the incommensurable value codes of radically different social orders. In Marxist terms, one might say the fetish is situated in the space of cultural revolution as the locus where the truth of the object *as* fetish is revealed.[33]

This is precisely Marx's point in the first chapter of *Capital* when he writes that "the whole mystery of commodities, all the magic and necromancy that surrounds the products of labour on the basis of commodity production, vanishes [or is revealed as fetishism] as soon as we come to other forms of production."[34] Marx's constant use of religious terminology to critically characterize commodity ideology was the expression of a comparative method for critically analyzing the value system of one type of society by framing it in terms of the value systems of societies with other modes of production. As I discuss in [chapter 5,] "Fetishism and Materialism," the rhetorical structure of this analytic method is evident in Marx's earliest uses of the term "fetish" (in 1842 after reading a German translation of de Brosses's book). As Lucio Colletti states in his criticism of the Marxism of the Second International, "Marx's theory of value is identical to his *theory of fetishism*."[35] The theory of fetishism is the theory of value articulated from that comparative standpoint located (if only in imagination as with the young Marx) at the point of encounter between the values and value consciousness of societies with different modes of production (say, at the point of conflict between peasant feudal privileges and bourgeois property rights in criminal cases concerning the "theft" of firewood in the Rhinelands, as judged from the value perspective of Afro-Caribbean society).[36]

In what sense, then, is there such a thing as a fetish? If "fetish" does name some specific "problem-idea," what is the truth it names? In a 1929 note on the sculpture of Giacometti, Michel Leiris speaks of "the fetishism that, from the most ancient times, dwells at the base of our human existence" and of the power of certain exceptional art works to respond to this "true fetishism."

> It is puzzling that, in the domain of works of art, one finds objects (paintings or sculptures) able to resonate just a bit with the needs of that true fetishism—that is to say, love, true infatuation with ourselves, projected from inside to outside and clothed in a carapace that traps it within the limits of a particular thing and location, like

a piece of furniture that we are able to use in the vast, strange room that we call space.[37]

The fetish is, then, first of all, something intensely personal whose truth is experienced as a substantial movement from "inside" the self (the self as totalized through an impassioned body) into the self-limited morphology of a material object situated in space "outside." Artworks are true fetishes only if they are material objects at least as intensely personal as the water of tears: "drops of water, pretty little liquid spheres able to call back at least the form, if not the drop, of our tears, and this moisture, this fluidity corresponds to the sweetness that flows in our limbs when we love or just when we feel touched."[38] The teardrop, or the fetish object, "corresponds" by "recalling" the amorous flow or sense of being touched within the embodied self as this was made conscious in singular moments of "crisis" in which the identity of the self is called into question, put at risk, by a sudden encounter with the life of the outside world. "There are moments which one can call the crises that alone are important in a life. These are moments when the outside seems abruptly to respond to the sum of what we throw forth from within, when the exterior world opens to encounter our heart and establishes a sudden communication with it."[39] These crisis moments of singular encounter and indefinable transaction between the life of the self and that of the world become fixed, both in places and things, and as personal memories that retain a peculiar power to move one profoundly.

Leiris continues:

> I have some memories of this order in my own life, and all relate to events which were, in appearance, futile and stripped of symbolic value and, if one wishes, gratuitous: in a luminous street of Montmartre, a Negress of the Black Birds dance troop holding a bouquet of damp roses in her two hands; a steamer on board which I found myself standing slowly separating itself from a quay; some snatches of song murmured at random; encountering in a Greek ruin a strange animal that seemed a sort of giant lizard. . . . Poetry expresses itself only out of such "crises," and only those works count which furnish their equivalents.[40]

The quality Leiris attributes to these four vivid memories of "crisis" is that of being "gratuitous," unmotivated and unearned, and in appearance "futile"—perhaps because such encounters lack any adequate formal code to transform them into meaningful communications or coherently narrativized interactions. Such a singularly fixating encounter is

Figure 1. Alberto Giacometti (1901–1966), *Gazing Head*, 1928–1929. Bronze; 15½ × 14½ × 2½ in. (39.3 × 36.8 × 6.3 cm). New York, Museum of Modern Art, Florene May Schoenborn Bequest. © 2022 Alberto Giacometti Estate / VAGA at Artists Rights Society (ARS), NY / ADAGP, Paris. Digital image © The Museum of Modern Art / Licensed by SCALA / Art Resource, NY.

"stripped of all symbolic value" and, paradoxically because of this degradation from any recognizable value code, becomes a crisis moment of infinite value that expresses the sheer incommensurable togetherness of the living existence of the personal self and the living otherness of the material world.

Such a crisis brings together and fixates into a singularly resonant unified intensity an unrepeatable event (permanent in memory), a particular object or arrangement of objects, and a localized space. Were one to elaborate a theory of the fetish, one might then adopt the following as fundamental categories: historicization, personalization, reification, and territorialization. The fetish is always a meaningful fixation of a singular event; it is above all a historical object, the enduring material form and force of an unrepeatable event. This object is territorialized in material space (an earthly matrix), whether in the form of a geographical locality, a marked site on the surface of the human body, or a medium of inscription or configuration defined by some portable or wearable thing. The historical object is territorialized in the form of a reification: some thing (*meuble*) or shape whose status is that of a self-contained entity identifiable within the territory. It is recognizable as a discrete thing because of its status as a significant object within the value codes proper to the productive and ideological systems of a given society. This reified, territorialized historical object is also "personalized" in the sense that beyond its status as a collective social object it evokes an intensely personal response from individuals. This intense relation to the individual's experience of his or her own living self through an impassioned response to the fetish object is always incommensurable with (whether in a way that reinforces or undercuts) the social value codes within which the fetish holds the status of a material signifier. It is in those "disavowals" and "perspectives of flight" whose possibility is opened by the clash of this incommensurable difference that the fetish might be identified as the site both of the formation and the revelation of ideology and value consciousness.

Each fetish is a singular articulated identification (an "appropriation," *Ereignis* in Heidegger's language[41]) unifying events, places, things, and people, and then returning them to their separate spheres (temporal occurrence, terrestrial space, social being, and personal existence) in such a way that certain structured relationships are established—some conscious, others unconscious—that constitute the existential-phenomenological fabric (the "flesh" in Merleau-Ponty's sense in *The Visible and the Invisible*) of immediate prereflective experience. As Deleuze says, "The fetish is the natural object of social consciousness as common sense or recognition of value."[42]

Fetishes exist in the world as material objects that "naturally" embody socially significant values that touch particular individuals in an intensely personal way: a flag, monument, or landmark; a talisman, medicine-bundle, or sacramental object; an earring, tattoo, or cockade; a city, village, or nation; a shoe, lock of hair, or phallus; a Giacometti sculpture or Duchamp's *Large Glass*. Each has that quality of synecdochic fragmentedness or "detotalized totality" characteristic of the recurrent, material collective object discussed by Sartre:

> When we say there are only men and real relations (for Merleau-Ponty I add things also, and animals, etc.), we mean only that we must expect to find the support of collective objects in the concrete

activity of individuals. We do not intend to deny the reality of these objects, but we claim that it is parasitical. . . . Marxism remains uncertain as to the nature and origin of these "collectives." The theory of fetishism, outlined by Marx, has never been developed; furthermore it could not be extended to cover all social realities. Thus Marxism, while rejecting organicism, lacks weapons against it. . . . It is necessary to take up the study of collectives again from the beginning and to demonstrate that these objects, far from being characterized by a direct unity of a consensus, represent perspectives of flight. . . . For us the reality of the collective object rests on recurrence [repetition of the same property within the members of a series]. It demonstrates that the totalization is never achieved and that the totality exists at best only in the form of detotalized totality. [In the sense, as Sartre writes a few pages later, that "a city is a material and social organization which derives its reality from the ubiquity of its absence. It is present in each of its streets insofar as it is always elsewhere."] As such these collectives exist. They are revealed immediately in action and in perception. In each one of them we shall always find a concrete materiality (a movement, the head office, a building, a word, etc.) which supports and manifests a flight which eats it away. I need only open my window: I see a church, a bank, a cafe—three collectives. This thousand-franc bill is another; still another is the newspaper I have just bought. . . . Marxism has never been concerned to study these objects for themselves; that is, on all levels of social life.⁴³

If the fetish, theorized out of the entire history of the term itself, can be taken as a name for the total collective material object, at once social and personal, then Merleau-Ponty is right in saying that "every historical object is a fetish." But this may be read in the sense that the fetish is that special type of collective object which reveals the truth of all historical objects, just as for Heidegger the work of art reveals and hence is the truth of "the thing."⁴⁴

The fetish might then be viewed as the locus of occurrence of a sort of originary carnal rhetoric of identification and disavowal which establishes conscious and unconscious value judgments connecting territorialized social things and embodied individual persons within a series of singular historical fixations. It would thus be the site of articulation both of ideological reification and hypostasis, and of impassioned spontaneous criticism. Leiris speaks of the "true fetishism" while in the same breath criticizing the "bad fetishism" of "the meager phantoms that are our moral, logical, and social imperatives . . . a fetishism transposed, falsely resembling the one which profoundly animates us."⁴⁵

The discourse of the fetish has always been a critical discourse about the false objective values of a culture from which the speaker is personally distanced. Such was the rhetorical force of negative revaluation when Portuguese Catholics named African religious and social objects *feitiços*, and such was the force when commodity-minded Dutch, French, and English Protestants identified African religious objects and Catholic sacramental objects as equally "fetishes," thereby preparing the way for the general Enlightenment theory of the fetish. This negative critical force continued as an implication of the word throughout the various nineteenth- and twentieth-century discourses about the fetish. "Fetish" has always named the incomprehensible mystery of the power of material things to be collective social objects experienced by individuals as truly embodying determinate values or "virtues," always as judged from a cross-cultural perspective of relative infinite degradation, "stripped of symbolic value."[46] Fetish discourse always posits this double consciousness of absorbed credulity and "degraded" or distanced incredulity. The site of this latter disillusioned judgment by its very nature seems to represent a power of the ultimate degradation and, by implication, of the radical creation of value. Because of this it holds an illusory attractive power of its own: that of seeming to be that Archimedean point of man at last "more open and cured of his obsessions," the impossible home of a man without fetishes.[47]

The Historical Field of the Fetish

The preceding section presented a preliminary theoretical model of the fetish put together from the diverse themes found to be fundamental to the history of fetish discourse. From the theme of the essential materiality of the fetish—that is, the fetish is precisely not a material signifier referring beyond itself and rather acts as a material space gathering an otherwise unconnected multiplicity into the unity of its enduring singularity—the category of territorialization was established. From the fetish's essential power of singular fixation and ordering repetition there emerged the peculiar historicity proper to the fetish. The term "reification" formalizes the fundamental theme of the institutionalized or routinized codes of social value between which a given fetish provides a determinate structure of mediation.[48] And "personalization" provides a name for the dimension of the reified objects' power to fix identifications and disavowals which ground the self-identity of particular embodied individuals.

The usefulness of this model depends on its applicability outside the historical field of fetish discourse as presently constituted. Even if this conception of the fetish as an analytic model proves unsatisfactory, the historical project stands on its own. This theoretical introduction to the study of the historical problem of the fetish concludes with a delineation of the historical field to be studied.

This field is defined first of all by the usage of the word itself. As I have already argued, this is the only approach that preserves the specificity of the problem, since it does not reduce the notion of the fetish to one or another (particularist or universalist) metacode. This historico-linguistic approach makes it impossible to say whether a given object is or is not a "fetish" in any simple, ahistorical sense. For instance, it is only from the perspective of twentieth-century medico-juridical discourses about sexual fetishism that Restif de la Bretonne can be considered a fetishist. While for these discourses Restif was the classic shoe fetishist (to the point that some psychiatric dictionaries of the second quarter of the twentieth century preferred the term "Restifism" to "fetishism"), the usage of *fétichisme* during Restif's lifetime did not denote sexual perversities of the sort that characterized Restif's desire. Our approach, then, must respect the specific sense of the term in any given period or situation in order to grasp the theoretical implications of the term's specific usages within an overall totalizing perspective on the history of fetish theory.

Despite the necessary methodological restriction to the history of the word itself, the unifying principle of the notion of the fetish does not derive from the ground of discourse, of the "logos." Rather, this chapter argues that the problem-idea of the fetish arose within and remains specific to a particular type of cross-cultural experience first engaging European consciousness in ongoing situations on the West African coast after the fifteenth century.

Within these philological and historical parameters, objects traditionally considered "fetishes" such as the famous Kongo nail fetishes or the *suman* of the Akan-speaking peoples of West Africa must be situated in the cross-cultural problematic proper to the application of the term "fetish" to these objects. But this approach also requires that objects at times termed "fetishes" which were produced specifically within these cross-cultural situations be equally considered. Examples include, from the non-European side, such productions as the Akan goldweights and, from the European side, objects such as the fifteenth-century *padrões* of the Portuguese King John II. Both, at least in some instances, were accepted as "fetishes" by those on the other side of the cultural barrier. The Akan goldweights were a direct cultural response to the impact of gold-seeking European (and Arab) traders, and to the resulting quasi-monetization of the domestic Akan economy through the circulation

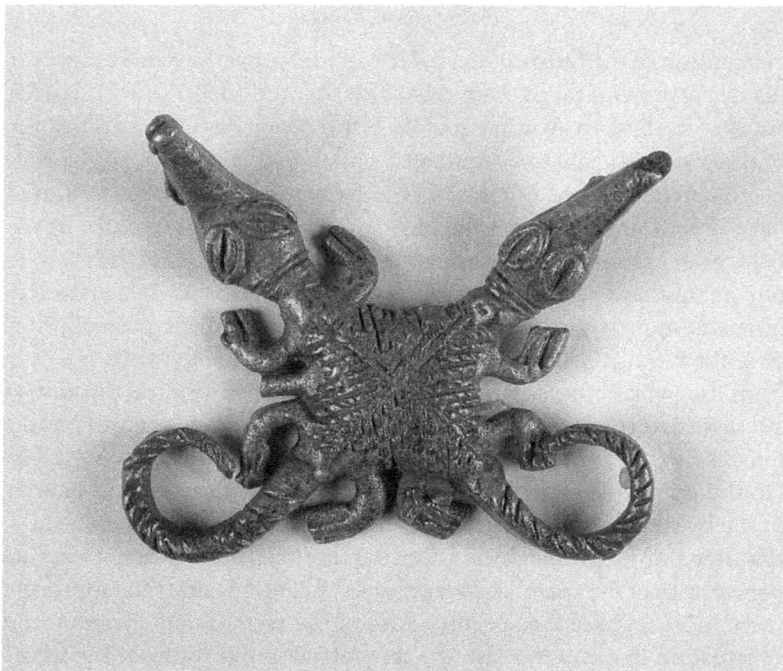

Figure 2. Akan weight in the form of a two-headed crocodile, eighteenth to late nineteenth century. Cast copper alloy. Smithsonian Institution, National Museum of African Art, gift of Mr. and Mrs. Robert Bevill, Mr. and Mrs. Alan Bresler, and Mr. and Mrs. Gilbert Schulman, 75-22-402.

Figure 3. Akan weight in the form of a coiled puff-adder snake biting a hornbill bird, eighteenth to late nineteenth century. Cast copper alloy. Smithsonian Institution, National Museum of African Art, gift of Mrs. Emil J. Arnold in memory of her husband, 75-3-318.

of gold dust as a measure and store of value. In a fine study of the little brass figures used as counterweights in gold weighing, Timothy F. Garrard writes:

> The primary purpose of goldweights was for use in trade, but some of the figurative weights could serve other purposes. They were occasionally worn by sick children to restore them to good health, and also as charms or amulets to bring good fortune or to preserve the wearer from harm. . . . In Ghana it is sometimes said that these weights could be sent to a person as "messages," the particular proverb associated with the form of the weight serving as a reminder of some debt or obligation, or as a warning, a piece of advice or a token of friendship.

Garrard quotes the following explanation of a local man:

> As a white man writes a letter, so do we send these weights to one another. [For example, the weight known as] the Crab's Claw. As you know, the crab is a very tenacious animal, and what he once holds with his claw he will never let go; even though it becomes severed from the body, it will still hold on, until crushed to atoms. If I were to send this to another chief, who had done me an injury, he would at once know what I meant, without a long palaver, and if he meant to compensate me, send me some suitable weight in return, if not, another crab's claw, then that meant that we would have to fight.[49]

The goldweights' function, then, was to relate incommensurable social values, those from traditional Akan culture as expressed in proverbs or traditional healing, with the newer market values introduced from outside. The brass figures constituted a new cultural territory reifying the possibility of movement across diverse value codes: the weights were singular productions of Akan artists (students of these objects often remark on the seeming infinity of different forms given to these figures) which could function in the market activity of gold weighing, could communicate the traditional wisdom of some native proverb, or could be endowed with power to protect or to heal sick individuals when worn upon the body.

A comparable example from the European side is the fifteenth-century *padrão dos Descobrimentos*.[50] In 1482, with the revival of Portuguese exploration of the African coast under John II, Diogo Cão made his first voyage, reaching the Congo and Angola for the first time. The *padrões* were monumental stone markers carried on board ship and set

Figure 4. Padrão of Saint Augustine, erected by Diogo Cão in 1482 on Cape Saint Mary, Angola, now located at the Lisbon Geographical Society. Image from Antônio Baião, Hernani Cidade, and Manuel Murias, eds., *Historia da expansão portuguesa no mundo* (Lisbon: Ática, 1937–40), vol. 1, between pages 374 and 375. Courtesy of Biblioteca Acadêmico Luiz Viana Filho.

up on newly discovered river mouths and capes both as claims of possession and as navigational landmarks.

In Prince Henry's time the voyagers had sometimes marked their discoveries with wooden crosses or carvings on trees, but these were perishable monuments. Diogo Cão's *padrões* were made of lioz, a kind of limestone marble quarried near Lisbon. A cross surmounted the pillar, but the most important part was the shaft, because on it would be found carved the discoverer's name, the date of discovery, and the name of the king sending out the expedition. Much of the *padrão* could be prepared before leaving home, but a few details, such as the date, had to be left until the time of erecting the pillar. Needless to say, it was planted firmly enough to withstand all foreseeable weather conditions.[51]

For example, at Cape Saint Mary in Angola, to mark the farthest south-ward point of his voyage, Cão set up the *padrão* de Santo Agostinho, a pillar with an inscribed square capital: the side facing north bore the arms of the royal house of Portugal, the west face situated the moment of erection in time reckoned in relation to the death of Christ, the south face situated the moment of the pillar's fixing in the time of the reign of John II, and the east side declared the act of fixing the pillar in place to be the deed of the Portuguese noble Diogo Cão. The *padrão* thus functioned to territorialize the codes of Christianity and Portuguese feudalism into the African landscape, thereby "reifying" this space in terms of these value codes through the singular noble act of founding by Cão. As in cases such as that of the *padrão* de S. Jorge set up at the mouth of the Congo, a pillar might come to be accepted as a mark of enduring Portuguese presence by local Africans; the Europeans understood that the Africans had come to regard the *padrão* as a "fetish."

Another historian records the fate of this particular "fetish": "[the *padrão*] of St. George at the mouth of the Congo served as a fetish until 1859 when some British seamen, attempting to remove it, dropped it overboard."[52]

I have concluded with these two examples—the Akan goldweights and the Portuguese *padrões*—simply to indicate some of the less familiar objects proper to the historical field of the fetish. Adequate discussion of these objects must await their treatment within the complex historical context which will be explored in the next chapter.

CHAPTER 2

The Origin of the Fetish

In the last chapter, I argued that the terms "fetish" and "fetishism" have marked a specific problem-idea for social theory—and spirituality—since the Enlightenment. Despite the use of this terminology in a variety of disciplines that claim no common theoretical ground—ethnography and the history of religion, Marxism and positivist sociology, psychoanalysis and the clinical psychiatry of sexual deviance, modernist aesthetics and continental philosophy—there is a common configuration of themes among the various discourses about fetishism. Four themes consistently inform the idea of the fetish: (1) the untranscended materiality of the fetish; "matter," or the material object, is viewed as the locus of religious activity or psychic investment; (2) the radical historicality of the fetish's origin; arising in a singular event fixing together otherwise heterogeneous elements, the identity and power of the fetish consists in its ongoing capacity to repeat this singular process of fixation and focus, along with the resultant effect; (3) the dependence of the fetish for its meaning and value upon a particular order of social relations, which it in turn reinforces; and (4) the active relation of the fetish object to the living person (self and body) of an individual; a kind of external organ directed by active powers outside the affected person's conscious will, the fetish represents a subversion of the ideal of the autonomously determined self. (That is, "fetishism" presumes the self as necessarily and in essence embodied.)

If the history of the idea of fetishism that I am exploring has any interest, it is due to the appropriation of this word as theoretical term by many of the major social thinkers of the nineteenth century (a "long" nineteenth century extending from Kant to Freud, that is, from Enlightenment to Modernism). The human sciences that constituted themselves in this period (sociology, anthropology, psychology) did so in part by taking a position in the ongoing debate over the history and nature of religion proposed in the theory of fetishism. This theoretical term was well established in European intellectual discourse by 1800, having been formulated during the period of the Encyclopedists (the 1750s and 1760s). A study of the theoretical use of "fetish" and "fetishism" should illuminate in a fresh manner the mentality of nineteenth-century cosmopolitan social theorists and the distinctive problematic expressed in their arguments regarding materialism, history, value, and culture.

In this chapter, I trace the origin of the distinctive notion of the fetish. The eighteenth-century intellectuals who articulated the theory of fetishism encountered this notion in descriptions of "Guinea" contained in such popular voyage collections as Ramusio's *Il viaggio di Giovan Leone e le navigazioni* (1550), de Bry's *India Orientalis* (1597), Purchas's *Hakluytus Posthumus* (1625), Churchill's *Collection of Voyages and Travels* (1732), Astley's *A New General Collection of Voyages and Travels* (1746), and Prévost's *Histoire générale des voyages* (1748). The configuration of themes and explanatory concepts peculiar to the idea of the fetish originated on the coast of West Africa—especially along the coast from present-day Ghana to Nigeria—during the sixteenth and seventeenth centuries. The idea first appears in the pidgin word *fetisso*. Basically a middleman's word, it brought a wide array of African objects and practices under a category which, for all its misrepresentation of cultural facts, enabled the formation of more or less noncoercive commercial relations between members of bewilderingly different cultures. Out of this practical discourse about *fetissos* and "fetish-oaths," Protestant merchants visiting the coast elaborated a general explanation of African social order as being based on the principles underlying the worship of *fetissos*.

The alienness of African culture, in particular its resistance to "rational" trade relations, was explained in terms of the Africans' supposed irrational propensity to personify material (and especially European technological) objects, thereby revealing a false understanding of natural causality. A complementary principle said to characterize Africans was their supposed attribution of causal relation to random association. This intellectual error of understanding causality through principles of chance encounter and personification (more generally, anthropomorphization) was considered responsible for the Africans' supposedly distorted manner of valuing material objects, their superstitious religious practices, and their perverse social order which (especially after the emergence of the African slave-trading "gunpowder empires" in the late seventeenth century) was perceived by Europeans to be based on fear, credulity and violence. The fundamental question that determined both the perception of the problem and the terms of its explanation concerned how material objects as such could embody any sort of religious, aesthetic, sexual, or social value at all (i.e., any value not expressing the material object's "real" instrumental and market values).

The idea of the fetish originated in a mercantile intercultural space created by the ongoing trade relations between cultures so radically different as to be mutually incomprehensible. It is proper to neither West African nor Christian European culture. Given that our interest in the idea concerns its significance for European social theory, in this book I focus on the distinctiveness of the notion in European discourse. (I am not concerned here with the relation of the fetish idea to the actual conceptions of West African culture.) I do this by tracing the etymology of the word "fetish" itself from Latin *facticius* to Portuguese *feitiço*, attending in particular to its usage in Christian theology and jurisprudence. By considering Christian notions of idolatry, superstition, and witchcraft, it will be easier to show the novelty of the idea of the *fetisso* which developed on the West African coast. While the notion of the *fetisso* centered on the concepts of personified things and chance conjuncture, Christian notions of witchcraft centered on concepts of manufactured resemblance and voluntary contract. I conclude by examining three phases of the development of the novel idea of the fetish: the coming of the Portuguese to West Africa in the fifteenth century and their initial application of *feitiço* and *feitiçaria* to African objects and practices; the development of the pidgin *fetisso* by middlemen groups outside the Portuguese empire during the sixteenth century; and the treatment of the term in Protestant—especially Dutch—texts in the seventeenth century, culminating in the influential 1704 account of Willem Bosman.

Facticius in Christian Theology: Idolatry and Superstition

The terms *feitiço*, *feiticeiro*, and *feitiçaria*, which were part of the vocabulary of the fifteenth-century Portuguese who sailed to West Africa, referred, respectively, to the objects, persons, and practice proper to witchcraft. To understand the Christian idea of witchcraft, it is necessary to consider its relation to the notions of idolatry and superstition as these were elaborated within the essential ideological tension determined by Christianity's central concepts of Creation, Incarnation, and Salvation. The Christian theory of witchcraft, as it related to fetish objects, was determined by theological explanations regarding the false sacramental objects of superstition. These explanations were integrated with only partial success into the Church's general theory of idolatry, whose logic required that material "idols" have the status of fraudulent manufactured resemblances. The descriptive inadequacy of the discourse of "idolatry" led to the development of a distinct terminology of witchcraft (*fechicei-ria* in Iberian languages of the time) in the Middle Ages.

Since I am also tracing the etymology of the word "fetish" itself, I begin with its development prior to its entry into Christian discourse about idolatry.

The pan-European word whose English version is "fetish" derives lin-guistically from the Latin *facticius* or *factitius*, an adjective formed from the past participle of the verb *facere*, "to make." The past participle *factum*, of course, means "made." *Facticius* was formed by joining the past participial stem *fact-* to the adjectival suffix of condition, quality, or state *-icius*, which is an enlarged form of the usual adjectival suffix *-ic*, and seems to have been used to stress the enduring, substantial, or final character of the completed action named by the verb; the suffix was also added to certain substantives denoting building materials—*caementicum* means "made of *caementum*" (a crude cement) and *latericus* "constructed of brickwork." These terms, like *facticius*, appear to have developed in Roman mercantile discourse pertaining to the manufac-tured commodity.

The adjective *facticius* seems to have gained currency as a term in Ro-man commercial language around the Augustan period—so, at least, its early appearance in Pliny (c. 23–79 CE) would indicate. In Pliny's *Natu-ral History*, *facticius* means "manufactured." It characterizes "man-made" commodities in contrast to goods produced through purely natural pro-cesses (that is, goods merely collected and sold without being shaped or otherwise altered by human effort). For instance, Pliny distinguishes between two types of ladanum (an aromatic gum): the first type, from Arabia, he terms "natural" (*terrenum*) since the gum was produced from certain plants which at times dripped sap onto the ground below, where the fluid coagulated and could be collected in solid form. These dusty lumps of Arabian ladanum were distinguished from the cakes made in Cyprus, where the juice was sweated out of the plants that had been rolled into bundles and tied with strings. Pliny terms these Cyprian cakes "artificial" (*facticium* rather than *terrenum*).[1]

In a slightly different usage, the adjective designated the character of the product itself rather than the fact of its artificial production. Natural and manufactured varieties of the same commodity might differ in cer-tain particulars: for example, natural ladanum was friable, Pliny tells us, whereas artificial ladanum was tough. Difference in qualitative appear-ance could mean difference in substantive value as well: "some people distinguish in two-fold fashion between the mined [*fossile*] flower of copper and the manufactured [*facticium*], the latter being paler than the former and as much inferior in quality as in color."[2] Here a difference between natural and artificial production causes differences in appearances (color) of the thing produced, and this visible difference is itself the index of a difference in value (or "virtue" in that word's original sense) between the two varieties of the good.

But if it is possible, in such cases and more generally, for appearance to be the index of value of a useful substance, it is consequently possible for an unscrupulous entrepreneur to "manufacture" a commodity, not in its substance, but in its counterfeited appearance. That is, in commodity exchange, appearance as the signifier of useful value can become a value in itself in the special case of commercial fraud. The final meaning of *facticius* found in Pliny pertains to such cases. In discussing the reddish "flower of salt" normally found along the Nile or on the surface of certain springs, Pliny cautions: "It is adulterated too and colored by red ochre, or usually by ground crockery; this sham is detected by water, which washes out the artificial [*facticium*] color, while the genuine [*verus*] is only removed by oil."[3] Here *facticium* means "artificial" in the sense of "materially altered by human effort in order to deceive"—that is, "factitious" as opposed to "genuine" (*verus*). The morally neutral opposition between "man-made" and "naturally produced" now becomes a valuative contrast between "natural" (in this sense of "authentic" and "true") and "artificial" (in the sense of "unnatural" and "deliberately false").

In short, in its original commercial usage *facticius* had three distinct but related senses. In its simplest sense, the word meant "manufactured" as opposed to "naturally formed." Somewhat more complex was the use of *facticius* to distinguish the "artificial" from the "natural" varieties of some commodity. The second sense of *facticius* indicated an equivalence in substance or function among the varieties, but a difference in manner of production and also in quality and value. Finally, the word could mean "factitious" or "fraudulent" as opposed to "genuine"—the "unnatural" fabrication of appearance, of the signifiers of exchange value, without the substance or use value which the appearance promised.

The nuances of meaning in the word embody some of the necessary distinctions and categories of the commercial mind; it was with this dialectical set of meanings that *facticius* was subsequently appropriated into Christian discourse by Tertullian and Augustine.

Outside mercantile discourse, *facticius* was not a familiar word in preChristian Roman culture. From the concordances, we learn that it was not a term in general use—politicians such as Julius Caesar did not employ it; nor did historians such as Livy, Tacitus, or Suetonius; nor poets such as Virgil, Horace, or Ovid; nor moralists and rhetoricians such as Cicero, Seneca, or Quintilian. Nor was it a theoretically significant term in the special usages of classical materialist philosophy, whether the atomistic materialism of the Epicureans or the corporealist materialism of the Stoics. Given the new significance the term takes on in Christian religious discourse, it is especially worth noting that *facticius* is not the word Cicero employs when he distinguishes in his *De Divinatione* between natural kinds of divination (such as occur through dreams, necromancy, and prophecy by the inspired or possessed) and artificial (*artificiosum*) forms of divination such as augury.[4] Nor is that most famous deceptive cult object of classical literature, the Trojan horse, characterized as *facticius*; that "fraudulent device" (*dolus*) which the *fabricator* Epeos built guided by the *divina arte* of Athena would be termed *artificiosus* rather than *facticius*.[5] *Artificiosus* means "skillfully made"; it lacks the specific emphasis on making through human (as opposed to divine) power, and on the material status of the thing worked upon, which *facticius* connotes. It is just these connotations which make the term occasionally useful to Christian writers of the third and fourth centuries, the period in which the Latin vocabulary for Christian ideology and the essential doctrinal and liturgical components of the Catholic Christian Church were developed and institutionalized.

The basic ideas in *facticius* appear in a new and radically different light when displaced into the Christian cosmology of a God-created natural world, a man- (and devil-) willed fall into sin, and true ecclesiastical and false idolatrous paths to salvation. We find the term used by Christian writers in three contexts. First, in theological discussions of the natural human body as divine image, whose willful alteration constitutes idolatry. (That is, as the one material object in some sense bearing a nonfraudulent resemblance to God. Given the fundamental Christian beliefs in a single transcendent personal divinity, a material Creation where evil tends to rule, and the saving Incarnation of Christ—the question of how the material human body could in any sense be a divine image was a particularly vexing problem, as illustrated by early Christian heresies. The fourth-century Audians, referring to Genesis 1:26–27, held that God himself had the human form; they were condemned for anthropomorphism. The Gnostic Valentinians, on the other hand, argued that Christ was a purely spiritual being with no real body, yet with real humanity. The Marcianists, holding that matter was worthless, denied the resurrection of the body. The Apollinarians and the Paulianists held that Christ did have a body and was thus a mere man but that the impersonal power of God's divine word dwelled within him. The most important heresy, Arianism, claimed that Christ assumed a human body but not a human soul and, as a created being, was a secondary divinity inferior to God. The Adamite sects of early modern Europe illustrate the persistence of such issues.) Second, we find the term *facticius* used in arguments concerning the human soul as an immaterial substance which is the only locus of nonsuperstitious spiritual activity. And finally we find it in discussions of the simultaneously personal and ecclesial status of legitimate sacramental objects. The general theory of idolatry was articulated in the course of resolving problems relating to these three topics of body, soul, and sacramental object, problems both created and solved by the fundamental Catholic tenets regarding Creation, Incarnation, and ecclesiastical Salvation.

The first of these topics appears in Tertullian's *De Spectaculis* when he denounces bodybuilding and the spectacle of wrestling as idolatry because these activities attempt to produce "an artificial body so as to surpass God's work" (*facticii corporis ut plasticam dei supergressa*).[6] Tertullian situates the problem involved within the framework of Christian creationist cosmology: since God created the natural world, including Adam's body, and gave all natural things to man for him to use, how can any use of any natural object be other than good? Tertullian responds that simply because certain material objects can be used to commit murder, this does not mean murder is good or permissible—indeed, God made a commandment to the contrary.

> Moreover, who but God, the Maker of the world, put in it gold, brass, silver, ivory, wood and all other materials used in the manufacture of idols [*fabricandis idolis material*]? Yet has He done this that men may set up a worship in opposition to Himself? On the contrary, idolatry is in His eyes the crowning sin. What is there offensive to God which is not God's? But in offending Him, it ceases to be His; and in ceasing to be His, it is in His eyes an offending thing. Man himself, guilty as he is of every iniquity, is not only a work of God—he is His image [*opus dei, verum etiam imago est*], and yet both in soul and body he has severed himself from his maker.[7]

Tertullian argues that any misuse of the material objects of the natural world constitutes idolatry (in effect murdering one's soul), even though the constituent elements of an idolatrous act of fabrication are not themselves evil. Later theologians would elaborate a theory of the divine status of "the law of nature"; willful interference in a natural process or willful alteration of a bodily form otherwise determined by natural type was held to be sacrilege. The only truth of which a natural body was capable was the achievement of a form bearing a true resemblance to its natural species type.

In Christian theory, reasoning about material bodies consistently appealed to the principle of resemblance. Unlike the Greek philosophic tradition, Judeo-Christian discourse holds resemblance to be an essentially material relation and as such inherently improper for representing spiritual models. The resemblance of a material individual to its eternal species form may, as in Greek thought, serve as the measure of the degree to which a given individual succeeds in embodying the virtues of its type. But the Christian distinction between the material human body (which is merely matter and not essentially human—but which somehow "resembles" God) and the spiritual substance of the immaterial soul (which acts voluntarily out of itself, not the will-less body) makes the idea of manufactured material resemblance essentially a negative one. There is no Christian Daedalus; skillful making is not a divine art. Christianity replaces the idea of such inspired artifice with the idea of mere manufacture in order to distinguish all human craft from the true divine mode of production: creation. The "unmotivatedness" of the act of creation is conceived on the logocentric model of free verbal utterance, while created matter and physical manufacture are assigned to the contrary principle of resemblance. In Genesis 1:26–27, God says "Let us make man in our own image and likeness" (*Faciamus hominem ad imaginem et similitudinem nostrum*), and "God created man in His own resemblance" (*Et creavit Deus hominem ad imaginem suam*).[8] Here, resemblance is the relation Adam bears to God, whose creation of Adam through a spoken command to be (as in Genesis 1:3 when "God said [*dixit*], 'Let there be [*fiat*] light,' and there was [*facta est*] light") was neither an act of generation nor of manufacture. Man, on the other hand, is capable only of the manufacture of *facticii dei*, and these are forbidden. The God of the burning bush appears to Moses without any "likeness" (*similitudinem*) in order to discourage idolatry: "Lest ye corrupt yourselves and make you a graven image [*sculptam*], likeness [*similitudinem*], or any image of male or female [*imaginem masculi vel feminae*]" (Deuteronomy 4:15–16). This latter phrase again indicates that the human image bears a special relation of resemblance to God. Humans can manufacture *facticii* images as idols, but they cannot endow them with any true relation to God in the manner that the divine resemblance of Adam's body (by its unity with the soul) is a true relation. Humans can manufacture but not create, and they cannot endow a body with a soul. Hence Isaiah writes, "for they were not gods [*deos*], but the work of men's hands [*opera manuum hominum*]" (Isaiah 37:19). The only instance of human ability to make a material object embody a spiritual substance is the Eucharist (and the power behind this ability is the divine power of Christ); this is neither manufacture nor creation but "transubstantiation"—that is, the original material substance of the object worked on does not remain, at least according to Catholic doctrine. Luther's notion, of course, was precisely that of "consubstantiation" in opposition to the notion of transubstantiation. In the 1520s Zwingli and the Swiss theologians adopted the more radical view that denied the power of the Eucharist entirely (sometimes referred to as the doctrine of the "real absence"). To reject the power of saints and sacramental objects as mediating agencies was to challenge the authority of the Church itself as the legitimate earthly agent of mediation between man and God. This was precisely the theological significance of the iconoclastic dimension of the Protestant Reformation, introduced by Zwingli and Calvin. In his commentary on the commandment in Exodus 34:17, "And thou shalt make no molten gods" (*Et deos fusiles ne feceris tibi*), Augustine interprets "molten gods" to be a synecdoche (*locutio est a parte totum significans*) for the true genius of "images or any sort whatever of manufactured gods" (*genus simulacrorum aut qualiumcumque facticiorum deorum*).[9] Idols and all nonecclesial sacramental objects were characterized as at once semblances ("images," or *simulacra*) and manufactured (*facticii*). As "images," they were mere external forms, likenesses, lacking essential truth and inner spirituality. As *facticii*, they were purposefully altered material bodies, and, from a spiritual viewpoint, vain acts of the will.

Idolatry, in the narrow sense, was defined as the humanly willed manufacture and worship of artificial varieties of sacramental objects whose true essence was spiritual fraud. Augustine interpreted "idol" to mean any manufactured cultic image not addressed to the true God. Tertullian had already proposed a far more general significance for the category of idolatry. Since salvation in this world could only occur through the Church, Tertullian argued, there could be no greater wrong than actions which ran counter to Catholic forms of worship by setting up cults of idols. So important was this that "idolatry" became the general term for all deviant religious activity:

> The principal crime of the human race, the highest guilt charged upon the world, the whole procuring cause of judgment, is idolatry. . . . The essence of fraud, I take it, is that any should seize what is another's, or refuse to another his due; and, of course, fraud toward men is the greatest crime. Well, idolatry does fraud to God [*idololatria fraudem deo facit*] by refusing to Him, and conferring on others, His honors. . . . In idolatry all crimes are detected, and in all crimes idolatry.

But even otherwise, since all faults savour of opposition to God, but there is nothing which savours of opposition to God which is not assigned to demons and unclean spirits [*daemoniis et immundis spiritibus*] whose property idols [*idola*] are.[10]

All crimes, indeed, all wrong actions, were thus a species of Tertullian's new Christian supercategory of idolatry. Wrong deeds were idolatry because, at the least, they violated the will and commandment of God, and, at the most, they served the will of some false god, one of the fallen angels or their chief, the devil. The fabrication of a material cult object in order to worship a false god (whose "property" the material idol object became) was thus merely the most exemplary instance of various types of wrong acts—all deviation from God's will and law—which could rightly be classed as demonically inspired idolatry.

The final theoretical elaboration of the idea of idolatry concerned the inappropriateness of material bodies as such to be the medium of devotional activity. Surely the most vivid illustration of this argument was Augustine's discussion of eunuchry. In this discussion, he used the term *facticius* to distinguish false acts of faith (which take as their object part of the world of material bodies, specifically, the sexual organs of the human body) from the voluntary acts of true faith (such as renouncing sexual desire), which proceed from and affect the soul. In commenting on Christ's distinction in Matthew 19:12 between three types of eunuchs, Augustine labeled *nativum*, he who was born a eunuch (belonging to the order of generation); *facticium*, he who was physically made a eunuch by men (belong to the order of manufacture, of human artifice); and *voluntarium*, he who had made himself a eunuch for the kingdom of heaven (belonging to the order of creative action, of free will).[11] Augustine explained this latter good form of eunuchism to mean "the youths of both sexes who have extirpated from their hearts the desire of marriage."[12] By a purely voluntary and spiritual act, such good eunuchs thereby transferred desire from the sexual organ of the physical body to the soul, the organ of free will and faith. The *facticius* type of eunuch, who defeated sexual desire by direct action upon the material body, rather than by means of the soul, thus omitted the voluntary component necessary in all redeeming acts of true faith. It was precisely the absence of any material effect that testified to the authentic spirituality of an act of faith: the natural body, the material image, most properly remained unaltered from the form determined for it by God in the original Creation.

The general theory of idolatry elaborated the meaning of the first two commandments in accordance with the cosmological implications of Creation by a transcendent divinity. Willful alteration of material bodies

for religious purposes was idolatrous insofar as it disfigured their God-
given natural forms, turning them into images of a fraudulent spirituality; moreover, the realm of matter as such was an improper medium for
acts of worship.

The problem of the *corpus facticium* was generated by the cosmological
core of Christian ideology and was resolved by the general theory of
idolatry. The issue of the *anima facticia* concerned a problem in Christian ontology, specifically the problem of the substance of the human
soul, and was resolved by subsuming the idea of superstition under the
general category of idolatry.

Throughout the history of Christian theology, conceptual problems
regarding the incarnate status of man—as an embodied spiritual agent in
a cosmos where spirit and matter are completely distinct substances—
have been resolved through interpretations of the nature and powers of
the soul. In his debate in 392 CE with his former friend, the Manichean
Fortunatus, Augustine denies that the human soul can itself be God,
since it is sinful whereas God is not. When asked from what substance
the soul is made if not out of God's own divine substance, he replies:

> I deny the soul to be the substance of God as I deny that it is God:
> but nevertheless [I say] that it is out of God its author because it has
> been made by God [*ex Deo auctore esse, quia facta est a Deo*]. He who
> makes is one thing, that which is made is another [*Aliud est qui fecit,
> aliud quod facit*]. He who made is wholly incapable of corruption;
> that which He made, however, is wholly incapable of being the equal
> of He who made it.[13]

It is to this argument that Fortunatus responds: "I did not say the soul
was similar to God [*similem Deo*]. But rather I said the soul is made
[*factitiam esse animam*], and is nothing other than God; I ask whence
God took the substance of the soul [i.e., if not from His own divine
substance]?" Augustine responds, of course, that God created the substance of the human soul out of nothing (*de nihilo fecerit*).[14] The human
soul, according to Christian doctrine, is not manufactured (*facticius*)
out of the material of God's divine substance but is a distinct substance
created ex nihilo with its own human nature distinct from God's divine
nature (hence the mystery of Christ's embodiment of both divine and
human natures in one). God, then, created not only the natural world
of matter, which includes Adam's body as the divine image, but also the
human soul, a distinct substance which was neither manufactured from
preexisting (divine or spiritual) material, nor generated out of God's

own substance (only Christ, the Son of God, bears a genealogical relation to God), but rather created ex nihilo as a distinct type of entity specific to humans.

The human soul consists of created spiritual substance whose essence is to be united with the material body of the individual human being. Angels—including the fallen angels called "gods" by the heathens and known to be demons by Christians—also consist of created spiritual substance, but this is distinguished from that of humans by its lack of relation to a material body. Since the soul is understood to be the principle of life, it becomes necessary as well to distinguish between the human soul and the souls of other animate embodied beings. In the Christian worldview, plants and animals do not have immortal souls; being animate, they must have souls, but the substance of these souls is corporeal rather than spiritual. "For while the souls of brutes are produced by some power of the body, the human soul is produced by God."[15] As the forms of their bodies' life-function, such souls are subject to the principle of generation and decay that rules all beings which exist in nature. Nature is a region of creation logically distinct from that of spirits with free wills; the substance of the latter cannot be material because, even though such souls are created, they are also eternal.

While arguments about material bodies were guided by the trope of resemblance, arguments concerning the soul appealed to the category of the free action of faith. Whereas in Neoplatonism the soul united with the godhead through reflection on its substantial resemblance to God until it realized its status as in essence an emanation of the One, Christian salvation unites a man's soul and God through the radical act of the soul's free will, which constitutes the fact of faith, along with the equally freely given grace God may bestow on a human soul. In Platonic thought, resemblance expresses the relation between material entities and their eternal ideal forms. In Christian thought, the logic of image and resemblance explains the truth within the material half of Creation only (with the single exception of the human body, which is in God's image because of its unity with divine reality through having as its soul an eternal spiritual substance). In Christian theology, resemblance neither expresses the true relation between the earthly and the divine, nor does it describe the logic of the spiritual half of Creation (which is explained by a logic of identify and voluntary relation—even notions of the "imitation" of Christ are based on the idea of enacted identification rather than mimetic reflection). Faith is the act of the soul's free will (analogous to God's acts of creation in its undetermined freedom), whereas the body's acts can at most manufacture a semblance or simulacrum of spiritual action. In discussions about the proper spiritual activity of hu-

man souls, the concept of idolatry was extended to cover any religious
practice which attended to external forms rather than inner faith. It was
in this way that the category of idolatry came to be related to traditional
conceptions of superstition (*superstitio*).

The theory of idolatry concerns the objects of sacrilegious worship;
the theory of superstition concerns the forms of worship caused by improper religious attitudes. Specifically, *superstitio* referred to that religious sensibility which produced exaggerated or excessive, and hence
superfluous, cult practices. In *De Natura Deorum*, Cicero mentions as
the traditional example of superstition: "Persons who spend whole
days in prayer and sacrifice to ensure that their children should outlive them."[16] Since *religio* referred to a person's sense of how rightly to
achieve a true bond with divine power, the fundamental definition of
superstitio, formulated by Lactantius, was *"religio veri cultus est, superstitio falsi"* (religion is the cult of the true [God], superstition that of the
false).[17]

Elaborating this idea in *De Doctrina Christiana*, Augustine argues that
false religious attitudes could lead to two distinct forms of idolatrous
worship: "The arrangements made by men for the making and worshipping of idols are superstitious, pertaining as they do either to the worship of what is created or some part of it as God, signs and leagues with
devils [*consultationes et pacta quaedam significationum cum daemonibus*],
such, for example, as are employed in the magical arts [*magicarum ar-
tium*]."[18] Augustine goes on to distinguish between these idolatrous
forms of superstition and those which came to be termed "vain observances" (vain in the sense of superstitious practices which cannot bring
about the intended effect). In its full development, the Christian theory
of superstition distinguished four basic forms of superstitious worship:
superstitiously exaggerated practices within the true religious worship
of the Church; idolatrous worship (i.e., formal cults) of false gods; and
two types of noncultic superstition (divination to gain knowledge of the
future and "vain observances" to bring about good effects or ward off
bad ones). Divination was understood always to have for its object demonic spirits whose oracular utterances were sought. Intercourse with
demons was conceived in terms of verbal rather than physical action:
incantation, invocation, conversation, oracle, and pact. Such essentially
verbal action was voluntary in a manner, in the Christian perspective,
proper to spiritual rather than material activity. Christian logocentrism
attributed all voluntary action to immaterial spirit. "Vain observances,"
on the other hand, were conceived as physical actions which sought
means whereby humans could interfere with the processes and laws of
nature. The term "magic" might be applied to either of these latter two

classes insofar as they claimed to be systematic procedures based on knowledge (*ars*); in Christian usage, "magic" almost invariably implied demonic invocation.

The degree to which vain observances constituted idolatry was something of a gray area (a "hard case"); for some, the absence of explicit invocation of demons suggested that the simple superstitious customs of the lower classes were to be tolerated; for others, the superstitious search for nonnatural power other than the power of God was idolatrous and damnable—even if no demons were invoked, vain observances were forms of religious self-deception, and the true author of all spiritual fraud was the devil. Whatever position a particular thinker took, the material objects involved in such superstitious practices were always understood in terms of illegitimate sacramental objects.

The distinction between the immaterial acts of the soul proper to true faith and the merely external acts of superstitious idolatry was theoretically grounded in orthodox doctrine regarding the spiritual substance of the human soul. This view of faith might seem to imply that only aniconic forms of worship were legitimate (a position taken by "protestants" from Adelphius to Muhammad to Calvin). However, almost from the beginning of the Church, cults of relics and saints were accepted. Gregory the Great's later affirmation of the educational value of images as the "books of the illiterate poor" authorized the use of figurative art for its anagogic value. Moreover, a material object became the focus of the central sacramental ritual of the Church itself. For this reason, a clear theory regarding true and false sacramental objects was needed. Such a theory was achieved by extending the notion of divine incarnation to the institution of the Church.

Christ was the sole incarnation of God on earth and, through his sacrifice, the only means to Salvation. However, at the Last Supper he endowed his disciples with the divine power of Salvation and the ability to confer this power on others. Thus began the unique priestly lineage who form the officers of the Church; by reference to the bread of the Last Supper, the wafer of the Eucharist celebrates the unique fact of Christ's incarnation and reenacts the power of the Church to save human souls which flowed from it. As became perfectly evident during the Protestant Reformation, to deny divine power to any material object per se was to deny the rightful power of the Catholic Church as the mediating agent of human Salvation in the material world.

While the bread of the Eucharist is the principal sacramental object of the Church, there are many other sacred objects (small crosses, medals of saints, wedding rings, etc.) which, through the power of the Church, are considered to legitimately embody the power to bless and bestow grace on the user.[19] The Christian sacramental object, with its real efficacy, is distinguished from the sacramental objects of superstition and idolatry in two essential ways: the necessary voluntary component of personal faith, and the empowering of the object through the intercessory agency of the Church. In particular, it is only through the Church that material objects might become vehicles of faith and divine power.

All of these sacramental objects are, of course, manufactured objects (wafers, crosses, rings, images of saints); none are unfabricated natural things or places or animals. However, the act through which the Church endows these with sacred power is distinct from the act of their material manufacture. Anyone can manufacture an object intended for worship, but only the priestly lineage of the Church can empower them for the community of the faithful. All other such objects are idols (*idola*), a term used by Jerome in his late fourth-century translation of the Bible for a host of Hebrew terms. (The general category of the "idol" was itself a product of this formative Latin period of Christian ideology.)

As already discussed, the error of idolatry was understood to involve either the vain worship of mere material things and external forms, or the use of a material idol as the medium through which demonic spirits were invoked and conversed with. The degree to which the general conception of idolatry should be extended to "vain" superstitious practices was debatable. In an influential passage, Augustine distinguished between practices that were clearly damnable, such as magical consultations of demons by haruspices and augurs, and "the thousands of inane [*popular*] customs" (*millia inanissimarum observationum*), such as kicking something that passed between two friends who were walking along together. The text from *On Christian Doctrine* reads:

> To this class [of superstitious human institutions] belong, but with a bolder touch of deception, the books of the haruspices and augurs [*aruspicum et augurum libri*]. In this class we must also place all amulets and cures [*ligaturae et remedia*] which the medical art condemns, whether these consist in incantations [*praecantationibus*], or in marks which they call characters, or in handing and tying on certain articles or even dancing in a certain fashion, not with reference to the condition of the body, but to certain signs hidden or manifest; and these remedies they call by the less offensive name of *physica*, so as to appear not to be engaged in superstitious observances, but to be taking advantage of the forces of nature. Examples of these are ear-rings on the top of each ear, or the rings of ostrich bone on the fingers, or telling you when you hiccup to hold your left thumb in your right hand.
>
> To these we may add thousands of the most frivolous practices

[*inanissimarum observationum*], that are to be observed if any part of the body should jump, or if, when friends are walking arm-in-arm, a stone, or a dog, or a boy, should come between them. . . . To this class too belong the following rules: To tread upon the threshold when you go out in front of the house, to go back to bed if any one should sneeze when you are putting on your slippers; to return home if you stumble when going to a place; when your clothes are eaten by mice, to be more frightened at the prospect of coming misfortune than to be grieved by your present loss.[20]

All of his examples of "inane observations" involve superstitious performances (as opposed to productions of material objects); material objects like "ligatures and remedies" [*ligaturae atque remedia*] and various rings worn to assure health and safety are condemned as much as augury and incantation. Augustine denies the claim that such objects honestly try to take advantage of "the forces of nature"; since they appeal to powers other than those of nature, they are as damnable as are explicit attempts to invoke demons. Such a position begs the question of what powers were in fact contained in "the forces of nature." It was in this conceptually obscure area that the words *facticioso* and *factura* emerged in the Middle Ages as designations of certain superstitious practices and the objects they employed.

Feitiçaria in Christian Law: Witchcraft and Magic

Although based on the categories of idolatry and superstition just examined, the discourse about witchcraft and the word *feitiçaria* itself were developed (or, at least, adopted) by Christian law rather than Christian theology. Theological discourse was never able to conceptualize "vain observances" satisfactorily within its logic of material resemblance and voluntary verbal invocation and agreement. Nevertheless, insofar as any coherent theory of witchcraft was elaborated in the late Middle Ages, it was attempted in terms of idol worship and demonic pact. The constant appearance of conjunctive phrases like "idolatry and witchcraft" (*idolatria y feitiçari*) in the Portuguese voyage accounts and "superstition and witchcraft" (*supersticiones y hechicerias*) in sixteenth-century Spanish treatises on witchcraft indicates the conceptual failure of the theory of idolatry to determine the discourse about "witchcraft" (much less to explain the actual phenomena being designated).

There are three distinct phases in the history of Christian witchcraft law. The first consists of the laws promulgated under the first Christian emperors in the fourth and fifth centuries which were eventually collected in the Theodosian Code. The second consists of medieval European laws—at first episcopal laws and later, after the revival of civil law in the twelfth century, canon and royal law. The final phase is characterized by the granting of jurisdiction over witchcraft cases to the Inquisition (enabled by the identification of witchcraft as in itself heresy) and the adoption of scholastic inquisitorial ideas about witchcraft by secular courts.[21] The relevance of this final phase for the notion of *feitiçaria* carried to West Africa is minimal.

The Theodosian Code, the first Christian code of law, was promulgated in 438 CE. Several sections of the code record laws regulating religious and magical practices. Study of these laws helps situate the formulation of Christian theologians in the context of the struggles over religious politics in the period from Constantine to Theodosius. For instance, the theological interpretation of the gods as evil demons in effect delegitimated the public cults and traditional religious authority of non-Christianized Roman senators. Indeed this class was the principal object of Theodosian laws penalizing superstitious magical practices. (Laws regulating heresy were put in a different section of the code, since conflicts with "pagans" and conflicts with "heretics" were distinct issues.)[22]

The relevant section is entitled *De maleficis et mathematicis et ceteris similibus* (On magicians and astrologers and other like criminals).[23] Most of these laws concerned practices categorized as "divination" (*ars divinanda*) and were condemned as *maleficia*—literally meaning "evil deeds," hence the English word "malefactor." *Maleficia* is usually translated as "magic," "sorcery," or "witchcraft" because the term carries the implication that evil acts involve the supernatural agency of malignant spirits. As a legal category, *maleficia* entailed the religious crime of sacrilege. Under this category we find *augures*,[24] *haruspices*,[25] *sacerdotes*,[26] *harioli* and *vates*,[27] *mathematicii*,[28] *Chaldaei et magi*, interpreters of dreams, and various other practitioners of magical divinatory arts. (When the tolerant emperor Valentinian wished to permit haruspicy, he did so by denying that it was properly classed among the *maleficia* because it fell outside the category of religious superstition [*religionem genus*] and hence should not be considered sacrilege.)

While Theodosian religious laws were primarily concerned with regulating or forbidding the cult practices of the principal rivals of Christian political power, whose religious organs were the augurs and the haruspices, the category of *maleficium* covered more than just crimes of divination. Vain observances, too, might be sacrilegious, and there is one law of Constantine directed at such superstitious practices among the lower classes. This law draws a distinction between harmful magical practices and noncriminal "remedies" and fertility rites:

> The science of those men who are equipped with magic arts [*magicis artibus*] and who are revealed to have worked against the safety of men of have turned virtuous minds to lust shall be punished and deservedly avenged by the most severe laws. But remedies [*remedia*] sought for human bodies shall not be involved in criminal accusation, nor the assistance that is innocently employed in rural districts in order that rains may not be feared for the ripe grape harvests or that the harvests may not be shattered by the stones of ruinous hail, since by such devices no person's safety or reputation is injured, but by their action they bring it about that the divine gifts [of nature] and the labors of men are not destroyed.[29]

Augustine's theology condemned "remedies" and vain observances as superstitious appeals to unnatural powers. Early Christian law, however, denied their status as criminal sacrilege due to the absence of harm to "safety or reputation."

The Theodosian Code contains several lists of the highest, most unpardonable crimes; these lists include the distinct terms *veneficium* and *maleficium*. *Veneficium* refers to the art of poisoning, and more generally to sorcery exemplified by the use of herbs and magically powerful physical substances in the making of potions and philters to achieve some specific effect on another person (death, love). In translating the second book of Kings (9:22), Jerome uses *veneficia* to refer to the "witchcrafts" of Jezebel. The Vulgate's general term for what the King James Bible terms "witchcraft," however, is *maleficia*.[30]

Pharaoh's magicians in Exodus 7:11 and 8:18–19 are also termed *maleficos*. However, when a passage required a distinction between divination and "witchcraft," Jerome used the familiar Latin terms for the former and *maleficia* for the latter. For instance, Deuteronomy 18:10 reads: "Nec inveniatur in te qui lustret filium suum, aut filiam, ducens per ignem: aut qui ariolos sciscitetur et observet somnia atque auguria, nec sit maleficus / nec incantator, nec qui pythones consulat, nec divinos, aut quaerat a mortuis veritatem." The King James translators render this passage as: "There shall not be found among you anyone who makes his son or his daughter to pass through the fire, or that uses divination [*ariolos*], or an observer of clouds [but *observat somnia* in the Vulgate], or a fortune-teller [*auguria*], or a witch [*maleficus*], or a charmer [*incantator*], or one who asks after familiar spirits [*pythones*], or a wizard [*divinos*], or one who calls to the deed [which later witchcraft discourse usually termed necromancy]." Similarly, the second book of Chronicles 33:6, recounting the "abominations" of King Manasseh, states that he made his children pass through the fire: "also he observed times [thus the King James version, where Jerome has "*observabat somnia*"], used enchantments (*auguria*), used witchcraft (*maleficis artibus*), and dealt with a familiar spirit (*habebat secum magos*) and wizards (*incantatores*)."

The distinction between *veneficium* and *maleficium* was enabled by the obscurity of the line between effects caused by the little-known powers of natural substances and effects caused by immaterial spirits, and perhaps by the strength of the popular image of the *venefica* as a definite type.

The distinction between *maleficium* and *veneficium* was retained in the legal code of the short-lived Iberian kingdom of the Christian Visigoths. The *Codex Wisigothorum*, established around 654 when King Recceswinth converted from Arianism to Catholicism, created a legal system which promoted assimilation between the Gothic and the Romanized native populations of Iberia (until both code and kingdom were swept away in the Muslim conquest of 711). After the Christian reconquest, state-building kings of the eleventh century revived the Visigothic Code (translated into Spanish as the *Fuero Juzgo*).

Conforming to the Theodosian Code, the Visigothic Code's list of criminals disqualified from giving testimony included *malefici* and *venefici*.[31] The Spanish *Fuero Juzgo* translated these, respectively, as *sorteros* and *los que dan yervas* (those who give [others] herbal potions).[32] The section in the Visigothic Code covering crimes of magic made the same distinction in its title: *De maleficis et consulentibus eos, atque veneficis* (the *Fuero Juzgo* translated this as *Los Malfechores, e de los que los consulen, e de los que dan yerbas*). Here *maleficia* is associated with divination: *malefici* are *ariolos, aruspices, vel vaticinatores* (*adevino, encantadores* or *provizeros* in the *Fuero Juzgo*). As in the Theodosian Code, penalties are aimed as much at those who consult *malefici* as at the *malefici* themselves. The specific political concern of this law is made clear in the stipulation that the crime forbidden is the consulting of diviners regarding the health or death of princes or other such men (*principis, vel cuiuscumque hominis*). A separate section covers the various crimes of *malefici* themselves, whose evil is always brought about through the invocation of demons (*per invocationem daemonum*). A third section entitled *De veneficis* (*los que dan yerbas*) refers particularly to *venenatam potionum* (*las yerbas*)— that is, a potion drunk by the victim. A fourth and final section concerns evil done to people or to their animals or crops by "*maleficium, aut diversa ligamenta (por encantamiento o por ligamiento)*" (i.e., by enchantment and by ligature). Here ligatures are more closely associated with demon-invoking *malefici* than with *venefici*.[33] While the potion of the *venefica* is a preparation which exerts its force through being consumed, the ligature is a more permanent object, usually made to be worn (or, more generally, working by proximity), which exerts a constant force after its production.

The first use of a word deriving from *facticius* in this context that I have been able to find occurs in the *Forum Turolij* of 1176. This was the municipal code for Tervel in Aragon. (The law was the model for all subsequent royal charters of Aragonese and Castilian cities in this state-building period.) A part of the law dealing with crimes of women, such as the teaching of how to induce an abortion, has a section *De ligatricibus*, followed by a section entitled *De muliere facticiosa*.[34] The first section refers to women who *ligaverit* (make ligatures directed upon) men or animals or other things. The second section names women who are *erbolaria vel facticiosa*. *Erbolaria* clearly relates to *venefici* (i.e., *los que dan yerbas*). I am at a loss as to the specific meaning of *facticiosa*, which here appears as a synonym for *erbolaria* or else as a somewhat more general category containing *erbolaria* as a subset. Since the next section of the law is titled *De medicatricibus*, context would seem to imply some manipulation of materials in order to achieve a particular effect upon the physical state of an individual.

In his glossary of medieval Latin, Du Cagne mentions several related terms which seem to have arisen in popular speech. The term *factura* appears in a synodal text of 1311: "*Aut incantationes, sacrilegia, auguria, vel maleficia, quae Facturae, sive praestigiae vulgaritur appellantur*" (Either incantations, sacrileges, auguries, or witchcrafts, which are vulgarly called *Facturae*, or jugglery).[35] According to Du Cagne, *factura* was a synonym for *maleficium* or *sortilegium* in common speech. A popular Life of St. Bernard speaks of "*hoc malefica arte Facturae*."[36] The equivalent French word of the time was *faiture*. A *faiturier* was a *sortilegus* or *veneficus* (a sorcerer or witch), and *faicturerie* meant witchcraft. Similar terms developed in the Spanish of the time. The Spanish *Partidas*, which replaced the Visigothic *Fuero Juzgo* as the basic law of Castile in 1260, employs the terms *fechura* (the manufacture magical objects), *fechizo* (the object thus made), and *fechicero* (the person who makes them). The section of the *Partidas* dealing with magic is divided into three separate laws: the first refers to various sorts of diviners (*adevinos*); the second to *fechiceros*; and the third to *truhanes* (con artists). Under the *fechicero* law we find all magical practices aimed at achieving a concrete result (as opposed to gaining knowledge, the object of divination). Thus *fechiceiria* could involve the invocation of demonic spirits as means to achieve some tangible effect, the preparation of *yervas* to bring about amorous infatuation or death or illness, and "the making of images of wax, or metal, or other fetishes" (*fazer ymagines de cera, nin de metal, nin otros fechizos*).[37]

As the Spanish language developed, the "f" of *fechizo, fechicero,* and *fechiceiria* shifted to the "h" of modern Spanish words *hechizo, hechicero,* and *hechiceiria*.

In the late twelfth century, Portugal emerged as a kingdom, and Portuguese began to emerge as a distinct language. Between 1273 and 1282 the Spanish *Fuero Juzgo* as well as the *Partidas* were translated into Portuguese. The Portuguese words most often designating witchcraft were *feitiço, feiticeiro,* and *feitiçaria*. Especially after the witchcraft bulls of Pope John XXII in the 1320s and the resultant upsurge in inquisitorial witchcraft trials, more consistent national terminologies for witchcraft developed: *hechiceiria* in Spanish, *feitiçaria* in Portuguese, *sorcellerie* in French, *hexerie* in German, and witchcraft in English. *Maleficia* remained the learned Latin term. Competition over jurisdiction between ecclesiastical and secular courts was doubtless an important impetus promoting terminological regularity.

In Portugal, witchcraft law begins with the rise of the House of Avis in the social crisis of the 1380s. In 1385 the new king, John I, promulgated an antiwitchcraft edict in the capital city of Lisbon. Its aim was to purge the "grave sins which in this city of Lisbon have been practiced since very ancient times." The nature of these "idolatrous sins and wicked customs" is enumerated in some detail: "No person may use or effect fetishes [*obre de feitiços*], nor bonds [*ligamento*], nor summoning up of devils [*chamar os diabos*], nor incantations [*descantações*], nor casting spells [*obre de veadeira*], nor making cabalistic figures [*obre de carântulas*], nor evil spells [*jeitos*], nor interpreting dreams [*sonhos*], nor working enchantments [*encantamentos*], nor may he cast lots [*lance roda*] nor read fortunes [*lance sortes*], nor practice divinations [*obre d'advinhamentos*] in whatever guise that may be forbidden."[38]

In 1403 John established a more succinct national antiwitchcraft law entitled *Dos Feiticeiros*. This law was primarily concerned with establishing the illegality of using magical means to hunt for treasure. Adopted into the fifteenth-century code of Afonso V, this rather perfunctory statute was the principal national law regarding *feiticeiros* during the period of the first Portuguese contacts with West Africa. (Municipals laws, however, such as John I's 1385 law or the law in the 1543 *Constituiçoes* of the archbishop of Evora,[39] might go into considerable detail regarding the precise practices being outlawed.) Moreover, during this period, Portugal lacked an Inquisition. Indeed, the famous Inquisition of Portugal's principal Iberian rival, established by Ferdinand and Isabel in 1478, was itself more concerned with Jews and "New Christians" than with witches. Certainly in fifteenth- and sixteenth-century Portugal, witchcraft was not a burning issue, and this may be one reason for the eventual characterization of African religion as "feitiçaria" by Portuguese imperialists who, having failed to conquer Guinea, sought to exploit it through trade. (That is, one would not have traded with "witches" conceived in the strong sense of the word proper to the witch-craze.)

To summarize this admittedly lengthy preamble to the story of the origin of the fetish: The basic components of the idea of the fetish were not present in the medieval notion of the *feitiço*. The notion of the *feitiço*, as conceived within Church doctrine on witchcraft, did not raise the essential problem of the fetish—namely, the problem of the social and personal value of material objects. It failed to do this because the logic of idolatry displaced the status of the material object to that of an image, a passive medium affecting relations between spiritual agents according to a principle of resemblance; and it displaced the power of the bodily fetish-maker to create novel spiritual states of affairs onto the agency of the phonocentric free will, whose spiritually significant actions were the forming of verbal, contractual relations (whose spiritually significant effect was upon the status of the immaterial soul). The concept of the material image attributed no significance to the fetish object's unique origin—that is, to the historical process of its production. Based on a logic of resemblance, it was the likeness of the end product as image that mattered. In addition, the concept of voluntary invocation and linguistic contract blocked any attribution of free spiritual power and moral value to the material body itself. This is evident from the attribution of all new knowledge revealed in magical divination to the utterance of demonic spirits—whereas the powers of the physical productions of the *venefica*, the ligatrice, and the *feitiço*-maker were conceived as effects determined by the correctness of procedure in combining material ingredients (this was conceived "mechanistically" even when verbal formulas—spells— were involved). That is, the principle of novelty (i.e., of divine revelation and spiritual change) was attributed to immaterial verbal interactions and was excluded from physical productions. This conformed to the model of the Eucharist (and other legitimate productions of sacramental objects by the Church), in which there is no moment of indeterminacy to allow what Whitehead would call the "ingression of novelty" (Deleuze would call it "the repetition of difference"). The model for novel revelations of divine power was in essence linguistic—verbal prophecy and scripture—however much the medieval Church accommodated the different religious perceptions of subordinate groups by accepting the reality of physical miracles by God, Christ, and saints. In contrast to this paradigm, the model for the fetish idea involves the realization of novel divine power in material objects and bodily fixations within the contingency of worldly experience.

Beyond this, there was no problem in Christian medieval culture regarding the ability of material objects to embody social value and human-oriented power (which is the basis of the problem of the fetish). Material objects might bear such exceptional powers: (1) as true sacramental objects produced by the divine power of the Church, (2) from their use as vehicles by demonic spirits, (3) from astrological influences, and (4) from "natural magic" inherent in certain materials. This last means is often explained in terms of the alleged acceptance of "magic" by the medieval mentality. The fine Portuguese historian Oliveira Marques writes, "It must be emphasized that the age truly believed in the power of magic."[40] An example he gives is the "*linguero*" kept by many wealthy Portuguese among their dining utensils:

> *lingueros* [were] a sort of rod on which were suspended serpent tongues or a large number of rare stones (such as agate and serpentine), to which were attributed magical virtues. People believed that when these and other such talismans came near contaminated [i.e., poisoned] food, they would change color, become spotted, or even begin to bleed. The "Inventory and Accounts of King Dinis" enumerates certain stones, some with very strange names, which must have been used for this very purpose. It also mentions such items as a "scorpion's tooth" and a "bone suspended in the head of a silver stick."[41]

The general acceptance of such objects might seem to imply that, within the cultural horizon proper to the term *feitiço*, there was no sense that a material object as such excluded those "magical" influences which a later Enlightenment mentality would label as superstitious. However, it is unclear in what sense, if any, objects such as *lingueros* were considered "magical" by their uses. Torquemada himself, the ascetic zealot who was the first head of the Spanish Inquisition, who would surely not have dabbled in the black arts of "magic," allayed his obsessive fear of being poisoned by using the "horn of a unicorn" at each meal to detect envenomed food.[42] Rather than attribute a general belief in "magic" to medieval Europe, it is perhaps more accurate to speak of a historical logic or "episteme" based on principles of resemblance and analogic correspondence through which the medieval Christian intellect conceived the material world.[43] Within such an intellectual framework, objects such as *lingueros* and *feitiços* might well have been conceived as nonmagical, if by "magic" one means the violation of the "laws of nature" governing the action and powers of material entities. The conceptual obscurity in the late medieval mind regarding this issue is the same as that already encountered in early Christian theory regarding the religious status of "vain observances."

Between this fifteenth-century mentality and that of the eighteenth century that induced the Portuguese Inquisition, under the influence of Pombal, to rule that "malignant spirits cannot, through pacts with sorcerers and magicians, change the laws of Nature established by God for the preservation of the world,"[44] a fundamental change occurred in the conception of the natural powers of the material object. One place where the emergence of this new conception of material objects—identified by Enlightenment ideology as the attitude of scientific objectivity—can be studied is in sixteenth- and seventeenth-century accounts by merchant adventurers describing their experiences on the coast of "Guinea." In these texts, the truth of material objects came to be viewed in terms of technological and commodifiable use value, whose "reality" was proved by their silent "translatability" across alien cultures. All other meanings and values attributed to material objects were understood to be the culture-specific delusions of peoples lacking "reason." In the eighteenth century, this materialist attitude was combined with the earlier mechanistic and atheistic materialist ideology of the Epicureans (revived by Gassendi and others) to form the materialist view characteristic of the Enlightenment. The formation of the novel idea of the fetish on the West African coast, and its later elaboration into the general theory of fetishism, were expressions of a new historical problematic outside the horizon of Christian thought.

Feitiço in Portuguese Guinea

For the Portuguese who first reached the Senegal River and encountered Black African societies in 1436, there were two universal commonplaces about sub-Saharan Africa: that "Guinea" was a land of complete social orderlessness and that it was the source of the world's gold. Beginning with Herodotus, European literature had recorded tales of giant gold-digging ants in the forests south of the desert and of strange rituals involving silent trade with unseen peoples. Land of the mysterious origin of that most desired substance which embodied all wealth, its social chaos was said to be so great that it did not bear describing. As the tenth-century Arab geographer Ibn Hawqal stated: "I have not described the countries of the blacks in the West, nor those of Beja and other peoples of those latitudes because the characteristics of organized states, such as religious, cultural and legal institutions and stabilized governmental institutions, are utterly lacking among them."[45] Such lawlessness meant to Christian thinkers that the religion of such people was "idolatry." Indeed, a popular fourteenth-century Spanish survey of the peoples of the world (known as the *Book of Knowledge*) describes several sub-Saharan kingdoms, all peopled by "idolators."[46] Illustrations of the alleged flags of these states were even included: each showed some variation on a human-shaped statue, the popular image of what an "idol" looked like.

Perhaps the most significant aspect of the religious terminology of the fifteenth-century Portuguese who first sailed to West Africa was the distinction between *idolo* and *feitiço*. *Idolo* suggested a freestanding statue representing a spiritual entity (a "false god") while *feitiço* referred to an object worn about the body which itself embodied an actual power resulting from the correct ritual combination of materials. The notion of the *feitiço* stressed its use as an instrument to achieve a concrete, material effect, while the status of an object of worship was central to the idea of the *idolo*. In the early Portuguese voyage accounts, *idolatria* and *feitiçaria* often appear as distinct but paired terms characterizing the superstitious practices of Black African societies. While the religion of heathen peoples was automatically termed "idolatry" by medieval Christians, the greater descriptive accuracy of *feitiço* over *idolo* for characterizing the sacramental objects of African religion led in time to the classification of African religion as *feitiçaria* rather than *idolatria*. The use of a term meaning "witchcraft" to characterize the religion, and thus the principle of social order, of an entire people was unprecedented.

The first Black African societies actually encountered were ruled by Islamicized groups,[47] and the first religious objects described were little leather packets worn about the neck (containing a bit of script from the Koran), familiar to Europeans as *nominas*. (The same practice occurred in medieval Europe with Bible text.) It was especially in regard to non-Islamicized peoples, such as were first encountered in the 1450s, that we find the term *feitiço* employed. In his 1500 account of the 1486 discovery of Benin, the chronicler Ruy de Pina reports: "Moreover, he [the commander, Joham Affom da Aveiro] sent [to the king of Benin] holy and most Catholic advisers with praiseworthy admonitions for the faith to administer a stern rebuke about the heresies and great idolatries and fetishes [*grandes ydolatrias e feitiçarias*], which the Negroes practise in that land."[48] Those Portuguese—usually traders from the colonies on the Cape Verde Islands—who frequented the Upper Guinea coast on a regular basis in the sixteenth century, came to perceive the significance of *feitiços* for the ordering of African society. Pacheco Pereira, writing in 1505, declared that the "Boulooes" of Sierra Leone were "all idolaters and sorcerers and are ruled by witchcraft [*sam idolatres e feiticeiros, e por feitiços se Regem*], placing their faith in oracles and demons."[49]

Indeed, increasing familiarity and interaction led observers to view some groups as lacking in "idols" entirely. There emerged a perception that African religious and social practices were based on *feitiços* in a manner which fell outside the code of "idolatry." In a report included in a letter of 1585 sent by the Jesuit priests of Coimbra to the Jesuit General in Rome, Antônio Velho Tinoco declared of the coast of Upper Guinea: "All the people of the land along the seacoast are black. They are a harmless people, willing to communicate and trade with the Portuguese, and of a simple disposition, although they tend to be attached to magical practices [*inclinada a feitiços*]. . . . they have no organized religion, and do not worship the Sun or the Moon or any other Idols [*nem outros idolos alguns*]."[50] While the passage quoted from Ruy de Pina associated *feiticeiros* and their *feitiços* with demonic invocation, here the more tolerant view on "vain observances" is followed, stressing the "harmless" nature of these peoples despite their inclination to *feitiços*.

When highly organized non-Islamicized African societies were encountered, in Benin and the Congo, the objects and practices labeled by the Portuguese *feitiços* were treated as the heathen equivalents of the little sacramental objects common among pious Christians. Crosses for idols and crucifixes and images of saints for *feitiços* was the proposal of the crusading Portuguese. One such social conversion was believed to have happened in the Congo in the sixteenth century:

> The King [of the Congo] caused fire to be set upon the Idols, and utterly consumed them. When he had thus done, he assembled all his people together, and in stead of their Idols which before they had in reverence, he gave them Crucifixes, and Images of Saints, which the Portugals had brought with them, and enjoined every Lord, that every one in the Citie of his owne Government and Regiment, should build a Church and set up Crosses, as he had already shewed unto them by his own example. And then he told them, and the rest of his people, that he had dispatched an Embassadour into Portugall to fetch them Priests, that should teach them Religion, and administer the most holy and wholesome Sacraments to every one of them, and bring with them divers Images of Christ, of the Virgin Mother, and of the Saints to distribute among them.[51]

Some pages later the author sadly recounts how, once the Portuguese
hopes of finding mines of precious metals in the Congo were disap-
pointed, no priests were forthcoming and "the Christian religion waxed
so cold in Congo, that it wanted very little to be extinguished."[52]

This perception of substitutability and hence of cross-cultural equivalence endured in the usage of *feitiço* on the coast of West Africa. One
vivid example of how this equivalence across antagonistic social codes
came to take on concrete significance after complex cross-cultural social
spaces developed outside Portuguese imperial control is found in a 1625
anecdote of the Cape Verdean André Donelha. In the important trading
city of Casan, located on an island of the Gambia River, Donelha encountered a young African who in Portuguese eyes was a slave belonging
to an acquaintance of Donelha:

> I met a black Mandinga youth, by name Gaspar Vaz, who was a slave
> on this island of a neighbor of mine in São Pedro, a tailor, called
> Francisco Vaz. The black was a good tailor and button-maker. As
> soon as he knew that I was in the port he came to see me and paid
> a call on me with great enthusiasm. He embraced me, saying that
> he could not believe it was me he saw, and that God had brought
> me there so that he could do me some service. For this I gave him
> thanks, saying that I was very pleased to see him too, so that I could
> give him news of his master and mistress and acquaintances, but
> that I was distressed to see him dressed in a Mandinga smock, with
> amulets of his fetishes (gods) around his neck [*com nominas dos seus
> feitiços ao pescoço*], to which he replied: "Sir, I wear this dress because
> I am nephew of Sandeguil, lord of this town, whom the tangomaos
> call duke, since he is the person who commands after the king. On
> the death of Sandeguil, my uncle, I will be inheritor of all his goods,
> and for this reason I dress in the clothes that your Honour sees, but
> I do not believe the Law of Mohammed, rather I abhor it. I believe
> in the Law of Christ Jesus, and so that your Honour may know that
> what I say is true"—he took off his smock, beneath which he wore
> a doublet and shirt in our fashion, and from around his neck drew
> out a rosary of Our Lady—"every day I commend myself to God
> and the Virgin Our Lady by means of this rosary. And if I do not
> die, but come to inherit the estate of my uncle, I will see to it that
> some slaves are sent to Santiago, and when I have found a ship to
> take me I will go to live in that island and die among Christians." It
> was no small advantage to me to meet him in the Gambia, because
> he was of service to me in everything, and what I bought was at the
> price current among the people themselves, very different from the

price they charged the tangomaos. And he served me as interpreter and linguist.[53]

In this passage there is a shift in the usage of *feitiço* to denote the active divine powers evoked through material amulets; the English translator's gloss on *feitiços* of "gods" is clearly not quite right. As the subsequent discourse about *fetissos* makes explicit, the understanding of Europeans familiar with West Africa was that *fetissos* were not false gods in the traditional sense but rather quasi-personal divine powers associated more closely with the materiality of the sacramental object than would be an independent immaterial demonic spirit. Of greater moment, in any event, was the need to use *feitiços* and rosaries as marks of allegiance and social identity. Clearly Gaspar Vaz was a young man who used his multiple identity as slave in the Christian order and noble in the Mandinga order to his advantage in Islamic-ruled city of Casan. Whether Gaspar Vaz habitually went around with pagan amulets on the outside and Christian rosaries underneath his clothes, or whether, as is equally likely, he trapped himself out thus that day in order more easily to effect his acceptance by André Donelha as the latter's middleman in Casan, it is clear that such tokens were of practical importance in establishing social relations and performing commercial transactions in the complex social formation of the "Guinea" coast.

The complexity of this world is vividly evoked in a note on the above passage by P. E. H. Hair explaining the term *tangomaos*: "[*Tangomaos* were] Portuguese speaking adventurers and traders who made their home on the Guinea mainland, in defiance of the orders of the crown, and who married there and established mulatto families. Some were religious dissidents, especially Jews, some criminals escaping the law, some economic entrepreneurs from non-privileged parts of the Portuguese empire challenging the metropolitan centralism of the crown. They were particularly disliked by orthodox 'loyal' Portuguese because they cooperated with non-Portuguese white traders."[54] Transactions in this complex intercultural world, crossed by many different African and European languages but with no language of its own, were increasingly mediated by groups such as the *tangomaos*—whose very existence depended on their location between alien cultures. The pidgin *fetisso* developed out of this practical situation. By the time the first great wave of Dutch ships arrived on the Guinea coast in the late 1590s, a complex usage of *fetisso* combining descriptive and pragmatic functions had come into being. Lacking texts by the "middlemen" themselves, the formative process of the discourse about *fetissos* must be reconstructed through readings of subsequent European texts.

Fetisso: Origin of the Idea of the Fetish

In 1593 Bernard Erecksz returned to the Netherlands from captivity on the island of São Tomé, where he had learned of the lucrative trade in gold and ivory on the Guinea coast. In 1580 Portugal had been annexed by Spain. The Dutch had been in revolt against the Spanish Habsburg Empire since 1555. (Calvinism had been adopted as the official church of the Dutch Republic at the Synod of Antwerp in 1566.) The merchants sent to trade on the Guinea coast by the Dutch in the late 1590s and early 1600s were self-conscious agents of secular economic enterprise and national policy. ([Pieter de] Marees writes: "Troubles and warres in the Netherlands, constrained us to seek Traffique here also, and to undertake this voyage, by that meanes to put the Portugalls from it, which in the end we did."⁵⁵) Their writings express a mentality far different from those of the Portuguese crusaders (though not so different from earlier texts by merchants, such as the fifteenth-century account of the Venetian [Alvise] Cadamosto). Efficiently organized under the Dutch West Indies Company after 1621, the Protestant Dutch completely ousted the Portuguese from the Gold and Slave Coasts by 1642.

In the texts of these Calvinist Dutch, and in later English and French texts, we find the explicit assertion of identity between African fetishes and Catholic sacramental objects. It was Marees's text which introduced the term *fetisso* into the languages of northern Europe. In the years immediately after its publication in Dutch in 1602, a French translation appeared, and a Dutch version was included in de Bry's collection. The English translation in Samuel Purchas's *Hakluytus Posthumus* did not appear till 1625. In his 1602 text, Marees speaks of the *fetissos* of the Akan peoples: "They also hang divers Wispes of straw about their Girdles, which they tie full of Beanes, and other Venice Beades, esteeming them to be their Fetissos, or Saints [*hare Fetissos, of Sainctos*]."⁵⁶ These beads are also referred to by Marees as "paternosters." A century later another Dutch merchant, Willem Bosman, wrote: "If it was possible to convert the Negroes to the Christian Religion, the Roman Catholics would succeed better than we should, because they already agree in several particulars, especially in their ridiculous Ceremonies."⁵⁷ Following Bosman, the Englishman Thomas Astley wrote in the 1740s:

> it is certain that the *Whidah* Negroes [Whidah was the principal slave port for Dahomey] have a faint idea of a true God, ascribing to him the Attributes of Almighty Power and Omnipresence. They believe he created the Universe, and therefore prefer him before their *Fetishes*; but they do not pray to him, or offer him any Sacrifices, for which they

give the following Reasons: God, say they, is too high exalted above us, and too great to condescend to think of Mankind; wherefore he commits the Government of the World to our Fetishes, to whom, as the second, third, and fourth Persons distant in Degree from God, and our appointed lawful Governors, we are obliged to apply ourselves. And in firm Belief of this Opinion they quietly continue.

As this is the very same Apology which the *Romish* Church and Priests make for their Images, it is plain, as *Loyer* (1714) has already observed, that they consider their Fetishes, only as material Objects qualified with certain Virtues and Powers, by the supreme Deity, for the Benefit of his Creatures [i.e., as opposed to considering the fetish objects as themselves gods].[58]

Neither fully personal gods, nor fully impersonal charms or amulets, *fetissos* were, simultaneously, quasi-personal powers and material objects which were capable of being influenced both through acts of worship, such as making food offerings, and through manipulations of material substances. It was the distinction between "fetishes" and "gods," and a belief in the former's historical priority, that led Charles de Brosses in 1757 to coin the term *fétichisme* by way of contrast to the term "polytheism." In the seventeenth-century voyage accounts, this notion of the fetish tends to be set within a theoretical frame not quite suited to it, that of Protestant Christianity's iconoclastic repudiation of any material, earthly agency—whether a small religious object or the pope in Rome—that claimed to serve as an intermediary between the individual believer and his God.

This Protestant denial of any true religious function for any material object was a view well within the horizon of traditional Christian thought. This view, however, was just one of several factors contributing to the first and central theme of the fetish idea: its status as a value-bearing material object. In these voyage texts, one finds that the conception of the material object is influenced both by Protestant Christian ideas and by descriptive conventions peculiar to this form of literary production and to its immediate audience of merchants and sailors. In particular, as I hope to show [in the next chapter] in a more detailed examination of the text of Willem Bosman, the textual practice of these navigators-cum-merchants made three sorts of material objects paradigmatic for the conception of the true nature of material objects (and of nature itself). These were: (1) the Europeans' own relatively novel technological objects (above all, ships and navigational apparatuses, surveying instruments, and firearms), (2) native objects of various animate and inanimate sorts classifiable as potential commodities, and (3) entities of no economic value but significant due to the potential danger they represented to the European trader attempting to penetrate unknown territory to obtain goods and profits. As paradigmatic examples of the powers and operation of the material world, their most prominent aspects were conceived to be the impersonality of their mode of being and operating, and their perceived transcultural significance. (That is, a gun or a tiger does what it does regardless of the cultural preconceptions of its victim; just so, a bolt of cloth or a meat-yielding hog have a practical value independent of cultural interpretations and superstitious fancies). Although I do not have space in the present chapter to support my proposition, it was the resultant reinterpretation emphasizing the fundamental impersonality of material happenings which was the basis of the new "enlightened" definition of superstition as the personification of impersonal natural forces, accompanied by the attribution of end-oriented intentionality to chance events and to objects randomly associated in contingent experience. This in itself was not a new theory of superstition, as readers of Lucretius know; what is novel is the ideological function of this theory when conjoined to ideologemes arising from identification with new quantitative technologies like navigation and ballistics within a new commercial consciousness fostered by novel forms of economic organization (such as the Dutch West Indies Company).

Indeed, for seventeenth-century European merchants, the economically valuable material object often became the very basis and medium for social relationships; this occurred in limited liability trading partnerships, in which individuals were bound together through joint ownership of some asset for the duration of a given venture.[59] In associated developments in political and legal argument, material objects came to be identified as proper to economic as opposed to religious activity. So Grotius argued in 1609 when he denied the pope's right to grant Portuguese trade monopolies: "trade has only to do with material gains, and has no concern at all with spiritual matters, outside of which, as all admit, Papal power ceases."[60] This not only articulated the attitude of merchants such as Marees and Bosman, but it resonated with the specific problems they encountered in trying to trade with non-Christian African societies.

The key notion which was elaborated to explain perceived African confusion regarding the religious and economic value of material objects was that of the trifle. Early European voyagers were above all interested in trading for gold. Prior to the discovery of the Mina Coast, gold was obtained in the form of rings, bracelets, and other personal ornaments. In a typical passage, the fifteenth-century Venetian trader

Cadamosto recounts how "From the Negroes in canoes [at the River Jeba] we obtained some gold rings in exchange for some trifles [*di alcune cosette*], buying and selling without speaking to them."[61] The successful trading of "trifles" of little or no value for gold thematized the issue of differential value systems among different cultures. In the first chapter, I mentioned the Venetian merchant Cadamosto's puzzled remark concerning the West Africans of Gambia: "Gold is much prized among them, in my opinion, more than by us, for they regard it as very precious: nevertheless they traded it cheaply, taking in exchange articles of little value in our eyes."[62] Enciso's 1518 text (as copied by Barlow) says of the Mina trade: "To this castle [São Jorge da Mina] the negros bryng the golde that thei gather . . . and selleth it for trucke of cloth of colour and rynges of latyn, shells, and other tryfles."[63] While it was precisely such "false" estimation of the value of things that provided the desired huge profit rates of early European traders, it also evoked a contempt for a people who valued "trifles" and "trash." This became intensified in the texts of eighteenth-century slave traders.

Just as West Africans seemed to overestimate the economic value of trifles, so they were perceived to attribute religious value to trifling objects. Indeed at one point Marees refers contemptuously to the *Fetissero's* [or fetisheer's] "trinkets" (*cramerye*—in Dutch a *Kramer* was a peddler and his smallwares are *Kramerje*).[64] *Fetissos* are referred to by Marees as "trifles" (*beuzeling*), "apish," "foolish," and "childish toys" (*Apenspel, guychelspel,* and *Kinderspel*). Fetish worship is termed idolatry (*Afgoderie*) and superstitious (*superstitieus*). Subsequent writers followed the same line. William Smith (the very model of an unoriginal writer on Guinea) declared in 1744 that:

> the most numerous Sect [in Guinea] are the Pagans, who trouble themselves about no Religion at all; yet every one of them have [*sic*] some Trifle or other, to which they pay a particular Respect, or Kind of Adoration, believing it can defend them from all Danger's: Some have a Lion's Tail; some a Bird's Feather, some a Pebble, a Bit of Rag, a Dog's Leg; or, in short, any thing they fancy: And this they call their Fittish, which Word not only signifies the Thing worshipped, but sometimes a *Spell, Charm* or *Inchantment*.[65]

Smith's assertion that any trifling object might become a fetish if chosen by "fancy" introduces the second theme of the fetish, that of its radical historicality. Before moving to this theme, however, there is a final component to the theme of the material object and its valuation which must be considered.

In accounts imbued with a thoroughgoing mercantile ideology—such as that of Bosman—the alleged false religious values of African fetish worshippers were understood to cause the Africans' false economic valuation of material objects. Superstitious delusion (and its exploitation by wily, self-interested fetish priests) was seen to block natural reason and rational market activity. And this superstitious mentality was in turn explained through anecdotes illustrating the Africans' alleged propensity to personify European technological objects.

In his fifteenth-century voyage account, Cadamosto mentioned that Black Africans marveled at the Europeans' guns and said they must be "an invention of the devil's."

> They were also struck with admiration by the construction of our ship, and by her equipment—masts, sails, rigging, and anchors. They were of the opinion that the portholes in the bows of the ship were really eyes by which the ships saw whither they were going over the sea. They said we must be great wizards [*grandi incantatori*], almost the equal of the devil, for men that journey by land have difficulty in knowing the way from place to place, while we journeyed by sea, and, as they were given to understand, remained out of sight of land for many days, yet knew which direction to take, a thing only possible through the power of the devil. This appeared so to them because they do not understand the art of navigation, the compass, or the chart.[66]

Here is the first appearance in European voyage accounts of a figure of thought and type of argument which has ever since been employed to explain the primitiveness of the primitive and his difference from the civilized man: the Africans' ignorance of certain technology (later ideologized as the lack of a scientific mentality) leads to a false perception of causality. What to Europeans is a purely technical matter to be understood instrumentally is superstitiously apprehended by the primitive as involving supernatural agency. Another such anecdote is related by William Smith concerning the flight of villagers when he was engaged in surveying: "the foolish natives [his company slaves informed him] were all terrified at my surveying Instruments, being sure that I came there with a Design to bewitch them!"[67] Nineteenth-century accounts are full of such anecdotes.

In the discourse about fetishes, this impression of the primitive's propensity to personify technological objects—or to regard them as vehicles of a supernatural causality—becomes conjoined to the mercantile perception that the non-European gives false values to material objects. The superstitious misunderstanding of causality is understood to explain the false estimation of the value of material objects. From this developed a general discourse about the superstitiousness of non-Europeans within a characteristically modern rhetoric of realism, which recognized as "real" only technological and commercial values. This is what people like John Atkins (author of a 1737 account entitled *A Voyage to Guinea, Brasil, and the West Indies*) had in mind when they made such statements as "infant Reason cannot reach above a material God."[68] For merchants and secular intellectuals of the eighteenth century, reason was above all the capacity to apprehend the material world of nature as determined by impersonal operations (determined by mechanistic laws of causality). In this discourse, superstition is defined as the attribution of personal intent to the events of material nature.

We may trace the second theme of the fetish idea from the most commonplace judgment regarding Black African societies before and after the Portuguese voyages of discovery: that they were societies of complete chaos lacking any principle of social order, "without a God, lawe, religion, or commonwealth" as the English captain Lok wrote in his account of a voyage of 1554.[69] Usually no reason was given for this state of affairs in early accounts beyond the Africans' ignorance of the true faith.[70] Nevertheless, as I have already discussed, when Europeans became more familiar with African societies, they increasingly viewed fetish worship as the principle underlying the paradox of these societies which seemed to exist and endure without any law or true rule of social order.

As in William Smith's typical identification of the fetish as an overvalued trifle, it came to be argued that it was not reason (which produces "the rule of law") that determined African fetish worship and social order, but rather "fancy" or "caprice." "Their fetishes are diverse," writes Loyer in 1702, "according to the diverse fantasy of each."[71] In a later passage (217) he writes: "Each makes their own fetishes and chooses them at will."

Thus African society came to be understood as being organized by an *irrational* and *arbitrary* psychological principle of social order. Christian discourse viewed this as the product of man's following the "law of nature" in the absence of revealed knowledge of God; secular discourse viewed it as the product of fancy or imagination in the absence of natural reason. The baffling diversity of what Africans (or, more properly, interpreters and middlemen) termed "fetish" was thus simply a function of the infinite diversity of the human imagination unrestrained by reason.

The specific explanation of the disordered order of fetishes was articulated in accounts of the alleged manner of their origin, what we may term the "first-encounter" theory of fetish formation. Le Maire claims that non-Islamicized Black Africans of Sierra Leone "worship the first Thing they meet in a Morning."[72] The French merchant Barbot writes that "they make deities of any thing that is new to them, or extraordinary in itself, a large tall tree, the bones of a whale, high rocks, etc. so that it may be said of them, their gods are any thing that is prodigious."[73] More specifically this explanation, whose key category is "novelty," was elaborated in terms of the chance conjuncture of a momentary desire or purpose and some random object brought to the desirer's attention. The classic statement of this first-encounter theory is that of Bosman:

> He [Bosman's principal African informant] obliged me with the fol-
> lowing Answer, that the Number of their Gods was endless and in-
> numerable: For (said he) any of us being resolved to undertake any
> thing of Importance, we first of all search out a God to prosper our
> designed Undertaking; and going out of Doors with this design, take
> the first Creature that presents itself to our Eyes, whether Dog, Cat, or
> the most contemptible Animal in the World, for our God; or perhaps
> instead of that any Inanimate that falls in our way, whether a Stone, a
> piece of Wood, or any Thing else of the same Nature.[74]

African fetish worship (and hence African society) was thus revealed to be based on the principles of chance encounter and the arbitrary fancy of imagination conjoined with desire.

The preceding discussion has already introduced the third basic theme of the fetish, that of its relation to a particular social order. Some explanation of the significance of fetishes for social relations was especially necessary for Europeans striving to form trade relations with African societies. By the time of Marees's 1602 text, it was clear to Europeans that in African society the *fetisso* performed the functions of various European political, legal, and juridical institutions. In one passage, Marees discusses the function of a particular fetish ceremony involving a drink: "This Drinke among them is as much an Oath, and is called Enchionke-nou; which they make of the same green herbs whereof they make their Fetissos; and as they say, it hath such a force, that if a man drinketh it falsely, their Fetisso causeth him presently to die; but if he drink it inno-cently, then their Fetisso suffereth him to live."[75] To Marees the force of fetish oaths was clearly the reason for the stability of African social order. Indeed his first mention of *fetissos* concerns their use in trials involving a husband's accusation of adultery against his wife:

if he cannot learne that his wife hath committed such a fact, by information of other men, but presumeth it of himselfe, or suspecteth
that his wife hath laine with any other man, he chargeth her with it,
and making her eat certaine Salt, useth other Ceremonies of their
Idolatrous Fetissos [*andere beswerighe van haere Afgoderie of Fetissos*],
wherewith the woman knowing her selfe to be cleere, and not to have
committed adultry with an other man, willingly taketh her oath. But
knowing her selfe to bee faulty, she dare not take her oathe fearing,
that if she should forsweare her selfe, her Fetisso would make her die.[76]

Marees describes the use of *fetissos* as charms worn to protect against
disease and misfortune, as objects of pious offering, as oracles, as idols,
as good-luck tokens in fishing and in war, as well as oath vehicles. But
the function of *fetissos* in oath taking was of particular importance to
European merchants searching for the means to establish permanent
and trustworthy trade relations. Many early voyage accounts relate instances of Africans who required the Europeans to take an oath upon
some material object before they would agree to transact trade.

An example may be found in William Towerson's account of his 1555
voyage: "About nine of the cloke there came boates to us foorth . . . and
brought with them certaine teeth [i.e., ivory], and after they had caused
me the sweare by the water of the Sea that I would not hurt them, they
came aboard our ship."[77] Europeans often expressed frustration at the
unreliability of such pseudocontracts. Marees writes:

In their Promises or Oathes which they make unto us, they are unconstant and full of untruth, but such promises as they make among
themselves, they keepe and observe them well, and will not breake
them: when they make any Oathes or Promises, specially, when they
will shew it to our Netherlanders. First, they wipe their faces upon
the sole of your foot, and then doe the like upon their shoulders and
brests, and upon all their bodies, speaking thrice each to other, saying,
Iau, Iau, Iau, everie time clapping hands together, and stamping with
their feet upon the ground, which done they kiss their Fetisso, which
they have upon their legges and armes: some for the more assurance
of their Promises and Oathes, will drinke certaine drinke, as I have
said before: but he that should repose much trust therein, should
soonest find himself deceived, because they are not to be credited
further than you see them.[78]

It is clear, however, that European merchants and the heads of trade
forts on the coast frequently routinized the taking of fetish oaths in

cross-cultural transactions. "Captain Shurley," writes Thomas Phillips, "us'd to make his negros aboard take the fetish, that they would not swim ashore and run away, and then would let them out of his irons. His potion was a cup of English beer, with a little aloes in it to embitter it, which operated upon their faith as much as if it had been made by the best fetishes in Guinea."[79] Another slave trader, Snelgrave, recounts at one point in his narrative how, uncertain of his reception by a certain local king, he sent his surgeon ashore, who in the evening sent him a letter informing him that all was well: "For . . . the Lord of the Place had taken his Fetiche or Oath, in presence of a French and Dutch Gentleman: On his Assurance I landed the next Day, and went up to the Town."[80] There are several anecdotes regarding the regular use of the Bible as the vehicle for fetish oaths.[81]

In each of these three themes of the fetish idea, we see that explanatory concepts, which might be (and which by Enlightenment writers were) treated as abstract principles, in fact emerged out of concrete problems faced by merchants on the African coast. They were shaped and articulated with each other as much out of the practical experiences and presuppositions of these merchants as by these men's objective observations of the alien practices of African societies. The final theme that emerged as part of the fetish idea concerned the distinctive relation of the fetish object to the embodied self of its worshipper.

The fetish oaths described by Marees and others were characterized as depending for their power (thereby maintaining the fabric of social order) on the superstitious credulity and personal fear of the people. That a fetish was believed to have the power of life and death over an individual was a commonplace of European fetish discourse. This sanctioning power through magical belief and violent emotion was understood to take the place of the rational institutional sanctions that empowered the legal systems of European states (at least those free of "Romish" superstitions). Indeed the paradox of African society as it was understood in these texts was that social order was dependent on psychological facts rather than political principles.

In addition, what was most distinctive about fetishes was that they were worn about the believer's body or were consumed internally. It was not the spiritual state of the believer's soul but rather the physical state of his or her body that mediated the relation of the fetish worshipper to divine power. Thus fetishes were external objects whose religious power consisted of their status almost as personal organs affecting the health and concrete life of the individual. For instance, Marees gives a long list of fetishes worn by children:

The children being a moneth or two old, then they hang a Net about the bodie thereof, like a little shirt, which is made of the barke of a tree, which they hang full of their Fetissos, as golden Crosses, strings with Coral about their hands, feet, and neckes, and their haire is filled full of shels, wherof they make great account, for they say, that as long as the young childe hath that Net about him, the Devill cannot take nor beare the child away, and leaving it off, the Devill would carrie it away, for they say, the childe being so little, it would not bee strong enough to resist the Devill, but having the Net upon the bodie, it is armed, and then the Devill hath no power over it; the Corals which they hang about the child, which they call a Fetisso, they esteem much, for that hanging such a Fetisso about the childes necke, they say, it is good against vomiting; the second Fetisso, which they hang about his necke, they say, it is good against falling the third, they say, is good against bleeding; the fourth is very good to procure sleepe, which they hang about the necke thereof, in the night-time, that it may sleepe well; the fift, is good against wild beasts, and the unwholesomenes of the Aire, with divers other such like Fetissos, each having a name a-part, to shew what vertue it hath, and what they are good for.[82]

The fetish's special relation to the believer's body was thus evident both through its being worn like an ornament and through its power to protect physical health or to inflict illness or even death. Thus what was marginal to the Christian theory of idolatrous superstition—vain observances and *veneficia*—was central in the conception of the fetish.

The final stage in the articulation of the idea of the fetish consists of the gradual recognition that the worship of *fetissos* was addressed to earthly entities rather than "false gods" or demons. The elaboration by de Brosses of a theory of primitive religion as *fétichisme* in the mid-eighteenth century was precisely the identification of a widespread form of religion which was neither monotheist nor polytheist. The nontheistic materialism of fetish worship was gradually grasped in the series of accounts of Guinea which were the principal sources of first-hand information on fetishism. These were the texts of Marees in 1602, Villault in 1669, Loyer in 1702, Barbot in 1704, Atkins in 1737, and the critical synthesis of Astley in the 1740s. Bosman, otherwise the great authority, did not participate in this development, always speaking of "fetishes" and "false gods" interchangeably.

Marees presents the discourse about *fetissos* in all its complexity, but he offers no principles of explanation and mentions at least one incident of fetishism as devil worship when the apparition of a large black dog (a traditional form for the devil to take) is appealed to as an oracle under a certain fetish tree.[83] Enlightenment notions of superstitious delusion cannot come into play in a text which assumes the reality of the devil, since the devil is the cause of all spiritual delusion. Villault's text is still willing to characterize the Africans as fearing the devil, but the true origin of their religious delusion he reveals to be hypocritical priests. Villault tells an anecdote in which he performs an iconoclastic act, smashing a native fetish to show Black Africans it lacks any real power, while they claim he will die if he touches it. Although he smashes it and does not die, his interlocutors are not enlightened: "They said to me, 'You didn't die because you don't believe.' I said to them, 'Couldn't you do the same thing?' They told me, 'We could not, for the fetish would stop us.' 'Who is this fetish?' I asked them. 'It is a great black dog, which sometimes appears at the foot of a great tree.' 'Have you seen it?' I replied. 'No, it only speaks with our priests, who tell us about it.' Thus one can see their deception."[84]

The priest Loyer tells an almost identical anecdote about iconoclasm, making himself the hero, though he concludes not with hypocritical priests but with a remark on "these poor wretches, so pitifully enchained by the enemy of Humankind."[85] Still, it is Loyer who perceives the nontheistic status of fetishes; as a priest who believes in natural reason's intimation of the truth of monotheism, Loyer criticizes Villault for asserting "that the Negroes acknowledge the fetishes as gods" when in fact "the Negroes acknowledge one God, creator of all things, but the author in particular of the fetishes, which He sent to the earth to serve man."[86] "I cannot better explain these fetishes," says Loyer, "than to say that they do not regard them as gods, but as particular devotions of the faithful, for they respect and honor them only as a cult relative to God, who is their creator just as we honor images and relics, without comparison [of them to gods] in the true religion."[87]

Barbot testifies that the African fetish worshippers are not devil worshippers but rather the victims of priestly exploitation: "it is certain that these priests have no other conjuration than to delude the people, and get what they can by them, thro' a persuasion that what they do proceeds from a God; and their ignorance makes them swallow any fraud, as something above the common cause of nature."[88] Barbot tries to make a nice distinction by affirming that Africans worship neither gods nor the devil but that their fetish worship is still properly classified as idolatry since it involves acts of worship not addressed to the true

God: he likens this to the teraphim of Laban in the Old Testament and to the Lares of the Romans.[89]

It is the "enlightened" slave trader Atkins who stresses the materialism of this nontheistic worship:

> if infant Reason cannot reach above a material God, what I think would first and most naturally occur would be Objects about us, as they did us good or hurt, the Fetishes of the Negroes. The original Gods, obvious to the first and darker days of Reason, were in my opinion Stocks and Stones [i.e., inanimate objects], Serpents [as at Ouidah], Calves [as the golden calf in the Old Testament], Onions [as among the Egyptians], Garlick, etc. Not that these things appeared to them in the exalted Attributes of Spirit, Creator, Omniscience, etc., then inconceivable: No: they only could observe that all the parts of Nature were mysterious in their Essence and Operations, and therefore attracted their Esteem and Worship.[90]

Among the texts about fetish worship in Guinea, it is Atkins's which first fully articulates the theoretical notion of fetishism, and he does this in an argument whose obvious intent is to justify the slavery of Blacks by Europeans. Atkins makes this argument in five stages: "From the Negroes Religion may be drawn these Observations. First, the Foundation of All Men's Religions is taken from this Visible Universe, as ancient as the Creation"; (2) this condition is universal for all men lacking "Light and Knowledge"; (3) given "the Negroes Ignorance of Good and Evil," contact with Europeans has had a civilizing impact, as is proved, he argues, by the greater moral improvement of coastal West Africans (i.e., those conducting the slave trade) over the inland Africans brought to the coast for sale as slaves; (4) "the essential Point in all this, is to mend Men's Morals, to make them good and virtuous to their Neighbours, obedient to superiors, and where it fails, the true Politician will account it bad, by whatever Name denominated, the Faiths that cannot produce Good Works, are certainly faulty"; and (5) "Lastly, the Fear of the Fittish keeps them from injuring one another a little . . . but has little influence in respect to us, whom they rob, cheat, or murder, as best answers their Conveniences."

Astley synthesizes the arguments of Loyer and Atkins, explaining of Black Africans: "they consider their Fetishes, only as material Objects qualified with certain Virtues and Powers."[91] Following Loyer, he adds that the power of the fetishes is believed by the Africans to come from "the Supreme Deity." However Astley's text in other places relies on the psychological first-encounter theory of the origin of fetishes, in which not God but the "fancy" is the true origin of the fetishes: "An exact Account of Fetishes has already been given from Loyer, who blames those Authors, who say the Negroes worship them as Deities. All Authors agree, that these Things are of no certain shape; a Bone of a Fowl, a Fish, a Plant, a Feather, or any Thing, may serve for a Fetish, according to the Fancy of every Man."[92]

The novel idea of the *fetisso* which emerged out of the cross-cultural interaction on the West African coast was utterly alien to the ideas of the Christian theory of idolatry. Where Christian theory identified two distinct entities, the material idol and the demonic spirit invoked through it, the discourse of the *fetisso* spoke of the deluded personification of material objects whose true efficacy lay in physical and psychological rather than spiritual causality. The Christian idol was produced as an image, whereas the *fetisso* was a radically novel production associating things and purposes momentarily conjoined in a random event. The social principle of the idol was the pact verbally enacted between a human soul and a demonic spirit, whereas the social power of the *fetisso* lay in binding oaths enacted through physical acts and consumption of material substances more proper to *veneficia* than idolatry. Similarly, the power of *fetissos* to affect personal health and fortune followed the metonymic logic of amulets rather than the metaphoric logic of idols. Christian theory located the principle of freedom and novel interaction with divine power in the nonmaterial substance of the human soul; the novel apprehension of divine power in the *fetisso* occurred in the contingent events of the material world.

For the European merchant, the *fetisso* posed a double problem, a double perversion. First, the status of commercially valuable objects as *fetissos* complicated his ability to acquire them as commodities and seemed to distort their relative exchange value. This often led to transactions with an exceptionally high rate of profit, but it also caused difficulties since the locals often regarded the desired objects in a personal, social, or religious register rather than an economic one. Second, to effect economic transactions, merchants had to accept the preliminary swearing of oaths upon *fetissos*—a perversion of the natural processes of economic negotiation and legal contact. Desiring a clean economic interaction, seventeenth-century merchants unhappily found themselves entering into social relations and quasi-religious ceremonies which should have been irrelevant to the conduct of trade were it not for the perverse superstitions of their trade partners. The general theory of fetishism which emerged in the eighteenth century was determined by the problematic specific to this novel historical situation.

In the eighteenth century, the basic conception of the *fetisso* was elaborated into the general theory of primitive fetishism by Enlightenment thinkers such as de Brosses. The themes and problematic specific to the notion were shaped by the novel cross-cultural situation of the African coast in the preceding centuries. The central idea of the fetish concerned the error of worshipping material objects, an idea Tertullian and Augustine would have been thoroughly comfortable with. But the complex of themes focused around this central idea express a problem unrelated to Christian preoccupations: the problem of how any personal or social value could be attributed to material objects whose only "natural" values were instrumental and commercial. In the next chapter, I trace the characteristic Enlightenment ideologization of this problematic as it first appeared in articulate form in Willem Bosman's *Accurate Description of the Coast of Guinea* (1704) and subsequently taken up by theory building intellectuals of the period of the *Encyclopédie*.

CHAPTER 3

Bosman's Guinea and Enlightenment Discourse

One of the ways of extending the range of anthropology is traveling, or at least reading travelogues.

KANT, *Anthropology from a Pragmatic Point of View* (1797)

My last chapter traced the origin of the term *fetisso*. I argued that it came to express a novel idea whose fundamental problematic lay outside the theoretical horizon of Christian theology despite its linguistic derivation from Christian juristic discourse as the Spanish and Portuguese word for "witchcraft." In that chapter, the formation of the fetish idea in sixteenth-century Afro-European discourse was explored in terms of a shift in core concepts: the key Christian ideas about witchcraft were "manufactured resemblance" and "voluntary verbal pact"; whereas the central concepts of the *fetisso* were "personification of material objects" and "fixed belief in an object's supernatural power arising in the chance or arbitrary conjunctions." Indeed, I argued that what was most marginal and conceptually obscure for the Christian theory of witchcraft—"vain observances" and *veneficia*—became central in the notion of the *fetisso*.

In this chapter, I look more closely at the complex idea of the fetish found in the travelogues written by northern European merchants and clerics visiting West Africa, texts which were read and appropriated by radical intellectuals of what might be called the anti-Leibnizian moiety among champions of the Enlightenment (a category broad enough to include figures as theoretically diverse as Hume, Voltaire, de Brosses, and Kant). In the first two sections, I reconsider the original idea of the *fetisso*, not in order to contrast it with feudal Christian thought as in my previous chapter but in order to grasp its practical and ideological significance for the commerce-minded Europeans who authored the travel accounts. In particular, I focus on the 1703 text of the Dutch merchant Willem Bosman and on accounts of the serpent worship at the slave port of Ouidah, for these were, respectively, the great authority on Black Africa and the paradigmatic example of a fetish cult for eighteenth-century Europe.[1] For merchants like Bosman, as for the clerics who accompanied them, such as the French priest Loyer who first asserted the nontheistic status of African fetishes, the worship of fetishes represented the central institution of African culture and society and was the one most responsible for its perceived perversity. It was Bosman's explicit thesis that African fetish worship was founded on the twin pillars of "superstition" and "interest." African society, conceived according to the mercantile ideology of traders such as Bosman, was a world turned morally upside down by officially enforced superstitious delusion which suppressed men's reasoning faculties. The "fetish worship" examined in the first half of this chapter thus pertains not to the real West Africa of the eighteenth century but rather to Enlightenment Europe's image of "Guinea."

We might take the word "Guinea" itself as an emblem of a novel problem constitutive of the new discourse and theory characteristic of the Enlightenment. "Guinea" was the word used to designate Black Africa—a non-European, nonmonotheist land not covered by the histories and cultural codes of old Europe or classical antiquity. But "guinea" was also the word for the gold coin which, being the first machine-manufactured coin and therefore the first coin immune to debasement by clipping and shaving around the edges, helped bring about Europe's unprecedented monetary stability after 1726.[2] The connection between the two meanings of the word is, of course, not arbitrary; the coin was first struck in 1668 by the English Royal African Company from gold it imported from West Africa. It is almost as if between these two psycho-geographical poles of the distant strange land and the new mysteriously monetized Europe, all natural objects with commodity value appeared in a new, exotic light, almost a new field of consciousness. For "guinea" was also an adjective added to familiar nouns to name new things and species which now appeared in Europe as commodities imported from far-off lands: not just "guinea gold" but "guinea fowl," "guinea hens," "guinea corn," "guinea pepper," "guinea wood," and so on. Indeed the adjective "guinea" came to stand for any far-off land, not just West Africa. For instance, "guinea pigs" are from South America. And of course a "New Guinea" was discovered in the South Seas already in 1545. Finally, the word "guinea" connoted the greatest and most profitable of contemporary abominations: the African slave trade. A "guinea ship" was a slave ship, and a "guinea trader" a slave-dealer.

What I am calling "Bosman's Guinea" was imagined to be a world of public corruption and popular delusion created by the libertine and priest-ridden religion of fetish worship. For Enlightenment intellectuals, fetish-worshipping Guinea became the definitively extreme example of a society made immoral, a government made unjust, and a people kept irrational by the economically self-interested promulgation of religious delusion. The African fetish worshipper became the very image of the truth of "unenlightenment," as a reading of Voltaire's *Candide* in the next chapter argues. In the present section of the book, I trace the appropriation of the "travelers'" discourse about fetish worship by French intellectuals of the age of the *Encyclopédie*. It was in this period, the late 1750s and early 1760s, that the Burgundian *philosophe* Charles de Brosses first proposed a general theory of fetishism and coined the term *fétichisme*.

My particular concern in what follows is to trace both the continuity in descriptive and explanatory concepts of African fetish worship and the discontinuity in regard to ideological purpose found between two sets of texts: the first-hand accounts of Guinea and the philosophical writings of Enlightenment intellectuals. Continuous is the conception of fetish religion as the worship of haphazardly chosen material objects believed to be endowed with purpose, intention, and a direct power over the material life of both human beings and the natural world. This conception implied a type of materialistic cult incommensurable with traditional Christian categories: the alternatives of monotheism (with its three varieties of Christianity, Judaism, and Islam) or polytheism (an amorphous range of cult activity all classifiable as idolatry: the worship of false gods). Making this implication explicit in his original treatment of *fétichisme*, de Brosses's new theoretical terminology redefined the problem of historical religion from one of identifying the varieties of theistic belief to that of deriving types of belief from people's "manner of thinking" about causal powers in material nature. This shift displaced the problem from theological discourse to a psychological-aesthetic discourse consistent with the emerging project of the human sciences.

Also continuous between "travel" accounts of Guinea and theoretical Enlightenment writings was the idea that African fetish worship was an institutionalized religious delusion which functioned effectively in maintaining the (allegedly perverse) social fabric of African nations. The efficacy of fetish beliefs to sanction all forms of social obligation (from marriage and sexual fidelity to political loyalty and commercial contractual agreements) was understood to derive from its core religious delusion: that the fetish would supernaturally cause the physical death of those who broke faith. Fetishism thus represented a principle of social order based on an irrational fear of supernaturally caused death rather than a rational understanding of the impersonally just rule of law. It therefore revealed the true political principle (always supplemented by arbitrary despotic violence) that governed all unenlightened societies, since ignorance about the workings of physical causality—the very definition of a mentality lacking "enlightenment"—provided the ground of religious delusion necessary for this system of social obligation to work. As a fundamental principle of both individual mentality and social organization, fetish worship was the paradigmatic illustration of what was not enlightenment.

What is discontinuous in the text of fetish worship between the travelogues and Enlightenment philosophy is the implicit judgment regarding the moral value of "interest" as a motive. Bosman and other authors employed by the various national "Indies" companies presented a picture of African fetish worship as the perversion of that very rational self-interest which, in their view, should be the natural organizing principle of good social order. Intellectuals of the French Enlightenment reversed this interpretation, viewing exploitive fetish priests and greedy merchants as equal embodiments of the essentially antisocial motive of "interest." In this ideological reversal, the key explanatory concepts in the discourse about fetishes were displaced from their original historically specific, mercantile context to the abstract ground of psychological and aesthetic theory.

The theoretical term "fetishism" was invented and received widespread acceptance during the third quarter of the eighteenth century. By the end of the century, it was established as the name of a widespread but distinctive historical reality, and as a crucial term in learned debates about the history and nature of religion. Moreover, a certain rhetoric about fetish worship had become a commonplace for Enlightenment polemicists, especially those who valued empirical observation over rational deduction. The final claim of this chapter is that, by redefining the crucial problem of the history and nature of religion in an essentially empiricist and materialist manner, the idea of fetishism played a minor but significant role in establishing certain general preconceptions about human consciousness and the material world which were fundamental to the disciplinary human sciences that arose in the nineteenth century.

The Discourse about *Fetissos* on the Guinea Coast

In the second half of the fifteenth century, the Portuguese crown established a presence on the Atlantic coast of Africa from Senegal to Angola. Unable to conquer the mainland, despite their superior weaponry, the Portuguese abandoned their ambitions for outright territorial empire by the end of the century. This was in large part due to a mortality rate from yellow fever and malaria of about 50 percent for a European's first year on the coast, a rate which continued until the discovery of quinine in the mid-nineteenth century.

During the sixteenth century, under the quasi-feudal "contract system" of the Portuguese empire, trade monopolies (at least, in theory) were granted to three groups: Cape Verdean colonists were given the trade of Senegambia and "Upper Guinea"; the planters of São Thomé the trade of Congo and Benin; and, most importantly, a more direct imperial control was exercised over the Gold Coast trade organized around the mainland fort of São Jorge da Mina (literally, "St. George of the Gold Mine," St. George being the patron saint of Portugal). Founded in 1482 by the Portuguese crown after the agents of the Lisbon merchant Fernão Gomes, a sort of royal subcontractor, had discovered a source of significant gold trade among the Akan peoples, this most important European fort was later known as Elmina. These ostensible monopolies were frequently subverted by individual entrepreneurs and non-Portuguese interlopers, who stimulated the formation of an Afro-European cultural space outside the effective jurisdiction of the Portuguese empire. As historians have noted, "Until the end of the sixteenth century, the Portuguese dominated West African maritime trade in spite of sporadic rivalry from other European powers. During this period, a body of Afro-European commercial custom came into existence, with patterns of exchange and cross-cultural behavior that were to be remarkably stable until the second half of the nineteenth century."[3]

It was in the formation of this "body of Afro-European commercial custom" that the Portuguese word *feitiço*—meaning "an object or a practice pertaining to witchcraft"—came to designate a number of objects and practices which the Portuguese encountered among various African peoples. The constellation of old and new referents and meanings expressed in the word's usage formed a distinctive semantic field or, perhaps more accurately, a novel intensity or locus for reflection within the semantic field of sixteenth-century Afro-European interaction. As other European nationals came to the coast, and as cross-cultural traffic in this social formation came increasingly to be mediated by entrepreneurial African middlemen and mulatto populations, the pidgin *fetisso* took on increasing pragmatic and explanatory importance and theoretical suggestiveness.

Almost without exception, Europeans failed to learn African languages. Early ship-trade was affected by silent trade or outright pillage. From the beginning (in the 1440s), among the slaves taken by the Portuguese, some were sent back to Lisbon and trained as translators.

In addition to the noun *fetisso*, African priests were called *fetisseros*, or "fetisheers," and a very important verbal phrase "to make Fetiche" or "to take the Fetiche" emerged. The word *fetiche* itself was sometimes used as a verb. The formation and elaboration of this terminology constitutes the origin of the idea of the fetish.

The northern Europeans who ousted the Portuguese during the first half of the seventeenth century encountered the developed discourse of the *fetisso* in spaces of routinized cross-cultural transaction: among the Afro-Portuguese population of Senegal, in the Islamic-ruled trading towns up the Gambia River, in the Mende chiefdoms of Sierra Leone, among African populations living within the shadow of European trade forts on the Gold Coast, and around the trade enclaves of the Slave Coast. These Protestant merchants were especially struck by the apparent confusion of Christian, Islamic, "pagan," and even Jewish religious forms found among such populations. Visiting the coast in the seventeenth century, the Frenchman Le Blanc remarks that some African populations "have become subjects of the Portuguese, where they live in a manner so strange that it is hard to tell the idolater from the Christian."[4] Of the people of "Rio-Fresca" in Upper Guinea, Nicolas Villault remarks: "Their religion is extremely mixed: one finds there Catholics (outside of the Portuguese, who live there in great numbers), Circumcizers who come close to Judaism, Mahometans, and Idolaters. The latter have little sacks of leather hung from the neck, which they call FETICHES."[5] The medieval categorization of world religions according to the four "faiths" can still be found in voyage accounts and collections throughout the eighteenth century, although this theoretical framework was implicitly undermined in the practical discourse about fetishes and their centrality in African religion and society, as I discuss below.

Bewilderment at this complex religious mix was deepened by a perceived African confusion of religious with nonreligious matters. Indeed, a careful reading of accounts of the seventeenth and eighteenth centuries shows Europeans discovering in Guinea a strange conflation of six distinct kinds of value objects: religious sacramental objects (such as their own crosses and rosaries); aesthetic or erotic objects (i.e., objects the Europeans understood to be chosen for their "beauty," especially feminine ornamentation); commodifiable objects of economic value (especially gold pendants); quasi-medical, talismanic objects (i.e., charms for health, luck, and safety); objects used as oath vehicles (similar to European use of the Bible in courtrooms); and technological objects of the Europeans themselves (whose causal efficacy the superstitious Africans allegedly personified). Although a great range of ritual practices and species of living beings were identified as *fetissos* in Afro-European discourse, the paradigmatic image tended to be that of some inanimate material object: a wooden figure, a leather amulet, a gold necklace, a stone, a bone, a feather—by implication any material object at all, however useless or trivial. As Smith explains, a fetish can be "any Thing they fancy." [To repeat:]

> Every one of them have some Trifle or other, to which they pay a particular Respect, or Kind of Adoration, believing it can defend them from all Danger's: Some have a Lion's Tail, some a Bird's Feather, some a Pebble, a Bit of Rag, a Dog's Leg; or, in short, any Thing they fancy: And this they call their FITTISH, which Word not only signifies the Thing worshipped, but sometimes a Spell, Charm, or Inchantment. To take Fittish, is, to take an Oath; which Ceremony is variously perform'd in several Parts of Guinea.[6]

Such baseless consecration of mundane material objects as this text describes seemed to imply a condition of mental confusion so extreme and yet so habitual that it could be taken (and was so taken by Smith and other authors) to characterize the essence of the African mentality. Moreover, this confusion of religious values with material objects was compounded by the African confusion of the sacred with other dimensions of value (aesthetic, erotic, economic, medical, sociopolitical, and technological), which were also found attributed to these capriciously chosen and childishly personified inanimate material objects. The novel idea forged in the discourse about *fetissos* was formed from this very confusion—a confusion attributed to the African mentality by various middlemen addressing European merchants and by the Europeans themselves in the course of describing and explaining their immediate pragmatic reality on the basis of the objective phantasm of African culture produced by the discourse about *fetissos*. Out of the very difficulty in grasping the much-used word as a unitary concept, the term came to express a novel idea in European theoretical reflection and to thematize a novel general problem: that of the nature and origin of the social value of material objects.

The general problem of the nontranscendent origin and status of value was first posed in European theory around the time (end of the seventeenth century and beginning of the eighteenth) that the key texts on fetish worship appeared: Loyer's account in 1702 and Bosman's in 1703. Around this time, Petty and the mercantile economists first posed the theoretical problem of nonintrinsic economic value; Shaftesbury proposed the specificity and autonomy of aesthetic value; and Bayle and other "critics" set up moral values as an independent standard by which to judge the worth of different religions.

Here and throughout this work, I am approaching the history of theories of fetishism from the "standpoint" of what I understand to be dialectical materialism—an approach, as discussed by Adorno in *Negative Dialectics*, which affords no standpoint whatsoever (in the sense of a stable system of theoretical categories applicable to history from some ahistorical Archimedean point of abstract thought). The dialectical-materialist approach to the history of theory assumes that theory begins in the consciousness of contradiction which leads historical actors to reflect (i.e., to seek to generalize from the particular) within a concrete historical situation and in terms of the discourse and categories formed in the pragmatic interactions which form the essence of any concrete historical context. Theory develops in the effort to explain and resolve such experienced contradictions by transforming the essential terms of the discourse proper to a type of historical interaction into the non-contradictory concepts of a formal system.

Consider the first type of African religious object noted by fifteenth-century European voyagers: the small charms commonly worn about the neck in Senegal and Gambia. Also referred to as *nominas* or *gregories*, these were small red leather packets containing a scrap of paper on which a line from the Koran had been written. Such were the "*nominas dos seus feitiços*" worn by Gaspar Vaz mentioned in the previous chapter.[7] Also regularly called "paternosters" or "saints," these charms were explicitly recognized as the African equivalents of Christian rosaries, small crosses, and other personal sacramental objects by means of which an individual believer sought divine intercession through the mediating powers of the saints.

Moreover, to these leather amulets were often added colored glass beads or other objects which to European eyes were mere ornament, "trifles" or "trash" of no conceivable value, religious or other.

I have already discussed the frequent reference to fetishes as "trifles" and "toys." The utter worthlessness of fetishes was often expressed through descriptions of their filthiness; speaking of the Gold Coasters, Villault claims: "their Fetiches, for which they have superstitions which surpass all belief, although the better part of these Fetiches are inanimate things, and most often so filthy and vile that one would not wish to touch them. They all have some which they carry on them, certain ones are small ends of horns filled with ordure, other ones are little figures, animal heads, and a hundred other infamies which their priests sell them, saying they found them under the fetish tree."[8] Notice in this passage the true status of fetishes as valueless "inanimate things," and also the ubiquitous figure of the greedy, hypocritical fetish priests who are responsible for much of the false valuation of valueless objects (the other cause being, of course, the superstitious mentality itself).

The following passage by Nicolas Villault concerning the Sierra Leoneans expresses the characteristic bewilderment surrounding such objects:

> Their religion is diverse, and with the great frequenting of this place by the Portuguese, and the great number of them who live here, many have been converted, while the rest remain Mahometans and idolaters. They revere certain extravagant figures, which they call Fetiches and which they adore as gods, to which they make a prayer evenings and mornings; and if they have a nice morsel, be it meat or fish or palm wine, they throw some of it to the ground, or let some of it drop, in honor of their god.
>
> One day setting out for land [from his ship] in the canoe of a Moor, upon going aboard, I heard him mutter, and, as I distinctly heard the words *"Abraham, Isaac and Jacob,"* I asked him what he was saying. He responded that he was thanking his Fetiche for preserving him at sea, and that all the Moors did the same thing. They all carry these Fetiches in a little sack hung round the neck, or under their shoulders, giving them something to eat evenings and mornings, and ornamenting them with Rasade, or little beads of glass of all colors, which they believe most beautiful.[9]

The interpretive movement in the above passage—from religious confusion to a contemptuous clarity regarding the primitives' aesthetic taste for mere ornamentation empty of any real value—is one of the characteristic rhetorical slides within the discursive nexus of the *fetisso*. Also characteristic is the interpretation of fetish offerings of food and drink as performed in the deluded belief that the (personified) fetishes literally "eat."

Indeed Europeans became convinced that the African mind failed to distinguish between personal religious objects and aesthetic ornaments. By the eighteenth century this perception had reached the level of theoretical statement: "The Word *Fetish* is used in a double signification among the Negroes: It is applied to dress and ornament, and to something reverenced as a Deity (a Lake, a Stone, a Tree, etc.) both so far agree, as to be regarded as a Charm."[10] This perceived religious-aesthetic confusion is illustrated especially well in discussions of what was probably the most important referent of *fetisso*: the small gold ornaments of

the Akan. Marees speaks of the husband of a Gold Coast woman "fold-
ing her haire with many golden Fetissos, and Crosses, putting about her
necke a Ring of gold."[11] Bosman remarks on the elaborate hairstyles of
Akan women, "between which they wear Gold Fetiche's."[12] Astley, following Philips, writes of the people of the Gold Coast: "They have little
Pieces of Gold, exquisitely made, in divers Figures, which for Ornament
the Blacks wear tied to their Hair, and about their Necks, Wrists, and
small of the Leg; and these they call *Fatishes*."[13]

These ornamental gold figures were, of course, of intense interest to
Europeans since gold was the primary commodity sought (at least, until
the slave trade took clear precedence at the beginning of the eighteenth
century). Cast into elaborate and varied animal, vegetable, and mythic
forms with a mixture of gold and other substances, such charm ornaments in fact represented both a desired and an undesired commodity in
European eyes. *Fetissos* were one of three forms of gold available to European merchants, the others being gold dust and lumps of ore. Atkins
explains that gold is available either "in Fetish, in Lump, or in Dust. . . .
The Fetish-Gold is that which the Negroes cast into various Shapes,
and wear as Ornaments at their Ears, Arms, and Legs, but chiefly at
their Head, entangled very dextrously in the Wool; it is so called, from
some Superstition (we do not well understand) in the Form, or in their
Application and Use, commonly mixed with some baser Metal, to be
judged by the Touch-Stone, and skill of the Buyer you employ."[14]

The adulteration of the gold in *fetissos* with baser substances was a
cause of much consternation, to the point that "Fetiche Gold" became associated with "false gold" used in commercial fraud. Bosman asserts that
"the Negroes are very subtle Artists in the sophisticating of Gold: They
can so neatly falsifie and counterfeit the Gold Dust and the Mountain
Gold (i.e., nuggets), that several unexperienc'd Traders are frequently
cheated."[15] The falsity of "sophisticated" gold in economic transactions
inevitably echoed the religious falsity embodied by the gold fetish figures: "I have already informed you of the Signification of the word Fetiche, that it is chiefly used in a Religious sense, or at least is derived from
thence . . . all things made in Honour of their False Gods, never so mean,
are called *Fetiche*: and hence also the Artificial Gold."[16] This "artificial
gold" (gold mixed with silver and copper) cast into *fetissos* was, in Bosman's day, cut up into small pieces called *Kakeraas*. These functioned
as currency in domestic market activities, supplementing the elaborate
system employing gold dust, weights, and balances, which had developed earlier as internal markets grew out of trade with the Islamic cities
of the Sahel to the north. Such gold was relatively bad, devalued gold;
Bosman praises the gold of Accany because "Their Gold was never mix't

with Fetiches, like that of Dinkira, and therefore much more valuable."[17] Similarly, "from the Acrians we also have it very good and pure, without *Fetiche's* or *Kakeraas*."[18] The notion of debased or outright "sophisticated" fetish gold became a sort of synecdoche expressing all the distrust and suspicion of fraud, all the intense anxiety about judging the commercial value of material commodities, which attends trade across cultures.

Embodying the ultimate economic desire of the European merchants, such ornamental "fetishes" also became a focus of the more personal desires experienced by European men on the coast. Misperceptions of the status of women in polygamous African societies, in which women of royal households performed important public and police functions, as well as the frequent sexual relations between Europeans and Africans (in leaving at least one child on the coast, Bosman was not exceptional), added a powerful erotic dimension to the notion of the fetish as somehow the essence and explanatory principle of African society. In the text of the English slaver John Atkins, we find this semantic dimension of the erotically ornamental and feminine expressed in the verb "to fetish": "The Women [at Cape Coast Castle, the principal English trade fort on the Gold Coast] fetish with a coarse Paint of Earth on their Faces, Shoulders and Breasts, each the Colour they like best."[19] In another place, he writes of the women of the Grain Coast:

> The Women are fondest of what they call Fetishing, setting themselves out to attract the good Graces of the Men. They carry a Streak round their Foreheads, of white, red, or yellow Wash, which being thin, falls in lines before it dries. Others make Circles with it, round the Arms and Bodies, and in this frightful Figure, please. The Men, on the other side, have their Ornaments consist in Bracelets; or Manillas, about their Wrists and Ancles, of Brass, Copper, Pewter, or Ivory; the same again on their Fingers and Toes: a Necklace of Monkey's Teeth, Ivory Sticks in their Ears.[20]

Ignorant of the complex symbolism involved in the West African use of the color triad, as well as in rings and other ornaments associated with body openings, Europeans assumed a pure aesthetic activity in African "fetishing" practices.

The text of fetish discourse regularly used the aesthetic-psychological notions of arbitrary, capricious fancy and foolish vanity to explain these African forms of ornamentation. Loyer observed that the elaborate hairstyles of Africans varied endlessly "according to their fantasy and imagination."[21] They are always at their mirror, he says, "and all this to give pleasure and to inspire love, especially from the whites, to whom they abandon themselves willingly."[22] Similarly Bosman writes: "These Female Negroes, I can assure you, are so well-skilled in their Fashions, that they know how to dress themselves up sufficiently tempting to allure several Europeans; but their greatest Power is over those who make no difference betwixt White and Black, especially when the former colour is not to be found."[23]

Capricious fancy is the psychological ground of religious fetishes as well, according to Loyer: "Fetishes are diverse, according to the diverse fantasy of each."[24] "They make deities of any thing that is new to them, or extraordinary in itself."[25] Thus the subjective ground for the crucial role of chance association in fetish formation tended to be located in nonrational, aesthetic-erotic psychology, reinforced by the absence of a rational understanding of the nature of physical causality. This was evident, European writers argued, in the way West Africans chose as a fetish the very first object that happened to catch their eye after setting out upon a certain course of action. Speaking of the "inferior *Fetishes*" of the Ouidans (as opposed to the public, royal fetishes), Astley, following Atkins, says:

> this small *Fetish* is the first Thing they see after they are determined upon any Affair, or Business, and sometimes determines them to that Affair. . . . This agrees with a Relation which Bosman had from a sensible Negro of his Acquaintance, who told him, that if one of them is resolved to undertake any Thing of Importance, he goes out immediately to look for a Fetish in order to prosper his Design.[26]

This alleged aleatory procedure for the external determination of a subject's will by the contingent association of a singular material object with an individual purpose constituted the fundamental intellectual perversion of "fetish worship." The slavishness of the situation of the fetish worshipper lay in the infantile submission of his inner autonomous will to the random determinations of the mechanism of natural events.[27]

Frequent descriptions of the use of the fetish in divination only reinforced this opinion, for it located the determining ground of intellectual understanding and purposive decision in an amoral aleatory process proper to the material mechanisms of natural events rather than in the rational logic of human thought. Such an oracle fetish is pictured in the illustration of *fetissos* from Barbot that accompanies this chapter [figure 5]. Barbot describes it in the following manner:

> That Black's idol was in the shape of a large Bologna sausage, made of a composition of bugles, glass beads, herbs, clay, burnt feathers,

tallow, and threads of the consecrated tree, all pounded and moulded together, having at one end an antick, rough and mishapen human countenance, and was set up in a painted deep calabash, or gourd, among abundance of small stones and bits of wood, with kernels of small nuts, and bones and legs of chickens, and other birds, as it is represented in the cut. All which trash, I was told, served the Black to know the will of the idol, when he made any request of it, or asked a question, by observing the disposition of those several things, after overturning the gourd or calabash.[28]

This "odd idol" thus illustrates the two central concepts of the idea of the *fetisso*: capricious unification of heterogeneous ingredients and anthropomorphizing personification.

Such characterization of the essential slavishness of the African prior to actual enslavement by Europeans was a solution to the fundamental ideological problem of Guinea merchants. ("Ideological" in the modern sense of "how you have to *think* in order to *feel* morally good about yourself, given what you actually *do*.")

The interpretation of fetishes as ornaments, and hence as conforming to the (empty) values of a primitive aesthetic sensibility and premoral erotic desire, also provided a crucial conceptual ground for the general notion of the libertine capriciousness of fetish worship. Villault writes that African women "are much given to lust,"[29] and Astley, following des Marchais, speaks of the Ouidans' "Libertinism with regard to Women."[30] Even the brief entry in Gueudeville's *Royal Geography* on "*Les peuples de Guinée*" mentions that "The women there are most lustful" (*Les femmes y sont très-lubriques*).[31] This theme is especially prominent in discussions of the serpent fetish of Ouidah, as I will discuss in the next section of this chapter.

Europeans experienced the fetishes of the African women as a temptation simultaneously to promiscuity and to superstition. Atkins notes with contempt that the mulatto woman taken as wife by the English director general at Cape Coast was "always barefoot and *fetished* with Chains and Gobbets of Gold, at her Ankles, her Wrists, and her Hair." When the director general and some of their children fell ill, Atkins was disgusted that they ignored his own medical advice in favor of native superstition, "[giving] the preference of *Fetishing* to any Physical Directions of mine, wearing them on his Wrists and Neck. He was a Gentleman of good Sense, yet could not help yielding to the silly Customs created by our Fears and shews the Sway it bears in the Choice or Alteration of our Religion."[32] As Marees and others remarked, the small fetish ornaments worn by Gold Coasters threaded on wreaths of

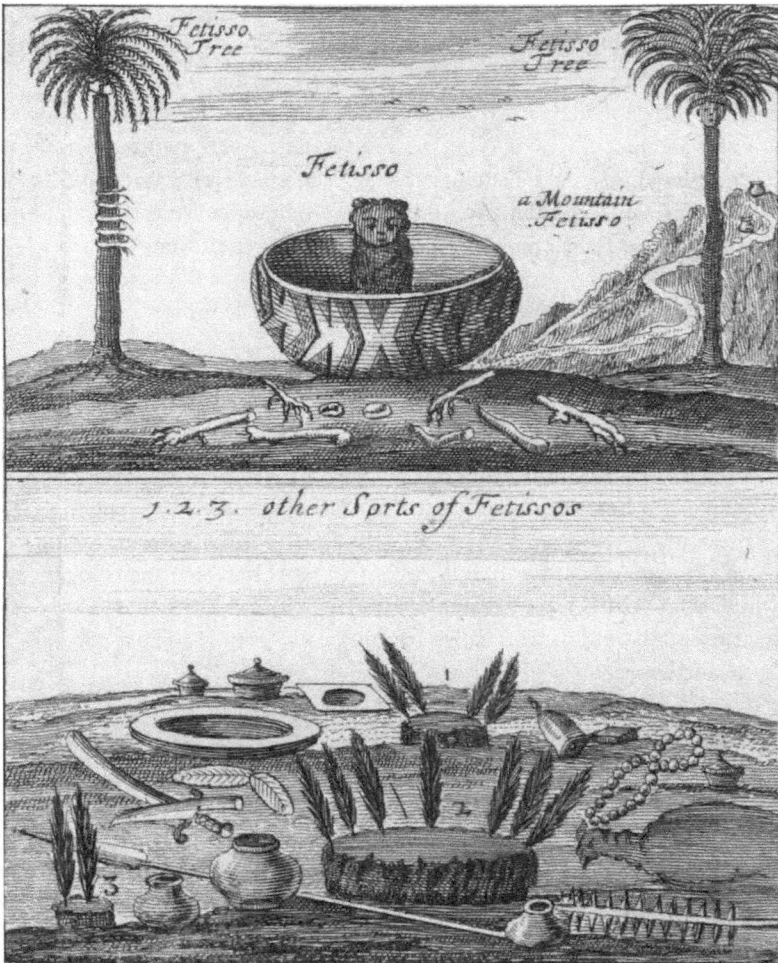

Figure 5. Illustrations of Akan fetishes. Image from John [Jean] Barbot, *A Description of the Coasts of North and South Guinea* (1732), printed in Awnsham Churchill and John Churchill, eds., *A Collection of Voyages and Travels*, 3rd ed. (London, 1746), vol. 5, between pages 104 and 105. Courtesy of Wellcome Library.

tree bark (the Akan *suman*) were also believed by the Africans to exert a protective power against disease and bad fortune.[33] Atkins inquired about this aspect of fetish belief from one of his principal "informants":

> Captain Tom, an honest Fellow among them [Blacks] (our Gold-taker) who, understanding a little *English* by being imployed in our Service, was a great Acquaintance of mine, and would, in the best manner he was able, always satisfy my Curiosity about the *Fetish*:

He believes it able to protect from Dangers, or recover from Sickness; so that, in Travail, or any Ailment, they never are without the Fetish about them, whom they constantly Dashee for Health and Safety. Tom wore his about the Leg, and at Sea, as constantly as he had a Dram, a Glass of Wine, or any Victuals, he dipped his Finger and gave the *Fetish* a Taste. It's the general Belief that it both speaks and sees; wherefore on any Action that ought to be done, the Fetish is hid within their Tomee, or wrapped in a Rag to prevent Tales.[34]

Barbot characterizes these protective fetishes as "baubles":

The palm-tree are the most peculiar sort they make choice of to consecrate into deities; especially that sort of them which they call Assianam [*asumani* is the plural of the Akan *suman*]. I suppose not only because the most beautiful, but by reason they are more numerous than any other; and accordingly there are very many consecrated in these parts, and scarce any Black will pass by them without taking off some strings of the bark, which they twist between their fingers and then tie them to their waists, necklaces, arms or legs, with a knot at one end, and reckon those baubles a protection against several misfortunes.[35]

Fetish priests were considered enlightened concerning the causality, but hypocritical:

In Sickness (in which they agree with all the rest of the World) they first have recourse to Remedies: However, not thinking them sufficient alone to preserve Life and restore Health, they apply their false and superstitious Religious Worship, as more effectual to those Ends; And what contributes to the promotion of this Custom, is, that he who here acts the part of a Doctor, is also a Feticheer or Priest; who consequently does not find it very difficult to persuade the Patient's Relations, that he cannot be recovered without some Offerings made to the False God in order to appease him.[36]

African women, on the other hand, are conventionally figures of superstition moved by irrational passions, as in the pathetic episode recounted by Bowditch concerning the medical value of fetishes:

The death of Quamina Bwa, our Ashantee guide, in the early part of the last week, creat[ed] an idle, but popular superstition that he had been killed by the fetish for bringing white men to take the country;

I was applied to in the King's name, to ameliorate this impression, by contributing an ounce of gold towards the custom to be made by the King for his repose. . . . Mr. Tedlie had brought Quamina Bwa (our guide) into a very advanced state of convalescence; but he so eagerly betook himself from low diet to palm oil soups, and stews of blood, that he soon relapsed, and a gathering formed on his liver, aggravated not a little by the various fetish draughts he swallowed. . . . Quamina Bwa was fetished until the last moment, and died amidst the howls of a legion of old hags, plastering the walls, door posts, and every thing about him, with chopped egg and different messes. I forget how many sheep he had sacrificed to the fetish by the advice of these harpies.[37]

Astley, following Roberts, mentions a group who "admired much the Hour-Glass and Fore-staff; and when he [Captain Roberts] told them their Use, they said, they believed all white Men were Fittazaers, (i.e., Conjurors)."[38] An example of this pertaining to writing is the remark of Richard Lander: "The natives of the regions traversed by Captain Clapperton and myself ever regarded our writing apparatus with mingled sensations of alarm and jealousy; and fancied, when they observed us using them, that we were making fetishes (charms) and enchantments prejudicial to their lives and interests."[39] On this latter point, the attributed native opinion was more accurate than the European colonialist might wish to acknowledge.

African belief in the power exercised by such objects over physical health and even over life and death was an important ground for interpretations of African fetish worship as based on a false, irrational understanding of the nature of causality. This was reinforced by the frequent anecdotes of European writers about how the superstitious Africans anthropomorphized their technological apparatus (surveyors' tools, navigational instruments, guns, and so on) as magical beings, or how they perceived the act of writing down observations on paper as a spell-casting "fetish."[40]

The protective function of fetishes was not limited to personal health or general good fortune, Europeans discovered. Loyer mentions the guardian function of certain fetishes. The king had fetishes to guard his hidden hoard of gold and another fetish which he set out to guard the fields at sowing time.[41] Marees mentions *fetissos* used for protection in war.[42] European writers were especially impressed by the "mumbo-jumbo" fetish, "a mysterious idol of the Negroes, invented by the Men to keep their Wives in awe."[43] (Holbach gave the "Mumbo-Jumbo Idol" its own entry in the *Encyclopédie*.[44]) For similar reasons, African wives were made to abstain superstitiously from eating certain fetish food "to guarantee faithfulness to their husbands, for they are obliged to continence [unlike unmarried women who, Loyer explains, are free to indulge in the greatest promiscuity], and believe that if they eat it, the fetish would kill them."[45] The excessive sexual passion of African women was understood to require such measures. At weddings, Loyer observes, "they all eat of the fetish, as a sign of eternal friendship, and of the fidelity of the new bride to her present husband, to which fidelity [he adds] the groom is not reciprocally pledged, having permission to take many wives."[46] Here, as in several other passages, Loyer, who elsewhere criticizes Villault, follows him closely: Villault writes that at a marriage bride and groom are assembled by the fetish-priest "who gives them Fetishes; and in the presence of all the bride swears to her future husband, and by her Fetishes, friendship and inviolable loyalty, whereas the husband promises to love her without being obliged [by the Fetishes] to be loyal." At trials, fetishes were drunk in oaths taken to ensure truth-telling, as in the case of a woman accused by her husband of adultery.[47] Loyer remarks: "The Negroes are very faithful observers of their word, when they have sworn by their fetish."[48]

Indeed, Europeans noticed that fetishes, with their credulously attributed lethal power, were used in all kinds of ceremonies and formal procedures involving obligatory oaths:

> Obligatory Swearing they also call, making of Fetiche's; If any Obligation is to be confirmed, their Phrase is, let us as a *farther Confirmation* make *Fetiche's*. When they drink the Oath-Draught, 'tis usually accompanied with an Imprecation, that the *Fetiche* may kill them if they do not perform the Contents of their Obligation. Every Person entering into any Obligation is obliged to drink this Swearing Liquor. When any Nation is hired to the Assistance of another, all the Chief ones are obliged to drink this Liquor, with an Imprecation, that their Fetiche may punish them with Death, if they do not assist them with utmost Vigour to Extirpate their Enemy.[49]

Fetishes were thus the ground of social order both in the private sphere of the family, and in the public sphere of state and civil society. This, together with the gold fetish as potential commodity, was where Europeans found themselves forced to enter into the reality of fetishes in a practical way, since commercial contracts and diplomatic treaties were inevitably put into the language of the fetish (as the vehicle for the creation of new interpersonal obligations). Thus, Smith describes how the first item in the peace terms sent by the British to the king of Sherbro was "that his Majesty would swear by his Fittish, that he would not for the future visit Sherbro Island [where the British trade fort was located] with more than twenty-four Attendants, and to them Unarmed."[50]

Typical formal diplomatic interactions in the period of British preeminence contained formulations such as the following quoted by Thomas Edward Bowditch in his *Mission from Cape Coast Castle to Ashantee* from a letter of the Asante king to the British governor of the Gold Coast: "The King thanks his God and his fetish that he had the Governor send the white men's faces for him to see."[51] The letter ends with the words, "and so again he thanks God and his fetish."[52] In a letter from Bowditch to the British governor he informs him: "The King intends your linguist De Graff, to take fetish with his five linguists, to be just to both the powers to be pledged to the treaty, and is convinced of his probity."[53] Bowditch reports: "All the King's linguists take fetish to be true to each other, and to report faithfully."[54] Another letter explains that "the King of Ashantee desires me to request you will write to all the Governors of English forts, on the African coast, to order the caboceers of each town, to send a proper person to Cape Coast, and that you will add one messenger yourself; that they may all proceed to Coomassie to take the King's fetish in his presence, that none may plead ignorance of the treaty concluded between his Majesty and the British nation."[55]

For Europeans, African fetish worship implied the direct intervention of superstition in political and commercial affairs. Difficulties and blockages which Europeans experienced as being imposed for no rational reason were explained by their interpreters as involving fetish beliefs.

Correspondence and reports of British agents during their period of predominance on the coast are full of more particular accounts of areas or types of interaction forbidden because they were "fetish." A typical minor incident is that reported by Richard and John Lander: "The king will not allow us to go to Jenna by the nearest beaten path, on the plea that as sacred fetish land would lie in our way, we should die the moment we should tread upon it."[56] And the Landers vent their annoyance at the petty problems created by irrational fetish beliefs: "in the centre of our yard grows a tree, round which several staves are driven into the ground. This tree is a fetish-tree, and these staves also fetish, and therefore we received a strong injunction not to tie our horses to either of them. Calabashes, common articles of earthenware, and even feathers, egg-shells, and the bones of animals—indeed, any kind of inanimate substance, is made fetish by the credulous, stupid natives."[57] Henry Meredith characterized the religion of the Gold Coast as "a mass of barbarous superstitions,"[58] and he expressed the same exasperation as the Landers. "Fetish is a word of great license, and applied in a great variety of ways: it frequently means anything forbidden. One man refuses to eat a white fowl, another a black one; saying, 'it is fetish!' There are places into which they do not wish a white man to enter; enquire, Why? They are fetish! To kill an alligator, or a leopard, is fetish in some places. If a person be poisoned, or unwell, in a way they cannot account for; it is fetish! In lieu of an oath to prove the truth of any assertion, they take fetish."[59]

Africans' perceived lack of truthfulness, honesty, reliability, etc. came to be understood by referring to the moral corruption caused by fetish superstition. Marees was only the first of many Europeans to claim that the efficacy of fetish oaths or, for that matter, "common sense" recognition of basic moral obligations, did not extend to outsiders: "In their Promises or Oaths which they make unto us, they are unconstant and full of untruth, but such promises as they make among themselves, they keepe and observe them well, and will not break them."[60] Explains Astley, "their Stupidity [in believing in fetishes] is attended with one good Effect, since the Fear of the Fetish keeps them from injuring such as are in the same Belief with themselves; although it has little or no Influence in respect to Strangers or Whites. whom they rob, cheat, or murder, as best answers their Conveniences."[61] This is a close paraphrase of Atkins.[62]

Desirable commodities were either adulterated or unobtainable because of their status as "fetishes." African society was seen to be structured and perverted by the core religious institution of fetish worship: an order of obligation based on the immediate fear of supernaturally caused death, rather than recognition of that rational rule of law and contract whose natural and universal transcultural order was becoming self-evident to the globe-trotting merchants in the age of Grotius. Bosman complains of the way one group of Africans attacked another group who were coming to the Dutch fort with commodities to trade: such an attack was "contrary to the Common Faith of Nations, when then they [the other group] came under our Protection to Market with their Goods. . . . Was not the Law of Nations herein violated in the highest Degree?"[63]

African "Fetish Worship" and Mercantile Ideology

The complex discourse of the *fetisso* mapped out a semantic field which brought together religious, aesthetic, erotic, commercial, and socio-political meanings. This semantic constellation was unified around the explanatory concept of the fundamental error in causal understanding evident in the medical and otherwise materially efficacious powers attributed to fetishes. Fetish worship was, therefore, a form of superstition which falsely attributed various sorts of values and powers to inanimate material objects, above all powers over material life: both natural abundance and individual human lives. Belief in such power provided the basis for an effective, though deluded and abused, system of social obligation: fear of supernatural death from the fetish for violating fetish oaths substituted for the apparently absent rational modes of social obligation: the subjective moral faculty and an objective legal order. "That excessive fear of death is what inflames their zeal in religious affairs," explains Barbot.[64]

For Europeans seeking to trade commodities and to establish reliable social relations to facilitate this commerce, the idea of the *fetisso* emerged as a pragmatically totalized and totalizing explanation of the strangeness of African societies and the special problems they themselves encountered in trying to conduct rational market activities with these benighted peoples.

Although he ignores the mercantile setting and function of the terminology, the pragmatic origin of the language of the fetish is recognized by Joseph Dupuis:

The application of the word Fetische, so commonly in use with Europeans and Negroes in this part of Africa, requires elucidation; yet it would, perhaps, be impossible to select from any known language a term of corresponding signification. Sufficient may be said, however, to explain its general import. Fetische is evidently a corrupt relic of the Portuguese, introduced to the country, probably, by the original explorers of that nation, and adopted by the Africans to accommodate to the understanding of their visitors, such things connected with religion, laws, or superstition, as could not be explained by the ordinary use of a few common-place expressions, and that could not be interpreted by ocular demonstrations. Religion, as we know, was a leading feature in the Portuguese and Spanish armaments of those days. Any exclusive power, or faculty in human nature, is deemed an inspiration of the Fetische, such as sleight of hand, necromancy, invocations of departed spirits, and witchcraft. The religious laws of particular sects or casts, (for they are probably as various in Africa as elsewhere) are described to Europeans, at the present day, under the denomination Fetische. The talismanic charms and sentences from the Koran, worn about the body, have the same appellation in common; and generally whatever is held as sacred, including trees, stones, rivers, or houses, whether ancient or of recent dedication to any invisible spirit or matter, are comprehended within that signification. Thus if a man should swear by the religious observances of his ancestors, an interpreter would say he called upon his fetische to witness the truth: and the same invocation may be applied to other cases, where the oath is upon trivial affairs. An invocation of the wandering spirits or Genii, which also bear the name Fetische, is considered inviolable.[65]

All the facets of this complex discourse of the *fetisso* appear in the text which was the authoritative account of West Africa for eighteenth-century Europe. I refer to *A New and Accurate Description of the Coast of Guinea* by the Dutch merchant Willem Bosman; as the title of this chapter implies, the Guinea known to the Enlightenment was above all Bosman's Guinea. Willem Bosman sailed to the Guinea coast at the age of sixteen in 1688; by 1698 he had become chief merchant for the Dutch West Indies Company, second in authority only to the director general on the Guinea coast. When his brutal superior was ousted by the company in 1701, Bosman was swept out with him and, at twenty-nine, found himself back in Holland, his career at an end. The book he wrote in 1702, which has been called "one of the most popular travelogues ever written,"[66] was addressed specifically to the board of directors of the Dutch West Indies Company, doubtless to remind them of his own value and unfair treatment, but also at least in part as an argument in favor of the gold trade and against the slave trade as the focus of company policy.

But Bosman's account found an audience that extended far beyond the directors of the Dutch West Indies Company. Upon its publication in Dutch in 1703, the book—because of its greater scope and detail, superior factual reliability, and skeptical empiricist spirit—at once displaced earlier authorities on the Gold and Slave Coasts of Guinea. French and English translations appeared in 1705, and a German translation was published in 1706. There was a second expanded Dutch edition in 1709 and three subsequent editions in 1711, 1718, and 1737. A second edition of the English translation appeared in 1721, and an Italian translation came out in 1752–54.

Another index of the success of Bosman's account is the frequency of its plagiarization in subsequent eighteenth-century accounts. While the most notorious of these was William Smith's *A New Voyage to Guinea*, Snelgrave, Atkins, and most eighteenth-century voyage authors "borrowed" from Bosman.[67] And while Labat's famous 1730 account of Guinea claimed to rely mostly on des Marchais, many of the facts, interpretations, and anecdotes about the Gold and Slave Coasts were drawn from Bosman, although because of nationalism and colonial rivalry in the area this often went unacknowledged. In 1743–47 there appeared the great English collection of voyage accounts by Thomas Astley, who attempted a critical edition of all the accounts in the earlier collections of Hakluyt, Purchas, and Harris. In his preface, Astley justifies the need for such a critical edition because authors so frequently copied or stole from each other, he writes, "not excepting *Bosman* himself."[68] Bosman is clearly the byword for an original and trustworthy author. In Astley's volumes on Guinea, Bosman is by far the leading authority. Astley's collection was translated, with additional material, into a famous French collection by the Abbé Prévost (in 1746–68) and into a German version by Schwabe (in 1747–74).

Beyond its high status among readers specifically interested in Guinea, Bosman's book gained the attention of the leading intellectuals of the day. We find copies of the French edition in the libraries of Newton and Locke and a copy of the English version in Gibbon's library. It is not listed among Adam Smith's books, but Smith had a thorough knowledge of the text and refers to it a number of times in his *Lectures on Jurisprudence* of the 1760s.[69]

It was Bosman's discussion of fetish worship in the tenth and nineteenth letters of his book that especially aroused the interest of eighteenth-century thinkers. Already in 1705 we find Pierre Bayle correcting Jacques Bernard's misinterpretation of Bosman's account of the nature of fetish religion and using Bosman's evidence to prove that heathen (and more generally all priestly) religion was grounded in mercenary motives and, far from promoting ethical behavior, systematically eradicated it.[70] Indeed it was Bosman's explicit thesis that African fetish religion in particular, and African social order in general, were founded entirely upon the principle of interest. "I have already informed you that the greatest Crimes committed at Fida are generally compensated by Money; and what followeth will convince you that their Religion seems only founded upon the same Principle, Interest."[71] Of Gold Coast society, Bosman states "the Richest Man is the most honored, without the least regard to Nobility."[72] In his much read collection, Astley begins his chapter on the religion of "Whidah" with the statement: "The Religion of Whidah, according to Bosman, is founded only on a Principle of Interest, and Superstition, above all he had ever heard of."[73]

Bosman is writing in one of the first modern European countries and during the first years when it is possible to dismiss out of hand the explanations of events in terms of supernatural, demonic causality. Bosman can mention to a knowing readership the name of Balthasar Bekker, whose scholarly *The World Bewitched* (*De betoverde weereld*) was the late seventeenth-century lightning rod for charges of heresy made by pious believers in miracles and demonic causality against those, like Bekker, who asserted the inviolability of the physical laws of nature. (Bekker himself, writing prior to Bosman, used the example of African belief in *fetissos*, to debunk superstitious beliefs in the operation of supernatural causality in physical nature.[74]) Bosman can express contempt for the popular author Simon de Vries because he "always brings the Devil in for a share of the Play"[75] and for "our European ridiculous Opinionists; who are persuaded no Conjuror can do any Feats without the help of the Devil."[76] Only because it was safe and acceptable to rule out absolutely the devil as a causal agent could a Bosman explicitly characterize African superstition as being based on ignorance of the fact (the knowledge of which was rationality itself) that natural events happened according to impersonal laws and chance conjunctures, not according to the intentional purposes of unseen spiritual agents. Bosman's Guinea is simultaneously a triumph of scrupulous observation and the new empiricist skepticism and a bizarre phantasm wherein the new forces and categories of the mercantile world economy then reshaping African and European societies alike were read into a foreign social order and locale. This phantasm itself originated in the intercultural spaces of the Guinea coast, and many of Bosman's reports and interpretations are derived from Black "informants" who dwelled in this space in alienation from their own societies.

For instance, Bosman recounts the following creation story as widespread among "Africans":

> the Negroes tell us that in the beginning God created Black as well as White Men to people the World together; thereby not only hinting but endeavouring to prove that their race was as soon in the world as ours; and to bestow a yet greater Honour on themselves, they tell us that God having created these two sorts of Men, offered two sorts of Gifts, viz. Gold, and the Knowledge of Arts of Reading and Writing, giving the Blacks the first Election, who chose Gold, and left the knowledge of Letters to the White. God granted their Request, but being incensed at their Avarice, resolved that the Whites should for ever be their Masters, and they obliged to wait on them as Slaves.[77]

Here we have a curious intercultural myth enabled by an axis of opposition between gold (as the material object of selfish, natural desire, preethical and presocial, hence immoral) and writing (an order of knowledge, hence social and moral). If we ask the dialectical question, "In what sense is gold itself already writing and in what sense is writing itself already gold?" (thereby reversing the terms and seeking the historical context from which the semiotic structure has been displaced), we are led to the ideas of the monetary values inscribed (written) on gold coins and of paper money (i.e., writing that "is" gold) and bookkeeping. That is, we are led to the new monetary system of commodity prices and cost calculations that had now become the self-conscious code and system of motives and actions for Europeans who came to the West African coast. The myth itself explains and justifies the most horrific problem created by this new logic—the enslavement of Blacks by whites, of humans by merchant capital—as punishment for African avarice, an interpretive reversal worthy of Freud's dreamwork theory.

Indeed Bosman's anecdotes function much as daydreams do in waking life, as wish-fulfillments revealing the desires and problems that underlie the interpretation of experience. Bosman's anecdotes about the serpent worship at the great slave port of Ouidah are especially of interest, since it was this snake cult that, beginning with Bayle in 1705, became the paradigmatic example of fetishism for the eighteenth century; and it is in these anecdotes that we can most easily examine the discursive structures that textualized and ideologized the earlier fetish discourse into the discourse that became part of the general language of the Enlightenment.

One often retold anecdote concerns the senseless massacre of a large number of hogs.[78] We find this anecdote repeated in Labat, in Astley, in Prévost, in the popular journal *The British Magazine*, in a 1765 article by Baron d'Holbach on the serpent fetish in the *Encyclopédie* itself, and we find the incident mentioned in the 1757 text of de Brosses in which the word "fetishism" was first coined and proposed as the general theoretical term for the primordial religion of mankind.[79] The anecdote runs as follows:

> In the Year 1697, my brother Factor Mr. Nicholas Poll, (who then managed the Slave Trade for our Company at Fida) had the Diversion of a very pleasant Scene. A Hog being bitten by a Snake, in Revenge, or out of Love to God's Flesh, seiz'd and devour'd him in sight of the Negroes, who were not near enough to prevent him. Upon this the Priests all complain'd to the King; but the Hog could not defend himself, and had no Advocate; and the Priests, unreasonable enough in their Request, begg'd of the King to Publish a Royal Order, that all the Hogs in his Kingdom should be forthwith kill'd, and the Swiny Race extirpated, without so much as deliberating whether it was reasonable to destroy the Innocent with the Guilty. The King's Command was Publish'd all over the Country. And in Pursuance thereof, it was not a little diverting, to see Thousands of Blacks arm'd with Swords and Clubs to execute the Order; whilst on the other side no small Number of those who were owners of the Hogs were in like manner arm'd in their Defence, urging their Innocence, but all in vain. The

Figure 6. "Many Pigs Killed at Fida on account of having Devoured a Serpent of the Idolators." Image from the Dutch edition of Willem Bosman, *A New and Accurate Description of the Coast of Guinea* (Utrecht: Schouten, 1704), between pages 168 and 169. Courtesy of University of Pretoria, Library Services.

Slaughter went on, and nothing was heard but the dismal sound of Kill, Kill, which cost many an honest Hog his Life, that had lived with an unspotted Character to his dying Day. And doubtless the whole Race had been utterly extirpated, if the King (who is not naturally bloody-minded) perhaps mov'd to it by some Lovers of Bacon, had not recall'd his Order by a Counter one, importing, that there was already enough of innocent Blood shed, and that their God ought to be appeased with so rich a Sacrifice. You may judge whether this was not very welcome News to the Remainder of the Hogs, when they saw themselves freed from such a cruel Persecution. Whereof they took particular Care for the future, not to incur the same Penalty.[80]

In this anecdote Bosman achieves the desired rhetorical effect by making ironic use of the literary genre of the fable. The fetish worshippers are characterized as believing literally in the sort of fabulous world in which animals talk and can act as purposeful moral agents, while the European author's heavy-handed irony ("the Diversion of a very pleasant Scene" and so forth) signals his realistic grasp of the natural world. The reader is addressed in the mode of fable as a child who can comprehend the true state of affairs by joining in the author's ironic contempt; and the reader is offered the chance to choose between reason and delusion in such locutions as the alternative explanations "in Revenge, or out of Love to God's Flesh" and in the concluding apostrophe, "You may judge whether this was not very welcome News" to the hogs. Far from conveying the edifying moral of a fable, Bosman's mock fable presents a world turned morally upside down.

Beyond this, the anecdote is textualized by certain discursive structures which occur throughout Bosman's book in his characterizations of the people and society of Guinea. These constitute the particular ideologization of the fetish discourse that Bosman encountered on the coast. One approach to ideology is to conceive it as the semiotic structuring of some real historical problem so that it appears to be a formal problem in which whatever counts as rational knowledge, on the one hand, and moral power, on the other, seem to have been separated, perverted, and set in opposition to each other.[81] Reason, sundered from the purpose of legitimate moral power, appears perverted by immoral motives, while public power, sundered from the guidance of rational knowledge, appears directed by violent, irrational purposes.

Bosman's anecdotes about the snake cult present us with a character system that has a familiar Enlightenment configuration. The immoral perversion of reason appears in the figures of the rational, economically self-interested priests of the cult who hypocritically manipulate the fears and superstitious credulity of the people. Bosman writes of the Gold Coast "Feticheers": "the Priests, who are generally sly and crafty, encouraged by the stupid Credulity of the People, have all the opportunity in the World to impose the grossest absurdities and fleece their Purses; as they indeed do effectually."[82] Of those of the Ouidan serpent cult, Astley summarizes: "their surest Revenue rises from the Credulity of the People, whom they impose on and fleece as they please; by a Variety of Cheats, extorting Offerings and Presents for the great Serpent, which they know how to convert to their own Use. Families are often ruined by these Extortioners."[83] The superstitious, terror-driven populace, who represent African society at large, embody the principle of irrationality combined with a state of complete political powerlessness (i.e., the lack of both knowledge and power). Astley speaks of "the blind Superstition of the People,"[84] following Labat's "the blindness of this poor people."[85] Another figure is the king, who represents the corruption of the public power (complementary to the people's absolute subjection), but who "is not naturally bloody-minded" and is therefore capable of hearing the voice of reason and becoming, at least momentarily, an enlightened rather than an Oriental despot. For the most part, however, the king appears as a passive beneficiary of the basic relation of exploitive delusion seen to exist between priest and common believer. Barbot, after discussing a phony oracle fetish palmed off on the gullible West Africans by the priests, declares:

> This instance of the simplicity of those deluded people, shews the subtilty and craftiness of their priests, who can so far blind them that they may not discover their palpable frauds, and keep them in an absolute submission to themselves upon all occasions, so to gratify their insatiable avarice or vanity, and lord it over them as well in civil as in religious affairs.[86]

An important character type associated with the snake cult that does not appear in Bosman's hog slaughter anecdote but which does appear in the others is the African woman. As I have already mentioned, African women were a great scandal and fascination to the Europeans, and they were invariably presented—not only by voyage account authors but by learned Enlightenment writers such as Holbach, de Brosses, Kant, and Castilhon—as at once absolutely powerless slaves to their husbands (in the domain of African family life) and as overpowerful intruders in the domain of political authority. For instance, see Baron d'Holbach's entry in the *Encyclopédie* regarding the panoptic "mumbo-jumbo" idol which the Mandingos "use to keep their women in submission" by persuading them the idol "watches their actions ceaselessly."[87] In 1764, Kant writes: "In the land of the black, what better can one expect than what is found prevailing, namely the feminine sex in deepest slavery?"[88] Yet for all their absolute subjection within the family, African women were imagined to have a correspondingly great power over the public, political sphere. For example, Jean-Louis Castilhon's libertine novel of 1769 entitled *Zingha, Reine d'Angola: Historie Africaine* was a source for de Sade at the end of the century. De Sade cites the work (identifying Castilhon as "a missionary"!) in *Philosophy in the Bedroom*.[89] It is conceivable that de Sade actually read the French translation of Bosman; at the beginning of the nineteenth letter, Bosman gives the following description of one type of capital punishment:

> Two Blacks, both executed for Murther in the same manner, viz. they were cut open alive, their Intrails taken out of the Bodies and burned; after which their Corps were filled with Salt and fixed on a stake in the middle of the Market-place, where I saw them on my first voyage thither.[90]

In *Juliette*, at one point the pope gives a long ethnographic list of institutionalized atrocities, including the following: "In Juida the belly is cut open, the entrails removed, the cavity stuffed with salt, the body hung out on a pole in the market place."[91]

In Ouidah, the king's wives were his principal executive force, and the women of the snake cult held high public status.

Bosman tells two anecdotes in which women play the role of the force of violent irrationality that perverts the public institutions and political power of society (a role played by the hog slaughterers in the previous anecdote). In the first, an African friend of Bosman is falsely accused of a crime; the king sends his women to raze the man's house and bring him to be executed; the man, who is friendly with Europeans and possesses such tokens of scientific rationality as a keg of gunpowder, stands with a blazing torch by the keg and threatens to blow up the women along with the house and himself. The women are daunted and return to the king, but the man beats them back to the palace and explains the situation to the king (who again is capable of hearing reason), who rescinds his judgment, and the man is saved. In the other anecdote, the wife of the same man, who is a priestess of the snake cult, has an attack of what de Brosses, retelling the anecdote in his book, terms *vapeurs hystériques* and which Bosman and others characterize as a ruse, a phony bout of religious enthusiasm, which women used to become masters of their husbands, and which the priests, who "cured" the women of their religious frenzy, used to extort yet more money from the populace.[92] Bosman relates that one day the man became fed up with his wife's fits, and instead of taking her to the cult temple to be cured, led her down to the shore in sight of a European ship, whereupon her terror that he was about to sell her into slavery cured her permanently of her deceitful hysterics and turned her into a dutiful wife. (Here, again, we see that most difficult of all wish-fulfillment reversals: the revelation of a positive moral function for the institution of European slave-taking.)

Des Marchais (i.e., Labat), the other great source for the Enlightenment knowledge of the Ouidan snake cult, even more explicitly characterized this African cult as the exotic equivalent of the libertine Catholic
nunneries that populated the French literary imagination in the eighteenth century. The priests of the serpent cult were greedy rascals living
off the offerings and payments extracted from a credulous population
to an amount which "depend[ed] on the fantasy of the [chief] priest,
the needs he finds himself to have, [and] his avarice, for all this turns a
profit."[93] From among the wives of the good husbands of the country,
the priests chose priestesses to serve the fetish serpent: "indeed, the
most beautiful young ladies were chosen to be consecrated to it."[94]

Whereas greed and sexual debauchery were the main aims of the
male serpent priests and their patrons, the purpose of the women who
became cult priestesses was primarily to reverse that state of absolute
slavery of wife to husband that was allegedly the norm in African society. Atkins writes: "They have Fetish-Women, or Priestesses, that live
separated with a number of Virgins under their Care, devoted to the
Snake's Service: I have heard, the rich Cabiceers do often buy the consent of these Women to debauch their Pupils."[95] When wives become
priestesses of the serpent, Labat tells his reader, "the poor husband is
obliged to honor them, to serve them, to address them on his knees, and
to permit them to live according to their fancy, and to give up to them
everything in the house."[96] Astley paraphrases this: "All other Women
[except those who become priestesses of the serpent cult] are obliged
to a slavish Service to their Husbands, but these [the priestesses] exert an absolute Sway over them and their Effects, besides which, their
Husbands are obliged to speak to and serve them upon their Knees."[97]
The cult of the snake fetish thus represented the absolute perversion of
private familial as well as public political order.

In Bosman's text, as in Labat's, Atkins's, and more, women tend to
embody that force of irrational passion for unregulated power and of
instinctive mendaciousness and lubricity which perverted all the institutions of legitimate authority. The exploiting priests, the irrational
women, the superstitious polity, and the despotic king constitute the
basic character system of Bosman's Guinea as a world that will remain
morally upside down until knowledge and power are reunited.

In the anecdote of the hog massacre, we can see the nature of Bosman's own underlying desire in the wish-fulfilling moment when "reason" and legitimate political power are reconciled by the emergence of
a new group produced by the general social crisis of the hog slaughter:
none other than the suddenly self-conscious and unified bourgeoisie
(in the form of the hog owners) who rise up to defend their property,

and who—in their identity as "lovers of Bacon" (rational consumers)—
catch the king's ear and avert a disaster to society as a whole (permanent
loss of an important food source) through the sovereign's exercise of his
absolute law-making powers.

The exemplary narrative of the cult of the Ouidan snake fetish as a
parable of the fate of societies that relied on irrational superstition for
their fundamental order was completed by Captain William Snelgrave,
who described the end of Ouidan Ewe independence from the great
Dahomean power to the north. The inhabitants of "Whidaw," as he calls
it, are "proud, effeminate, and luxurious."[98] Instead of defending the
crucial pass against threatening Dahomean troops:

> They only went every Morning and Evening to the River side to make
> Fetiche as they call it, that is, to offer Sacrifice to their principal God,
> which was a particular harmless Snake they adored, and prayed to on
> this occasion, to keep their Enemies from coming over the River. . . .
> There is a constant tradition amongst them, that whenever any Ca-
> lamity threatens their Country, by imploring the Snake's Assistance,
> they are always delivered from it. However this fell out formerly, it
> now stood them in no stead; neither were the Snakes themselves
> spared after the Conquest. For they being in great Numbers, and a
> kind of domestick Animals, the Conquerors found many of them in
> this manner: they held them up by the middle, and spoke to them in
> this manner: If you are Gods, speak and save yourselves: which the
> poor snakes not being able to do, the Dahomeans cut their heads off,
> ripped them open, broiled them on the Coals, and ate them.[99]

In the anecdote, Snelgrave adopts the same tone of mocking scorn found
in Bosman (expressed here by the realistic Dahomeans) at the superstitious personification involved in attributing speech and godlike powers
to dumb animals.

Throughout Bosman's book, fetish worship appears as the key to
African society considered as a theoretical problem. Bosman's explicit
thesis was that fetish religion was the perversion of the true principle
of social order: interest. Institutionalized superstition—the religion of
fetishes—was interpreted by Bosman as the specific social force that
blocked otherwise spontaneous and natural market activities that would
bring about a healthy economic and a truly moral social order.

Fetish religion was thus a priestly conspiracy; priests and merchants
acted from the same motives (economically rational self-interest), but
whereas merchants were honest and moral, priests were hypocritical and
immoral. Priestly exploitation was made possible by the superstitious

Figure 7. Front view of Janus (Bocio). Republic of Benin, Fon peoples. Nineteenth to early twentieth century. Wood, bone, metal wire, sacrificial materials; 19½ × 5¾ × 5⅝ in. (49.5 × 14.6 × 14.3 cm). New York, Metropolitan Museum of Art, purchase, Denise and Andrew Saul Philanthropic Fund Gift, 1984 (1984.190). Image © The Metropolitan Museum of Art / Art Resource, NY.

religiosity of the population. The anecdote of the hog massacre expresses the true situation by structuring the narrative around the opposition of snakes and hogs as natural objects with social value. The misperception of the value of snakes (i.e., absence of any real social value) through superstitious overestimation obscures the true value of hogs (i.e., potential bacon; rational economic value based on universal natural need). And this leads to violent collective conduct contrary to self-interest and, in addition, disruptive of political order.[100]

Bosman's use of the fable genre suggests an explanation of the mentality responsible for the religious delusion which blocks recognition of rational self-interest and social order: the alleged propensity of Africans to attribute personal intention to natural entities (expressed by the fable convention of animals that speak) makes them confuse the impersonal order of natural things with the moral order of human society. They anthropomorphize nature and believe that animals talk or at least exercise other spiritual powers (i.e., the supernatural powers of fetishes).

Just as they mistakenly attribute personality and intentional power to the impersonal realm of material nature so Africans are understood to import the mechanistic impersonality of nature into the human order of decision, purpose, and policy formation. Specifically, this is explained by the first-encounter theory of the origin of superstitious fixations—a sort of erroneous primitive empiricism.[101]

The general idea that African societies were ordered by mechanisms of chance rather than by morally principled intentions was adopted by leading minds of the eighteenth century. In his influential presentation of the characteristics of the four basic races of mankind, Linnaeus proposed that while the regulatory social principle of Europeans was law, for American Indians custom, and for Asiatics opinion, the social principle of Africans was "caprice."[102] Personification as the attribution of purpose and intentionality to natural objects proper to the order of mechanical or contingent causality, along with anthropomorphism as implying personification of impersonal material entities, thus becomes the characteristic mental operation of the superstitious mind cut off from that rational enlightenment provided by a scientific view of causality in the natural world (an interpretation which received its definitive theoretical expression in Hume's *Natural History of Religion*). This is a conception essential to the rhetoric of both social science and colonialist ideology for the next two centuries. It lies at the core of the idea of fetishism and provides a key, I would suggest, to showing a common conceptual ground among such diverse theorists as Kant and Tylor: the notions of purposiveness and of animism derive from the same problematic which engaged both thinkers in their writings about the problem of fetishism.

CHAPTER 4

Charles de Brosses and the Theory of Fetishism

In previous chapters, I examined the formation of the complex yet distinctive discourse about "fetishes" in the historical context of early modern Afro-European commerce. I argued that, among northern European merchants, the notion of *fetissos* and "fetisheers" provided conceptual ground for a popular rhetoric criticizing supposed African religious superstition, personal capriciousness, and social disorder according to preconceptions proper to the commodity form. This critical discourse, recorded in various "travel" accounts of Guinea, was appropriated by radical intellectuals of the eighteenth century, for whom anecdotes of immoral and socially destructive actions by fetish worshipping Africans, such as the anecdote of the hog massacre, provided concrete historical examples supporting their own arguments criticizing institutionalized superstition among Christians.

The term "fetishism" was itself first coined in 1757. The period of the Seven Years' War and the *Encyclopédie* was a climactic moment for religious criticism in France as Enlightenment intellectuals struggled and ultimately succeeded in ousting the Jesuits from control of the French university system. The word's rapid reception and widespread acceptance, at least in usage, and despite the less than enthusiastic—when not outright hostile—reaction to de Brosses's arguments and methodology, becomes comprehensible within this context of self-conscious cultural revolution. For the Enlightenment, the theoretical term "fetishism" was too handy to be dismissed: as the name for the most primitive type of historical religion, understood to be the direct expression of that "manner of thinking" responsible, not just for religious delusion, but for all forms of irrational belief produced by natural mentalities unguided by science and culture, fetishism represented the "other" of enlightenment itself.

De Brosses's Theory of Fetishism: The Hermeneutic of the Human Sciences and the Problem of Metaphor

The book that initiated this theory was Charles de Brosses's *On the Cult of Fetish Gods, or Parallel of the Ancient Religion of Egypt with the Present-Day Religion of Black Africa* (1760). While de Brosses's coinage of the term has been noted by historians of anthropology, his theoretical contribution to the rise of the human sciences has been considered negligible.[1] It is true that de Brosses was neither an especially original nor a thoroughly consistent thinker. But by inventing and justifying (both theoretically and historically) the term *fétichisme*, he established a problem-idea that became a sort of boundary stone for the human sciences of the nineteenth century.[2] For these new scientific disciplines, which claimed to ground social theory in an objective fashion (without appeal to any transcendent theological or metaphysical order), "fetishism" proved a suspect but indispensable term; in their inaugural moments, positivist sociology, social anthropology, Marxist political economy, and medico-juridical psychiatry each defined their central issues and explanatory concepts in part by coming to terms with the problem of "fetishism." For the general project of the human sciences, the discourse about fetishism marked a nexus of problems at the limits of the thinkable: interconnected problems relating to the purposive causality of material life, the libidinal grounding of social obligation, the external formation of personal identity, and the indeterminate singularity of historical time. These obscure but fundamental issues, thematized in controversies about fetishism, consistently troubled nineteenth-century theorists who sought a science of society proper to an age without illusions.

Such a claim for the historical significance of the problem of fetishism must surely at first sound implausible, especially given the common neglect of de Brosses's text by historians of the human sciences. The usual reason for dismissing the significance of de Brosses and his work on fetishism is that he stole the better part of it from Hume. The final third of his book—the section in which he explains the causes of that widespread religion of fetishism he had shown to exist among present-day primitives and ancient peoples alike—is as often as not a translation or paraphrase of Hume's *Natural History of Religion*, with de Brosses merely substituting his new word *fétichisme* wherever Hume had written "polytheism." (While *The Natural History of Religion* was first published in 1757, the same year de Brosses presented his fetish book before the Académie des Inscriptions et Belles-Lettres, it had circulated two years earlier among French intellectuals.[3]) De Brosses's reliance on Hume lent support to the opinion, formed by Diderot and others at the time, that the book was of little theoretical originality or interest.[4]

However, in contributing his new theoretical term to the controversy about the nature and history of religion, the historian de Brosses made a point substantially different from the one made by the philosopher Hume. The materialist perspective and ethnographic method legitimating de Brosses's conception of fetishism is much closer to the paradigm of the nineteenth-century human sciences than was Hume's explanation of polytheism. As for de Brosses's lack of consistency, his theoretical argument is indeed constructed around a conceptual blind spot regarding the status of figurative thought as the ground of personification. But this was not a mere failure of slipshod reasoning. Rather, it was a result of his fundamental methodological commitments to mechanistic materialism, empiricist historicism, and anti-universalist hermeneutics. Before considering this latter issue in detail, it is necessary to examine Hume's argument regarding the polytheistic nature of the earliest religion and de Brosses's appropriation of this argument.

As will become apparent, in following Hume on the particular issue of personification in the final section of his work, de Brosses contradicts the most fundamental claim about fetishistic thought made at the beginning of the book, a claim essential to the book's purpose as an intervention in the "politics of interpretation" of his day. What de Brosses intended to be new and scandalous in his essay (his hopes for scandal were gratified) was his radically empiricist assertion that historiography must be grounded in ethnographic observation; in affirming this method of historical inquiry, he intended to destroy the authority of all Christian and Neoplatonic allegorizing. However, in elaborating the notion of *fétichisme* in order to achieve this end, de Brosses failed to appreciate that the "materialism" implicitly problematized in the idea of the fetish, which he appropriated from the travelogues of Loyer and Atkins, undermined the mechanistic materialism he himself appealed to as the theoretical ground of objective explanation.

In the public culture of mid-eighteenth-century Europe, the traditional distinction between "revealed" and "natural" religion was still a necessary one for writers on the history of religion. "Natural religion" referred to whatever true knowledge of God was available to man through the "natural light" of his common reason, in the absence of any miraculous direct revelation. But from the start of the eighteenth century, the different problem of how man thought about religion in the primitive "state of nature" had been opened up by Bayle and Fontenelle.[5] Just as dissatisfaction with seventeenth-century models of the mind as disembodied rationality (Descartes and Locke) led to early eighteenth-century psychologies of sentiments, aesthetic feelings, and active imagination, so static pictures of man in the secular world of nature gave way to the idea of "natural histories." That is, the seventeenth-century dualism between man as inner rational thought just this side of perceptual experience and nature as external bodies moving at the invisible causal origin just beyond sensible apprehension was subverted by the discovery of man as a natural object ("human nature") and nature as accessible by historical study ("natural history").

The most influential work on this subject to appear in the eighteenth century was David Hume's essay *The Natural History of Religion*, a text which formed part of his overall project of grounding all sciences, including theology, in "human nature":

> There is no question of importance, whose decision is not compriz'd in the science of man; and there is none, which can be decided with any certainty, before we become acquainted with that science. In pretending therefore to explain the principles of human nature, we in effect propose a compleat system of the sciences built on a foundation almost entirely new. . . . The science of man is the only solid foundation for the other sciences.[6]

The fundamental claim of Hume's book was that polytheism was the first historical form of religion: "It seems certain, that, according to the natural progress of human thought, the ignorant multitude must first entertain some groveling and familiar notion of superior powers, before they stretch their conception to that perfect Being, who bestowed order on the whole frame of nature."[7] Adopting the deist notion of God as the power of objective rationality "who bestowed order on the whole frame of nature," Hume argued that polytheism was the original religion of mankind, because primitive peoples were especially subject to a multitude of sudden and capricious natural events, while they had yet to apprehend the unitary rational framework of nature. Polytheism, according to Hume, attributed "invisible, intelligent powers" (i.e., the gods) to natural things and events.

The polemical edge of Hume's essay, of course, cut against Christian theologians who believed that monotheism had to be the primordial form of religion, since God (being good, etc.) must have placed in natural man (prior to the coming of Christ and the possibility of salvation though the gospel) some intuition or propensity toward belief in the one true God—hence the missionary faith in the inherent receptiveness of non-European peoples to Christian dogma. For Christian orthodoxy, God the creator is precisely not a deceiver. For this natural tendency toward belief in the one true God claimed by Christian theorists, Enlightenment thinkers substituted a human propensity to personify the objects and events of the natural world, a hermeneutic act lacking any intuitive relation to truth. From the standpoint of "science," personification was the very psychological process giving form to delusory worldviews.

This false attribution of divine, personal powers to natural objects and events was due, according to Hume, to three distinct factors: ignorance of the true mechanistic causes of natural events; fear of one's helpless subjection to these unpredictable events; and, as I have just discussed, the human imagination's propensity to anthropomorphize natural objects.

> There is an universal tendency among mankind to conceive all beings like themselves, and to transfer to every object those qualities, with which they are familiarly acquainted, and of which they are intimately conscious. We find human faces in the moon, armies in the clouds; and by a natural propensity, if not corrected by experience and reflection, ascribe malice or good-will to every thing, that hurts or pleases us. Hence the frequency and beauty of the *prosopopoeia* in poetry, where trees, mountains and streams are personified, and the inanimate parts of nature acquire sentiment and passion. . . . Mankind, being placed in such an absolute ignorance of causes, and being at the same time so anxious concerning their future fortune . . . acknowledge a dependence on invisible powers, possessed of sentiment and intelligence. . . . In proportion as any man's life is governed by accident, we always find, that he increases in superstition.[8]

Mistaken belief in the causal power of imaginary personal beings (gods) is sustained, in Hume's view (as in Bosman's), by the passion of fear. The fear theory of superstition has, of course, a long and sustained history in the lineages of Western thought, extending at least as far back as Epicurus. For Hume, this fear, which is the ultimate cause of polytheistic religion, is, more specifically, anxiety (i.e., fear of the future) caused by unnecessary ignorance of the real causes of natural events. For Hume, against much of the previous Western tradition, science offers a true hope: a hope not generated by fear, a philosophical "cure" beyond consolation.

De Brosses follows (at times copying) Hume in arguing that fetishism rests on ignorance of true causes along with "the habit of personification" (*l'habitude de personifier*), which gives form to "superstition born from fear of accident" (*la superstition née de crainte des accidents*) proper to "the realm of chance" (*l'empire du hasard*). However, de Brosses claims that material objects are themselves superstitiously perceived as the causes of unforeseen outcomes and personal happiness or unhappiness, a view alien to Hume's conception. Hume's polytheism involves the positing of independent immaterial intentional powers (gods); de Brosses's fetishism proposes that particular material objects are themselves viewed as endowed with specific divine powers (fetishes). Hume's gods are "invisible powers"; de Brosses's fetishes are visible powers.

The following is the crucial passage in which de Brosses uses Hume to make this argument. This is also the basis of claims that de Brosses's theory is merely derivative of Hume's arguments.

Agitated by thoughts born from inner passions, man begins to cast his eyes about with a fearful curiosity concerning the course of future causes, and reasons—well or badly—about the principle responsible for the diverse and contrary events of human life. To the extent that these passions keep him hovering in anxiety over the uncertainty of future events which he can neither know nor control, his imagination applies itself to form an idea of certain superior powers who do what he cannot, themselves knowing and controlling the causes whose effects he himself has not the power to determine. We are familiar [now paraphrasing the first sentence of the Hume passage quoted above] with the natural propensity of man to conceive beings similar to himself and to suppose that exterior things have qualities he feels in himself. He attributes, easily and without reflection, benevolence and malice even to inanimate causes which please or harm him. The habit of personification, whether of such physical beings or all types of moral entity, is a metaphor natural to man, existing among civilized peoples as much as among savage nations. And although the latter, just as the former, do not invariably and truly imagine these physical beings—beneficial or harmful to man—to be in fact endowed with passion and feeling, this common use of metaphors cannot fail to prove that there is in the human imagination a natural tendency thus to figure them [*se le figurer*]. The nymphs of fountains, the dryads of the woods, are not imaginary personages for everybody without exception; in every country vulgar ignoramuses believe in good faith in the existence of genies, fairies, sprites, satyrs, specters, etc. Need one be very astonished if the same populace, among ignorant, crude peoples, proceeded to fancy [*se figurer*] that there existed in certain material entities, objects of his cult, a power, some genius, a fetish, a manitou; if in raising his eyes toward the luminous globes which adorn the heavens, he with even better reason imagined that the stars were animated [*animés*] by genies; if impelled by fear to presuppose the existence of invisible powers, and led by his senses to fix his attention on visible objects, he united two opposed and simultaneous operations by connecting the invisible power with the visible object, without distinguishing in the general framework of his reasoning the material object from the intelligent power which he presupposed—as it would have been a less unreasonable thing to do; if, finally, he imputed to this intelligent power the same feelings of love, hate, anger, jealousy, vengeance, pity, etc. by which he himself was moved? This manner of thinking [*façon de penser*] once admitted for certain objects, is easily generalized and extended to many others, especially in circumstances [once again paraphrasing Hume closely] where chance, that is, unforeseen accidents, have much influence; for it is then that superstition exercises a very great dominion over souls. Coriolanus said that the gods influenced particularly the affairs of war, where events are more uncertain than anywhere else. Our ancient Frenchmen entrusted the decision in especially difficult trials to a method of judgment very much in accordance with the manner of thinking of savages, which they most inappropriately called the judgments of God. A celebrated foreign writer [here, as others have pointed out, de Brosses acknowledges Hume without naming such a controversial philosopher in an already controversial essay], from whom I take part of these reflections, remarks that sailors—the men least capable of serious meditation—are at the same time the most superstitious of men. It is the same with gamblers, who imagine willingly that good or bad fortune attaches itself in an intelligent manner to a hundred frivolous little circumstances which fill them with anxiety. Before states were ruled by a good body of laws, by a methodical and unified form of government, the lack of foresight and good order rendered the realm of chance more dominant than it has since been: thus, accidents being more common in savage governments and epochs, that superstition born of the fear of accidents couldn't fail to exert a greater force and to multiply the invisible Powers believed to control the allocation of happiness or unhappiness to each individual. As in this manner of thinking it is natural to attribute [to these entities] only a power limited to certain effects [i.e., absent any conception of omnipotence proper to a monotheist mentality], although superhuman, it thereby became also natural to multiply their number so that they would be able to respond to the extreme variety of events and match so many effects of which they were regarded as causes. Hence so many local divinities, so many appropriated to certain particular little needs, so many amulets, talismans, and diverse fetiches.[9]

This distinctive conception derives from de Brosses's reading of voyage accounts a few years earlier while he was preparing his collection *Histoire des navigations aux terres Australes*, published in 1756, the year prior to his fetishism essay. The authorities he cites for his understanding of African fetishism are Atkins, Bosman, and des Marchais,[10] taking as the paradigmatic example of the fetishism of "Juidah."[11] It is above all from Astley that de Brosses takes his notion of fetishism; synthesizing the speculations of Atkins and Loyer, Astley explained of West Africans that "they consider their Fetishes, only as material objects qualified with certain Virtues and Powers."[12]

Following the French priest Loyer, the Englishman Astley adds that the power of fetishes was believed by Africans to come from "the Supreme Deity." But in other places, Astley relies on the psychological "first-encounter" theory of the formation of fetishes, in which not God but "fancy" is the originating power: "An exact Account of Fetishes has already been given from Loyer, who blames those Authors, who say the Negroes worship them as Deities. All Authors agree, that these Things are of no certain shape; a Bone of a Fowl, a Fish, a Plant, a Feather, or any Thing, may serve for a Fetish, according to the Fancy of every Man."[13]

This emphasis on the belief in the material "fetish" as itself the divine power was distinctive and novel enough to lead de Brosses (for reasons to be examined later in this chapter) to coin his new term *fétichisme* as the central concept in a new general theory of historical religions.

It is true that much of de Brosses's basic explanatory structure is identical to Hume's. Both adopt a conception of superstition familiar to us from European accounts of Guinea: superstition is itself an interpretive act of the mind—specifically, the act of personification which falsely attributes purpose and intention to the accidental outcomes of events. The implication of many travelogue anecdotes was that the primitive religions produced by such superstitious thinking constituted a culturally constructed and maintained delusory order of causality, which in turn blocked consciousness of the true, physical order of causality. This implication is, of course, made completely explicit in the philosophy of Hume, who not only raised the question of the objective ground of our knowledge of events in experience (the question of causality), but who demarcated the correlative subjective ground: the fear experienced by desire in its attempt to obtain gratification in temporal experience (the question of anxiety). In all this, de Brosses followed Hume.

But for de Brosses the central emphasis concerns the attribution of superhuman powers and religious values to material entities. The superstitious mentality for de Brosses is that "manner of thinking" [*façon de penser*, the phrase repeated on almost every page of the book] which makes fixed connections between singular visible objects and the causal powers which realize desired ends. Such a manner of thinking can produce not only "a system of credulity" (*un système de crédulité*) but "a method of judgment" (*une méthode de jugement*) underlying those political orders that lack an established rule of law.[14] The system proper to fetishism was a system lacking any universal principle (just as it lacked the idea of the one God); it was a system of fragmentation and connection in which particular desires were fixed upon singular objects.

Anti-universalist Hermeneutics

The fetishistic "manner of thinking" was the psychological ground of primitive religion. Its fundamental feature was the personification of a material object as the causal power controlling some desirable or undesirable event. De Brosses characterizes it in this final Humean section of his book as "a metaphor natural to man"—that is, as figurative thought. He uses the verb *se figurer* a number of times for this manner of thinking, and, in the above quoted passage, argues that this "*usage des métaphores*" "proves that in the human imagination there is a natural tendency to think figuratively" (*prouver qu'il y a dans l'imagination humaine une tendance naturelle à se le figurer*). The problem with this argument is that the definition of fetishism given earlier in the book by de Brosses is of fetishism as a "worship rendered directly, without figure, to animal and vegetable products" (*culte direct rendu sans figure aux productions animales et végétales*).[15] How can the primordial figurative thought of human nature produce, as the most primitive form of religion, a cult "without figure" (*sans figure*)?

To understand this, one must turn to the first two sections of de Brosses's book, in which he carried out the comparison of ancient Egyptian religion and contemporary African fetish worship announced in his title. The former was a commonplace puzzle for the eighteenth century, so common that even a relatively unlearned writer like the Guinea trader Barbot was familiar with it: "The Aegyptians, accounted the most rational and wisest of pagan nations, seem'd to have forfeited all common sense, in worshipping so many brutes as they did."[16] The unthinkable paradox here is that the most enlightened culture of its age also partook of the most debased sort of superstition—namely, zoolatry. While a voluntary act of humiliation in the submission before a god, a higher being, was rational in conception (even if mistakenly addressed to a nonexistent entity), worship of animals and plants—lower beings—was the ultimate self-degradation, inexplicable by any rational standard. De Brosses provocatively chose this most problematic and marginal of ancient cults as the focus for a general discussion of the nature of ancient religion; and even more provocatively, he proposed an answer to the riddle of the Egyptian animal gods by claiming to find its modern-day equivalent in the African worship of fetishes. Indeed, he argued that this method—of interpreting historical cultures by finding similar ones still observable in the present—was the only legitimate method for understanding the myths and cults of world history.

In his varied scholarly projects, as I have discussed elsewhere,[17] Charles de Brosses was above all concerned with finding methods that would permit a reconstruction of world history, a history which would include both classical antiquity and the newly discovered lands and peoples not included in classical history. This was a project admirably suited to both his intellectual radicalism and his political conservatism.

While I am concentrating in the following discussion on de Brosses's use of "Bosman's Guinea" and the notion of fetishism as a subversive intervention in the politics of interpretation of the age of the Encyclopedists, I should at least note here the role of the new global economic situation on de Brosses himself. Bosman had interpreted fetish worship in Guinea to be the principle underlying African social reality that effectively blocked natural market forces and mercantilist economic rationality. It was precisely this core ideological aspect which was repressed in Enlightenment fetish theory by intellectuals such as de Brosses. But it was nonetheless intensely present in the discourse and in the world of these intellectuals. For instance, de Brosses not only had estates and vassals in Burgundy and became president of the Burundian Parliament, but both he and his wife lost much of their capital in investments with the French Company of the Indies. In a letter of December 31, 1764, de Brosses complains bitterly of having spent most of the year in Paris attending to business matters of the company, finally pulling out at the loss of half his capital and two-thirds of his income.[18] We should remember that by the period of the Encyclopedists the "material objects" of Europe and those of the colonized areas of the non-European world were united in a common monetary code in a very real way. When Voltaire was negotiating to rent Tournay from de Brosses, land values had risen as investments flowed inland as a result of the loss of French colonies and markets during the Seven Years War.

In particular, his book on fetishism must be understood in the context of the quarrel between the ancients and the moderns: de Brosses's work, the term he coined, and the methodology he associated it with, constituted an assault against the champions of the ancients. When de Brosses presented his essay before the Académie des Inscriptions et Belles-Lettres in 1757, the members were sufficiently outraged to cause him to withdraw the work. (He published it anonymously in Geneva in 1760.) The scandal lay in his insistence that scholarly claims to what ancient peoples and cultures (i.e., those of classical antiquity) meant in their mythology and religion could be made with authority only on the basis of analogies to actually observable present-day peoples. The final sentence of de Brosses's book states "It is not in possibilities, but in man himself that one must study man: it is not a matter of imagining what he might or ought to have done, but of observing what he does."[19]

This first self-assured assertion of what James Clifford has termed "ethnographic authority" was taken by E. B. Tylor as the epigraph for *Primitive Culture*.[20] For de Brosses, direct observation of cultures and societies is the only basis for authoritative historical knowledge: "In general there is no better method to pierce through the veils of little-known antiquity than to observe when some aspect of it, or something approximately similar, occurs under our very eyes. . . . Let us therefore examine first what exists in this regard in the practices of barbarous peoples among whom the cult in question still exists in all its force."[21] De Brosses defined "fetishism" as "all religion which has for its object of worship animals or inanimate terrestrial beings."[22] The reason for defining fetishism in this way must be sought in what Hayden White would call the "politics of interpretation" of the time. De Brosses was above all interested in refuting the so-called figurism of Neoplatonic myth interpretation (he names Plutarch and Porphyry), which finds in the myths of "ignorant and savage nations knowledge of the most hidden causes of nature, and in the assemblage of trivial practices of a crowd of stupid and coarse men the intellectual ideas of the most abstract metaphysics."[23] Likewise de Brosses denounces critics who rely on Christian allegory to interpret pagan myths. It is the hermeneutic of theological or philosophical allegory itself, "the system of figurative meaning" (*le système du sens figuré*), which, de Brosses charges, leads to overblown interpretations which contradict logic and common sense, and which should have no place in an age of reason.[24]

While rejecting interpretation by the classical system of "figurism," de Brosses also explicitly rejects the euhemeristic view that myths and gods were the distorted commemorations of actual historical events and national heroes.[25] He wishes to locate the ground of interpretation, not in the history of events, but in a psychological "manner of thinking" on the one hand and mechanistic material structures on the other, just as his own historical investigations tried to combine direct material observation with the mimetic insights of style and taste.

De Brosses defined his object of study by distinguishing it from another type of cult, termed Sabianism—that is, cults of the sun and stars.

De Brosses's insistence that fetishism was the worship "of certain terrestrial and material objects" is intended to distinguish it from cults of
celestial phenomena, for these tended to be viewed as protodeist intima-
tions of the orderly frame of nature.[26] He yields to the deists in agreeing
that certain "Oriental" and Greek cults and myths originated from the
rational observation of the heavens and so expressed in symbolic form
scientific knowledge. But most ancient cults and myths, de Brosses argues, fall outside of Sabianism, and are properly classed under "the cult
that is perhaps no less ancient [than Sabian astral worship] of certain
terrestrial and material objects called Fetishes by the African Negroes,
and among whom the cult persists, and for which reason I will call
Fetishism."[27] His emphasis on the "terrestrial and material" status of
fetishes (which might be either living beings or inanimate things) was
also intended to indicate the non-rationality (in the onto-theological
sense) of the mentality proper to them. The instance of fetishism
de Brosses chooses as the paradigm appropriate for comparison with
Egyptian zoolatry, since it was also a cult centered on animal worship,
was the serpent cult of "Juidah":

> [Contemporary fetishism is best seen] among the Negroes, today the
> most superstitious of nations in the world, as were the Egyptians the
> most superstitious people of their day. I can't resist telling the story of
> the fetishism practiced in Juidah, a small kingdom of Guinea, which
> will serve as the example for everything similarly done in the rest
> of Africa; especially the description of the worship rendered to the
> striped serpent, one of the most celebrated divinities of the blacks.
> One will see how little it differs from that rendered by the Egyptians
> to their sacred animals, among whom there was perhaps no fetish
> more honored than these latter.[28]

Although not endowed with true theoretical genius, de Brosses had a
talent for making intellectually subversive connections. He next com-
pares the Guinean and Egyptian cults to the serpent worship described
in the suppressed fourteenth chapter of the Book of Daniel, scandalous
for its bold depiction of the debunking of a false god and its hypocritical priests.[29]

Having considered the original intention of de Brosses's book and the
point of his claim—made in the very act of defining "fetishism"—that
it is a cult of material objects "without figure," we can now see that by
"without figure" de Brosses meant "without being the expression of a
rational theological or philosophical system," such as the Greeks and the
Church Fathers of classical antiquity established. Although his usage of

"figuration" is conceptually inconsistent, it is clear that he saw no serious contradiction in claiming that the primitive manner of thinking responsible for superstitious beliefs was a natural mode of figuration, since such "metaphors" as personification had nothing to do with universalizing allegorical symbolizations proper to the rational logos. Moreover, for de Brosses the origin of figurative thought was not in itself a significant linguistic problem (as it was for other eighteenth-century thinkers, such as Vico and Rousseau, who discussed the relation of language and early religion). In de Brosses's bizarre and highly influential *Traité de la formation mécanique des langues* (1765), the origin of words depends on the physical anatomy of the vocal organs plus acts of onomatopoetic and pictographic mimesis. Tropes are of no theoretical interest whatsoever, since the physical structures of articulation (lips, teeth, tongue, etc.) form the primordial "letters" of the first language and provide the key to that "archaeological" science of etymology which will permit the scientific reconstruction of the dispersion of peoples over the face of the earth, which is world history itself.

In proposing the theory of fetishism, de Brosses hoped to accomplish a double subversion—namely, to shift the ground of the origin of popular religion from rational theology to irrational psychology and to establish a historical methodology that appealed to the authority of direct observation of social reality, thereby delegitimizing traditional allegorical hermeneutics. The idea of the fetish accomplished this for de Brosses because it implied a general category of primitive worship which included both beliefs in gods and nontheistic religious or magical beliefs: "all these ways of thinking have at bottom the same source . . . they are only aspects of a general religion spread far and wide over the entire earth."[30] In this way, de Brosses set the problem of primitive religion outside the limits of "theism" and universalist metaphysics.

[Yet the very methodological and epistemological radicalism of de Brosses's theory reveals one of the nonscientific presuppositions that enabled the general viewpoint of the new sciences of man and the new scientific object of "human nature." De Brosses's blindness to the contradictions in his treatment of the problem of figurative thought is something he had in common with many of the early modern theorists out of whose work the nineteenth-century human sciences emerged. The "modern" definition of physical matter and events as excluding all intentional and teleological causation redefined subjectivity as above all the immaterial locus of these qualities, and hence as the free (i.e., not determined by material externality) power to choose personal ends (i.e., to determine one's desire) purely by the power of the inner rational mind. (That is, it seems clear that the modern conception of subjectivity was decisively shaped by the modern conception of materiality.) Inner thought and feelings not originating or guided by "reason" are therefore, by definition, random or arbitrary occurrences lacking end-oriented meaning (and hence a sort of invasion of interior subjectivity by operations proper to the external material world, i.e., chance encounters). Personal subjecthood is defined in opposition to material "thinghood" by its future-oriented quality and nonaleatory operation. (This is why Kant's critique of teleological judgment focused on the true but inconceivable fact of those living organisms lacking man's power of rational will—material entities which yet exhibit end-oriented activity in their natural material development.)

One characteristic result of this fundamental conceptual structure was to repress figurative thought as an object of rational, systematic knowledge and as anything essential to "human nature." To take as an example the "father" of modern social theory, consider Hobbes's treatment in *Leviathan* of "the consequence or train of imaginations," which he terms "mental discourse."[31] Hobbes's basic distinction is between "unguided" and "regulated" trains of thought:

> The first is unguided, without design, and inconstant; wherein there is no passionate thought, to govern and direct those that follow, to itself, as the end and scope of some desire or other passion: in which case the thoughts are said to wander and seem impertinent one to another, as in a dream. . . . The second is more constant, as being regulated by some desire, and design.[32]

Desire's teleological quality is proper only to "regulated" thought; "unguided" thought merely "wanders" in trains of "impertinent" sequence. Hobbes's example of the latter shows how thoroughly figurative and literary thought have been submerged in the physicalist discourse of the new philosophy:

> in this wild ranging of the mind, a man may oft-times perceive the way of it, and the dependence of one thought upon another. For in a discourse of our present civil war, what could seem more impertinent, than to ask, as one did, what was the value of a Roman penny? Yet the coherence to me was manifest enough. For the thought of the war, introduced the thought of the delivering up of the king to his enemies; the thought of that, brought in the thought of the delivering up of Christ; and that again the thought of the thirty pence, which was the price of that treason; and thence easily followed that malicious question, and all this in a moment of time; for thought is quick.[33]

What is significant here is that the mental act of literary-historical analogy is brought into Hobbes's discussion of "wild ranging" "unguided"
thought. Hobbes can "perceive the way of it" but not by any "guided"
or rationally systematic method of interpretation. The literary-cultural
mode of thought is submerged as an unconscious in the physicalist-
associationist image of thought offered by the British empiricist. Analogy and figuration are necessarily characterized as "unguided" and unconnected to desire and purposive thought—a view one might trace
from Hobbes to Locke, Hume, and their French followers up to Kant
and the critical philosophers. This presupposition is brought out particularly vividly in theories of fetishism because they most foreground the
issue of the relation of subjectivity to material objects. The eighteenth-
and nineteenth-century identification of the superstitious mentality of
the primitive as a personifying "animistic" mentality is enabled by the
obscuring of all figurative thought as random association (the chance
conjunctions of "thought objects" in the space of the mind), unconscious mental events "below" the "level" of rational consciousness and
objectively realistic thought.]

The Rhetoric of Fetish Worship in the French Enlightenment

The success of de Brosses's term was immediate. Diderot, writing to de
Brosses in 1757 after reading the manuscript, agreed that fetishism was
"the first, general, and universal religion" (*la religion première, générale et
universelle*).[34] One reason why de Brosses's term was adopted so quickly
and generally during the 1760s and 1770s was that it redefined the terms
of the central argument in the history of religion as to whether the earliest religion had been monotheistic or polytheistic. De Brosses's new
term and mode of explanation made possible a discourse about religion
which displaced the problem from theology per se toward psychology
and aesthetics. And it did this by focusing the argument on the believer's
attitude toward material nature, rather than the nature of the divine.
Fetishism thus became a way of discussing the religious mentality in
terms of its adequacy or inadequacy for knowing the truth of nature
(as revealed under the observation of scientific reason). In this way, the
theoretical term "fetishism" was framed as an illustration of the state of
mind lacking "enlightenment."

We can find more or less identical principles of explanation, structures
of ideas, and systems of characters in exemplary Enlightenment texts.
For instance, in Voltaire's *conte philosophique* of 1759, there is a moment
when Candide and his worthy valet Cacambo travel from that best of all
possible utopias, El Dorado, back to a historical world in which reality

is marked by the constant eruption of violent events whose extreme randomness is matched only by the extreme misery and horror that are their human consequences. This passage involves an encounter with an enslaved African fetish worshipper whom Candide and Cacambo find stretched across the road that leads from El Dorado to Suriname. Beyond his near nakedness, this figure is striking to the travelers for his lack of a left leg and a right hand. The conversation that ensues conveys an authorial message whose ideas and sentiments we recognize as typical of Enlightenment discourse:

"Oh, good Lord!" said Candide to him in Dutch. "What are you doing there, my friend, in that horrible state I see you in?"

"I am waiting for my master Monsieur Vanderdendur, the famous merchant," the Negro replied.

"Was it Monsieur Vanderdendur," said Candide, "who treated you this way?"

"Yes, sir," said the Negro, "it is the custom. They give us a pair of cloth shorts twice a year for all our clothing. When we work in the sugar mills and we catch our finger in the millstone, they cut off our hand; when we try to run away, they cut off a leg; both things have happened to me. It is at this price that you eat sugar in Europe. However, when my mother sold me for ten pataçons on the Guinea coast, she said to me: 'My dear child, bless our fetishes, worship them always, they will make you live happily; you have the honor to be a slave of our lords the whites, and thereby you are making the fortunes of your father and mother.' Alas! I don't know if I made their fortune, but they didn't make mine. Dogs, monkeys, parrots are a thousand times less miserable than we are. The Dutch fetishes who converted me tell me every Sunday that we are all, blacks and whites, children of Adam. I am no genealogist, but if those preachers are telling the truth, we are all second cousins. Now you must admit that no one could treat his relatives in a more horrible way."

"Oh, Pangloss!" exclaimed Candide, "you had not guessed this abomination; this does it, at last I shall have to renounce your optimism."

"What is optimism?" said Cacambo.

"Alas," said Candide, "it is the mania of maintaining that all is well when we are miserable!" And he shed tears as he looked at his Negro, and he entered Surinam weeping.[35]

Not only has Candide, through his encounter with the fetish worshipper, passed back to the nonutopian real world, he has moved from delusion to enlightenment—liberated from the dogmatic optimism of Leibnizian systems theory whose premise of the necessarily harmonious unity of the existing world system enables Pangloss to demonstrate that noses exist to permit the wearing of spectacles, legs were created to fill up trousers, stones created to be shaped into castles for aristocrats, and pigs made to be eaten.[36] Candide's encounter frees him from this farcical faith that material objects were designed to serve human purposes and promote human happiness. Candide arrives at a new philosophical perspective personified by Martin the Manichean, who becomes Candide's traveling companion after the Dutch merchant Monsieur Vanderdendur has run off with the last of Candide's El Dorado wealth.

The ironic knowledge that the real world of events should be—but is not—a harmonious and unified rational system on the order of the Newtonian solar system, a mechanism such as a clock, or an ideal commodity market and monetary system, is of course a hallmark of Enlightenment thought. It was an idea crystallized in the historical imagination of the day in the form of the 1755 Lisbon earthquake (a natural catastrophe) and the Seven Years' War (a social catastrophe which was the first primarily colonial war between European nations).

Even more characteristic of Enlightenment thought than scandalized recognition of the chaos of events is the equating of obedience to custom and tradition in the social domain with superstitious credulity in the religious domain. We see this equation and its significance in the figure of the victimized African, whose blind obedience to custom (lying passively in the road, waiting for Vanderdendur) becomes, despite all the coercion and mutilation, a kind of self-incurred immaturity (to use Kant's famous phrase) derived from his credulous reverence for the African and European fetishes preached by his mother and the Dutch clergymen. Voltaire's point is that "fetish worship" keeps people happy, no matter how miserable they are. He is using the figure of the African fetish worshipper to have Candide (and the reader) look into a contemporary historical mirror in which he perceives his own misery and dupery in that of the other. And indeed Candide attains enlightenment when he understands that the rationalist optimism of modern scientism, which assumed a necessary built-in harmony between natural objects and human ends, is no less a fetishism than are primitive religion and Christian dogma. The fetish discourse of the Protestant merchants in Guinea already contained a double critical aim: against both non-European primitives and Roman Catholics. Enlightenment intellectuals like Voltaire used the rhetoric of fetish worship to criticize unenlightened moderns as well: inhumane exploiters of the new mercantile world (Vanderdendur) and self-deluded philosophers of the new worldview (Pangloss).

We also find in Voltaire's text the typical Enlightenment figures of the hypocritical clergymen (the Dutch "fetishes") and the immoral woman (the mother) who out of greed perverts the private domain of the family as thoroughly as the priests pervert the public domain of political order. The character system associated with the figure of the fetish worshipper in Candide is essentially that found in Bosman's account of the snake cult of Ouidah, with one significant difference: for Bosman the problem is the repression of the mercantile principle, while for Voltaire it is its unrestricted exercise.[37]

By the late eighteenth century, "fetishism" had been widely accepted as the name for the earliest stage of historical religion and for the general tendency of the unenlightened mind toward irrational beliefs (be these theistic or nontheistic, religious or nonreligious)—a tendency which formed the psychological ground for traditional feelings of social obligation and recognitions of moral duty. Reframing questions of religion in terms of the problem of "fetishism" helped establish the intellectual orientation out of which the science of sociology would later emerge.

Above all de Brosses's theory opposed those historical interpretations which viewed religions and myths as figurative expressions of the eternal truths of speculative metaphysics. By calling fetishism a cult of earthly objects, de Brosses set a materialist historical theory in opposition to the interpretive theories of the Western philosophical and theological tradition. In the course of doing this, and despite de Brosses's own disinterest in the issue, metaphor and anthropomorphization became located outside the rationalist logos and within a nontranscendent material world and the "irrational" mental operation of connecting particular desires to singular events that was proper to such a radically historical world. This fundamental break with Western metaphysics in favor of a materialist and (historically and ethnographically) scientific method represents the theoretical articulation of concepts implicit in that pragmatic cross-cultural mercantile situation in which the discourse about fetishes developed.

The theoretical discourse about fetishes established itself in European learned conversation during the third quarter of the eighteenth century along with a certain polemical rhetoric about fetish worship. The latter aimed at debunking all forms of superstition and unenlightenment without necessarily appealing to the arguments and explanations of the theory of fetishism found in scientific writers concerned with the "natural history" of the religions of the world. At the same time, the practical descriptive discourse about African fetishes continued and gained a new virulence among Europeans directly involved in the slave trade. By 1800, a synchronic Foucauldian look at the "archive" of authoritative utterances using the terminology of the fetish would be complex indeed.

From the standpoint of our interest in social theory, we find a somewhat more manageable state of affairs. By 1800 "fetishism" was a controversial but widely accepted term. The form of religion it described seemed recognizable among many past and present-day peoples, and the scientific argument concerned whether "fetishism" was truly the first, most primitive form of religion, or whether it was a late, degenerative form (the latter position being taken especially by those who accepted the primacy of a revealed monotheism). In addition to this historical-descriptive dimension of fetish theory, the concepts drawn on in the superstition-debunking rhetoric about the fetishism of non-Europeans, Catholics, and rationalist system-builders marked a basic theoretical problem for ideologues and other social psychologists and philosophers concerned with the creedal needs, as it were, of national populations deemed incapable of worshipping reason per se, but perhaps able to be liberated from theological superstitions through some sort of aesthetic or sentimental education.

Both the historical-descriptive and the political-psychological dimensions of the theoretical discourse about fetishism were taken up in the 1790s in Germany—the moment of late Kant and early Hegel. In the writings of these thinkers, we find a fourth object of criticism proper to the terminology of fetishism: the fetishism of (abstract) reason itself. In theorizing about this fetishism of formal systems, the problem of irrational figurative thought raised in de Brosses's conception (though not in his articulated argument) of fetishism as the nonallegorical personification of material objects becomes a central theme. A further chapter would have to examine this moment in the history of fetish theory, when Enlightenment rationality itself comes to be understood as fetishism from the standpoint of critical philosophy. Having completed that examination, one could then begin to write the history of fetish theory in the age of the human sciences.

CHAPTER 5

Fetishism and Materialism:
The Limits of Theory in Marx

Poststructuralism has made for real theoretical advances in many areas, but it has not helped us read Marx. Indeed its principal contribution has been a certain semiological reading of Marxian theory that impedes any fruitful engagement with Marx's writing. The notion of fetishism has figured prominently in this poststructuralist revision of Marx since it is the locus within Marxian discourse for questions about the relations of science, ideology, consciousness, and the cultural construction of social reality—questions that have come to the fore in efforts to theorize the radical potential of nonproletarian identities, new social movements, and cultural politics. The problem with the semiological reading of fetishism that seems to have won the day among left cultural critics—whether in its Baudrillardian, Derridean, or Lacanian variants is that it eliminates from Marxian analysis that materialism which most distinguishes it and which is, in my opinion, its greatest asset as a critical method. Marx's materialist method is better comprehended through the very approaches—existential phenomenology, dialectical analysis, quantitative social science—that poststructuralist semiology rejects. For this reason, it seems worth prefacing this exposition of Marx's appropriation of the nineteenth-century discourse about fetishism with a discussion of the interpretation that I intend to oppose.

The Semiological Reading of Marx

One can trace the semiological interpretation of Marx, not surprisingly, to the discussions in Ferdinand de Saussure's *Course in General Linguistics*, in which linguistics and economics are identified as kindred sciences, sciences of "value."[1] But it was in the context of 1950s anti-Stalinism and in the wake of Claude Lévi-Strauss's famous essay "The

Structural Study of Myth" that Roland Barthes wrote what might be termed the "History and Class Consciousness" of the semiological reading of Marx, his 1957 essay "Myth Today." Lévi-Strauss had concluded his own essay with the claim that "the same logical processes operate in myth as in science."[2] Mythical thought (what used to be called the "primitive mind") and scientific reason obey the same laws, laws that also structure social organizations such as kinship systems. Different social structures, be they communicational systems like languages or concrete institutions, reflect the fundamental organizational structures of a given society like so many mirrors positioned around the walls of a room, each reflecting the same furniture from different angles with a "timelessness" that poststructuralism will identify with the timelessness Freud attributed to the "unconscious."[3] The "furniture" in Lévi-Strauss's image is not, of course, real furniture existing in the phenomenal space of lived experience and embodied movement but rather the general rules—the mental furniture—that inform a particular mode of social organization without themselves being objects of consciousness (people speak and marry without knowing the linguistic or kinship rules they use in performing these actions; hence such structures constitute a social unconscious shared by all members of a given culture). Dialectic, according to Lévi-Strauss, is simply the unlimited capacity of these mirrors to totalize all aspects of social experience through representation (an argument opposing Jean-Paul Sartre's privileging of the dialectical form of human temporality and historicity). But the metaplay with structures expressed in myths is really more combinatory and rhetorical than dialectical in any Marxian sense. Myths are likened to the dream-riddles decoded by Freud; indeed, structuralists identified the different processes of the "dreamwork" described by Freud with the different types of rhetorical figures, tropes, whose poetic operation had been classified in classical rhetoric. The psychic processes of the unconscious theorized by psychoanalysis were identified not only with the poetic structures theorized in linguistics but also with the performative rules of social organizations posited by structuralist social science. The result was a conception of general "cultural logics" whose rules were held to structure both social institutions and a collective ("political") unconscious. The poststructuralist critic of culture could then conceive a politics as a sort of radical analysis of these cultural logics analogous to Freud's psychoanalysis of individuals. This enormously flattering conception of the critical activity of intellectuals is theorized in the poststructuralist semiology inaugurated by Roland Barthes.

In the essay that Barthes himself claimed initiated semiological analysis, he identifies the structural dynamic of premodern myths theorized by Lévi-Strauss as also that of modern ideologies, and he understands ideology as language whose terms are mere images that have been "de-politicized" through their removal from the context of their praxis.[4] Barthes thereby rereads *The German Ideology* through Lévi-Strauss in a manner that allows him to condemn Stalinist repression while preserving a mystical belief in "revolution," conceived as nonideological action fusing productive activity and operational language:

> If I am a woodcutter and I am led to name the tree which I am felling, whatever the form of my sentence, I "speak the tree," I do not speak about it. This means that my language is operational, transitively linked to its object; between the tree and myself there is nothing but my labour, that is to say, an action. This is political language: it represents nature for me only inasmuch as I am going to transform it, it is a language thanks to which I "act the object"; the tree is not an image for me, it is simply the meaning of my action. But if I am not a woodcutter, I can no longer "speak the tree," I can only speak about it, on it. My language is no longer the instrument of an "acted-on tree," it is the "tree-celebrated" which becomes the instrument of my language . . . a second-order language, metalanguage in which I shall henceforth not "act the things" but "act their names."
>
> There is therefore one language which is not mythical, it is the language of man as producer: wherever man speaks in order to transform reality and not to preserve it as an image, wherever he links his language to the making of things, metalanguage is referred to a language-object, and myth is impossible. This is why revolutionary language cannot be mythical. Revolution is defined as a cathartic act meant to reveal the political load of the world: it makes the world; and its language, all of it, is functionally absorbed in its making. . . . The bourgeoisie hides the fact that it is the bourgeoisie and thereby produces myth; revolution announces itself openly as revolution and thereby abolishes myth.[5]

Among the many reasons why this passage has not aged well is the point, stated dryly by Jacques Rancière in another context, that "the idea of revolution is fairly ideological."[6] While subsequent semiology (Maoists aside) moved away from belief in the semantic transparency of revolutionary action, it never seriously questioned the assumptions that allowed Barthes's untheorized elision of politics with labor and of operational linguistics with the phenomenology of embodied action. Instead of opening the question of the relation between political repre-sentation and productive activity, and between semiosis and embodied

experience,[7] poststructural semiology, in rejecting Jacobin revolution-
ism and the mystique of direct action, also rejected any conception of
consequential action, use value, or material production as something
usefully distinguished from sign exchange and communicative activity.
In doing this, it failed to confront fetishism as a problem distinct from
that of ideology.

One can distinguish three particularly influential semiological ar-
ticulations of the theory of fetishism. One of these was Jean Baudrillard's 1970 essay "Fetishism and Ideology: The Semiological Reduction," which was written as part of his project to develop "the political
economy of the sign" and abolish "the artificial distinction between the
economic and the ideological."[8] His essential move—Fredric Jameson
refers to it as "virtually the paradigm gesture of the new production
process"[9]—was to collapse the distinction between exchange value and
use value, developed in the abstract discussion of the commodity form
in *Capital*'s opening pages, with Saussure's distinction between the signifier and the signified.[10] The logic of ideology thereby becomes the
internal logic of the commodity and the sign alike. A material commodity's relation to its use is conceived as the paradigmatic relation in a sign
wherein the phatic vehicle that is the sensible signifier refers to some
"real thing" (the signified, an object outside the signifier's own coded
medium). Exchange value is identified as the syntagmatic dimension
wherein different commodity-signifiers circulate through exchange circulate through exchange transactions that equate their economic value,
rather the way words in a poetic text are substituted for each other
through metaphorical equations of meaning. Such circulation itself
produces novel value representations (meaning-effects) because the
exchange values borne by commodities have a certain independence
from their alleged use values (their "proper meanings"). Market value
is viewed as a function of the structure of differential relations among
commodities as exchange values, apart from any relation to use or labor
values, just the way word meaning is internal to signifiers and distinct
from their objective reference (their significance). Moreover, notions
such as "need" and "use value"—and the concepts of labor power and
production related to them—are, contrary to what Marx said, the most
ideologically constructed notions of all.[11] The presumption of a realm of
production distinct from that of exchange is the illusion of an essentialist anthropology that would ground both in an order of consumption
composed of unchanging needs and the natural use values that satisfy
them. Baudrillard thus arrives at the central claim of the semiological
reading of Marx: the claim that Marxian theory of labor value tried to
anchor the exchange value of commodities in a primary order of mate-

rial production in just the same way that structuralist linguistics tried to anchor the meaning-effects of signifiers in a foundational order of the signified. Poststructuralist semiology thereby completes both the critique of signs begun by the structuralist linguistics and the critique of political economy begun by Marxism by overcoming their essentialist objectivism and humanism. In doing this, it reveals capitalist fetishism to be nothing other than the semiologist's own fascination with signs:

> If fetishism exists it is thus not a fetishism of the signified, a fetishism of substances and values (called ideological), which the fetish object would incarnate for the alienated subject. Behind this reinterpretation (which is truly ideological) is a *fetishism of the signifier*. That is to say that the subject is trapped in the factitious, differential, encoded, systematized aspect of the object. It is not the passion (whether of objects or subjects) for substances that speaks in fetishism, it is the passion for the code.[12]

According to Baudrillard, contemporary consumer society increasingly reveals—through the technological forms of its own self-spectacle—the degree to which commodities are no longer objects (those posited, but absent, signifieds) but rather image signifiers, "simulated" objects existing in a "hyperreal" social order that has been schizophrenically freed from all fixed investments of individual personality and particular desire. In postmodern society (so it is said), it is no longer the material use of products that is the object of our consumption so much as their commodified meaning—the content of their form, their exchange value—now revealed as autonomous forces in packaging and advertising. The post-Marxist theory of ideology suited to contemporary society is precisely that "semiology of images" proposed by Barthes, but now understood as the capitalist mode of production itself.

From the perspective of the history of theories of fetishism, Baudrillard's position is that of a postmodern Kantianism in which the free-acting subject's subordination to and reification by objective social forms is driven not by superstitious ignorance and fear, as in Kant's Enlightenment philosophy, but by fascination and the desire for pure formalism itself.[13] The other influential semiological versions of Marxian fetish theory are more Hegelian than Kantian.[14] Whereas Baudrillard would view fetishism in terms of the desire to inhabit self-contained formal codes that overcome all internal ambiguity and external materiality, Derridean post-Marxists would locate the fetish in semantic indeterminacy and the ambivalent oscillation (hence no dialectical resolution) between contrary determinations, a "space" where codes and their logics break down in a materiality that is conceived in terms of pure difference, contingency, and chance.[15]

More influential than deconstruction's fetish was the conception, developed from Louis Althusser's appropriation of Lacanian psychoanalysis, of the fetish as the ideological object itself. In this theory, ideology is premised on the impossibility of knowing the historical real: since the larger historical and social world in which we live can never, as such, become an object of direct experience for individuals, we substitute for this unexperienceable and unrepresentable reality an imaginary representation of our relation to history and society—a picture of the "whole earth," say—just the way a child, at the moment when self-consciousness first dawns, unable to experience his or her own subjectivity perceptually, substitutes for it the representable image of the self he or she sees pictured when looking in a mirror. "Ideology," writes Althusser in the formulation that has become a postmodernist article of faith, "*is a 'Representation' of the Imaginary Relationship of Individuals to their Real Conditions of Existence.*"[16] Moreover, "*Ideology Interpellates Individuals as Subjects. . . .* the category of the subject is constitutive of all ideology."[17] The subject—that aggressively self-protective emptiness, always already traumatized and primally antagonistic to all definiteness of desire—can no more be the object of concrete experience than can the historical real. In its absence, to console and defend us from the terror of our constitutive formlessness, we substitute personas, mirror selves, from our socially defined subject-positions. Both society and the self are, so this line of argument goes, imaginary totalizations, false universals that exist in the form of images, ideological signifiers of holistic closures we can never truly know or be, fetishes. But there is a problem. How can the antidialectical poststructuralist avoid conceiving this process of false semiotic objectification as a Hegelian dialectic that traces the story of the self-representations of self-consciousness without at the same time turning it into what Althusser called Hegel's materialist "mirror image"—"*economism* and *even technologism*"?[18] Either move constructs a vision of historical inevitability upon a teleological narrative. In the former, contradictions in ideological consciousness (in the ethico-political "superstructure") determine those of the economic base, and hence the historical process; in the latter, contradictions in the material infrastructure determine all ideological superstructures, along with the course of history. Either way, one accepts a reified dialectic whose monocausal explanations fail to account for the historical fact of heterogeneous social formations and "uneven" development. The solution is found in the concept of a historical movement whose determination is both multicausal and incomplete—partly determined by many economic, political, and ideological structures, yet still retaining a bit of contingent indeterminacy. This conception is articulated by Althusser in the notions of "overdetermination" and, in a timely footnote praising Antonio Gramsci, "hegemony."[19] For semiological post-Marxism, the notions of overdetermination and cultural hegemony resolve the fundamental contradiction in Marx's own argument: that between his historical determinism—his theory that the contradictions in the capitalist mode of production's own system must themselves drive it to dissolution—and the subjectivist voluntarism of his appeal to conscious class struggle in making the revolution.[20] Freed from the residual scientism of Althusser, Lacanian post-Marxists can affirm the presence, in the historical field of events and in ourselves as agents, of indeterminacy and contingency as the open horizon that makes possible radical action and social change. Ernesto Laclau and Slavoj Žižek have identified this "radical indeterminacy" as the ground of a "pure antagonism" able to challenge oppressive orders.[21] Yet, for all this, the Lacanian strand of post-Marxist semiology culminates in the announcement of a return to dialectic and to Hegel as "the first post-Marxist."[22] In his book *The Sublime Object of Ideology*, Žižek maintains that "the most consistent model of such an acknowledgement of antagonism is offered by Hegelian dialectics,"[23] and he proposes a "kind of 'return to Hegel'—to reactualize Hegelian dialectics by giving it a new reading on the basis of Lacanian psychoanalysis. The current image of Hegel as an 'idealist-monist' is totally misleading: what we find in Hegel is the strongest affirmation yet of difference and contingency—'absolute knowledge' itself is nothing but a name for the acknowledgement of a certain radical loss."[24] Žižek makes this argument by way of a rereading of the theory of fetishism in which the Hegelian dialectic is rediscovered in the movement whereby ideological universals are produced through a process that converts the experience of objects lacking adequacy as expressive signifiers into the experience of them as objective signifiers of that very lack, and therefore, in some less finite sense, sublimely adequate. This is, indeed, the true Hegelian move: materiality, exteriority, resistance, is always the same, always the necessary mediating otherness through which abstractly subjective concepts are actualized as ideas in a process of reconciliation to existing reality which is their own process of historical becoming. Žižek's great contribution is to reveal semiological criticism and poststructuralist theory as, at best, a form of the sort of left Hegelianism that Marx began his own intellectual development by criticizing. In these semiological readings of Marx, the concept of materiality is always either replaced altogether by a concept of objectified form, of the pure signifier, or else abstracted on a textualist model as sheer heterogeneity and contingency, as the "outside" of preexisting codes where semantic effects are produced by aleatory play among homologous structures and homophonic forms. In this way, all dualities between form and content, sign and referent, exchange value and use value, subject and object, difference and contradiction, are "overcome," as is the need for dialectic. Marx's text itself can then be read rhetorically, and the Marxian notion of fetishism can be interpreted as a rhetorician's theory of ideology.[25]

In opposition to such approaches, the present chapter searches for a more Marxian, materialist theoretical perspective by examining Marx's conception of economic fetishism in the light of his appropriation of the learned discourse about religious fetishism that was part of the intellectual context of nineteenth-century European scholarship. In this regard, Etienne Balibar is simply wrong when he argues that the discourse about fetishism occurs in Marx only during the writing of *Capital* and that it should be understood in terms of the problematic of "ideology," with "fetishism" conceived as Marx's attempt "to think both the real and the imaginary within ideology."[26] On the contrary, the problem of fetishism was very much present in Marx's thought (and writing) for twenty-five years prior to the publication of the first volume of *Capital*. Moreover, "fetishism" expresses a problematic distinct from that of "ideology," one with its own historical and conceptual specificity, concerned with articulating a materialist conception of theory.[27] In contrast to semiological post-Marxism, it is the Marxian view that the production of theoretical discourse is always an attempt at once to make intelligible and to complete (in a functional sense) some already institutionalized social reality. Theory always arises as a supplement not to the logic of a text but to a particular social practice; its analysis is best pursued not through deconstructions of intertextuality and aleatory play but by articulating the contradictions between institutional practices and the theories by which they explain and justify themselves and each other.[28] Indeed, such a materialist analysis of ideological theories is expressed in the notion of fetishism that Marx developed in the course of his writings: revisiting Marx's theory of fetishism is a way to reopen the question of materialist criticism. As Robert Meister has written,

> Without the premise of materialism the Marxist critique of ideology would tend to portray the concrete social formation as a hall of mirrors [alluding to Lévi-Strauss's image]. All essences would be reduced to appearances, and all appearances to the mutual reflection of overlapping social practices or "discourses." A Marxism lacking a dynamic material process such as "accumulation" could never explain why the patterns and outcomes of institutional overlap change over

time. We would be left with a series of static pictures of the range of institutional contradictions that make political action possible at any given moment. Instead of showing a path of development, historical argument would consist of demonstrating the discontinuities between these pictures, suggesting always that particular outcomes are "contingent" rather than necessary. . . . Materialism provided Marx with a path out of the hall of mirrors.[29]

Insofar as the present chapter arrives at any sort of general conclusions, they are the following. The Marxian theory of fetishism may be described as a critical, materialist theory of social desire. It presents modern political economy as a real social metaphysics (an institutional objectification of human temporality in the form of labor power, surplus value, and credit-money) and, at the same time, as a fantastically alien misrepresentation (an inhuman, doubly inverted vision of the collective life of individuals as "civil society"). Its method is that of a historicizing, dialectical phenomenology of social reality complementary to class analysis and giving concrete theoretical expression to what I believe Meister rightly terms Marx's *political materialism*.

Marx and the Discourse about Fetishism

In his mature thought, Marx understood capital to be a species of fetish. A factory machine, a wheat field, a pension fund, and other "things" reckoned as capital by accountants and political economists are fetishes, in Marx's view, not in their physical existence or concrete functions per se but in their reality as material forms ("part-objects") of a distinctive type of social system. The truth of capital, for Marx, is found in its social essence as an organizing principle, as the universal form for social processes aiming at the formation and accumulation of precisely this sort of materialized value: that odd type of "sensuous supersensuous thing" (*sinnlich übersinnliches Ding*) called capital.[30]

Fetishism is the term Marx used to characterize the capitalist social process *as a whole*. At the very least, his employment of this word was a vivid way of suggesting to his readers that the truth of capital was to be grasped from a perspective alien to that of bourgeois understanding, which knows capital exclusively through its own categories. One of the claims of this chapter is that Marx appealed to the language of magic and theology in general, and fetishism in particular, as a way of evoking the materialist imaginary proper to a communist mode of apprehending capitalist reality. At the most, Marx's mature discourse about fetishism expresses a dialectical and materialist critique of both religion and political economy—one which identifies political economy as an atheological "religion of everyday life" and which revalues both in terms of their effective relation to exploitive divisions of social labor.[31] That is, the discourse about fetishism redescribes both religion and political economy from the perspective of class struggle.

Marx's use of "fetishism" has a deliberately strange effect of erudition and vulgarity: when he speaks about capitalist fetishism, he is being theoretically serious and polemically satirical at the same time. In accepting "fetishism" as a historically scientific term, Marx was simply conforming to the learned opinion of his time; throughout his writing, Marx spoke of the fetish worship of "primitive" peoples as historical fact, often employing the term as a synecdoche for primitive religion in general (with Christianity taken as its modern counterpart). But Marx also recognized—in a way Feuerbach did not—that fetishism was a crucial category for the materialist critique of religion and, indeed, of philosophical idealism. As with all his key words, Marx's usage of "fetishism" enacts a dialogic subversion of the way his predecessors and contemporaries theorized social reality. Marx took advantage of the radically historical, materialist problematic implicit in the Enlightenment discourse about fetishism to travesty the idealist and, at best, abstractly materialist social philosophies of his time by means of their own deepest preconceptions. Although Marx's materialism and his social theory went far beyond those of Enlightenment thought, his synopsis of the historical progress of religious consciousness from primordial fetish worship to an ironic deism that was the next best thing to atheism ("from the African's fetish to Voltaire's supreme being"[32]) bears an eighteenth-century pedigree. This theoretical narrative of the world history of religion was established in European intellectual culture by the end of the eighteenth century, although the very word "fetishism" was coined only in 1757 by Charles de Brosses. Historians of religion around the turn of the century, especially Germans such as Christoph Meiners and Philipp Christian Reinhard, but also French writers such as J. A. Dulaure, discussed fetishism extensively as the earliest stage of religion.[33] Although the notion was controversial in circles where theological faith confronted the new history of religion (scholars argued whether fetishism was historically prior to polytheism and monotheism or was merely the most debased form of degenerate religion), popular and learned writers alike generally accepted that the worship of terrestrial, material objects (as de Brosses had defined his neologism) was the most primitive moment of religion.[34] Invented by a French philosophe and popularized in German texts, "fetishism" is referred to by English writers as early as 1801.[35] The use of the idea by English humanists already appears in 1809 when

Coleridge condemned vulgar empiricism by likening it to primitive fetish worship: "From the fetisch of the imbruted African to the soul-debasing errors of the proud fact-hunting materialist we may trace the various ceremonials of the same idolatry."[36]

In the 1840s, the founder of sociology, Auguste Comte, published a theory of fetishism so elaborate and so important to his theory of positivism that subsequent writers in the emerging social sciences were forced to react against his conception of fetishism if they were to approach the problem it named at all.[37] The principal alternative theories subsequently elaborated—around the time the first volume of *Capital* appeared—were E. B. Tylor's "animism," which offered an idealist psychological explanation of fetishistic beliefs, and J. F. McLennan's "totemism," an institutional theory that subordinated fetishism to ancestor worship and kinship organization.[38] In the last decades of the century, there was both an upsurge in "ethnographic" descriptions of primitive fetishism (a result of the colonialist scramble of those years)[39] and increasing distrust of the notion among social scientists,[40] although historians of religion still tended to treat the notion as unproblematic.[41] Meanwhile, the rise of the discourse about sexual fetishism developed by sexologists in the 1880s only intensified the association of the idea (already stressed by such writers as Hegel and Benjamin Constant in the 1820s) with the arbitrary and the idiosyncratically individual, and hence with psychological rather than sociological processes. Added to its association with the scandalous founder of sociology, Comte, this new usage encouraged the fathers of respectable sociology, Emile Durkheim and Max Weber, to avoid the term. In anthropology, while less "scientific" writers such as James Frazer and Wilhelm Wundt continued to use the term, we find it decisively rejected by Marcel Mauss in 1906.[42]

Marx's own appropriation of the theoretical discourse about fetishism began in the 1840s in the context of a repressive, antiliberal German political regime and the philosophical infighting over the legacy of Hegel. It is to this intellectual moment that a study of Marx's theory of fetishism must first turn.

Religious Fetishism and Civil Society: The Critique of Hegel

In a newspaper article of July 1842, the twenty-four-year-old Marx, claiming the authority of philosophy, defined fetishism as "the religion of sensuous desire" (*die Religion der sinnlichen Begierde*).[43] Although the remark is made in passing in order to expose the scholarship of the editor of a rival journal as mere "penny-magazine erudition," he was not just writing off the top of his head. Earlier that year, Marx had studied the notion of religious fetishism in depth, making extensive excerpts from the book in which the term was coined, Charles de Brosses's *Du culte des dieux fétiches* (1760), and from two more recent works, Karl August Bottiger's *Ideen zur Kunst-Mythologie* (1826) and Benjamin Constant's *De la religion* (1824).[44] In one apocryphal incident excerpted by Marx from the book by de Brosses in which the word "fetishism" was coined, we are offered the image of an apotropaic potlatch improvised by "savages" to ward off the barbaric agents of "primitive accumulation": "The *savages of Cuba* considered gold to be the fetish of the Spaniards. So they celebrated it with a feast, danced and sang around it, and threw it into the sea, in order to be rid of it."[45] This was not the first time that Marx had found some insight in an anecdote in which social conflict was expressed through the contradictory value orders of money and religion. The year before, Marx had concluded his doctoral dissertation with a reflection on the relationship of imagination to social reality, in which the theistic beliefs of ancient cultures and the monetarized relations of secular societies are understood through each other:

> Take for instance the ontological proof.[46] This only means: "that which I conceive for myself in a real way (*realiter*), is a real concept for me," something that works on me. In this sense, all gods, the pagan as well as the Christian ones, have possessed a real existence. Did not the ancient Moloch reign? Was not the Delphic Apollo a real power in the life of the Greeks? Kant's critique means nothing in this respect. If somebody imagines that he has a hundred talers, if this concept is not for him an arbitrary, subjective one, if he believes in it, then these hundred imagined talers have for him the same value as a hundred real ones. For instance, he will incur debts on the strength of his imagination, his imagination will *work in the same way as all humanity has incurred debts on its gods.* The contrary is true. Kant's example might have enforced the ontological proof. Real talers have the same existence that the imagined gods have. Has a real taler any existence except in the imagination, if only in the general or rather common imagination of man? Bring paper money into a country where this use of paper is unknown, and everyone will laugh at your subjective imagination. Come with your gods into another country where other gods are worshipped, and you will be shown to suffer from fantasies and abstractions. And justly so. He who would have brought a Wendic god to the ancient Greeks would have found the proof of this god's nonexistence. Indeed, for the Greeks he did not exist. *That which a particular country is for particular alien gods, the country of reason is for God in general, a region in which he ceases to exist.*[47]

Such problematizations of religion through economics and economics through religion run throughout Marx's writing. This was not merely a rhetorical conceit, a superficial analogy—embellishing Marx's arguments and unrelated to the real problems he sought to address. Religion was as serious a problem for Marx as economics; together they delineated a thematics in whose terms he strove to articulate the social theory and critical method proper to a materialism that was neither mechanistic nor deterministic but emerged from the vital tension in his dual commitment to social scientific objectivity, on the one hand, and, on the other, to a moral responsiveness toward those untheorized historical forces grounded in lived experience and personal suffering (a tension that locates the material limit and historical ground of theory itself).

Marx's first definition of fetishism as "the religion of sensuous desire" came in an article attacking the editor Karl Heinrich Hermes, an anti-Semitic Catholic who was urging severer censorship of religious criticism. Because religious belief is the basis of civic morality, and hence of the state, Hermes argued, the national heritage of theological ideas that lead people to such faith requires special public protection: "Religion is the basis of the state and the most necessary condition for every association."[48] That it is, he reasoned, is demonstrated by the fact that even "in its crudest form as childish fetishism, it nevertheless to some extent raises man above his sensuous desires."[49] Marx knew that Hermes's view did not accord with that of the authorities of his day, since he had recently investigated the notion of fetishism while writing an essay on religious art.[50] "Fetishism is so far from raising man *above* his sensuous desires," as Hermes claimed, wrote Marx, "that, on the contrary, it is *the religion of sensuous desire*: Fantasy arising from desire [*Die Phantasie der Begierde*] deceives the fetish-worshipper that an 'inanimate object' will give up its natural character in order to comply with his desires [*seiner Gelüste*]."[51]

This notion of the fetish worshipper's desire-driven delusion regarding natural objects, his blindness to the unprovidential randomness of physical events, was an element in de Brosses's original theorization of *fétichisme* as the pure condition of unenlightenment [see pp. 100–101, 113 in this book]. To be enlightened, as Voltaire and Kant both stressed, is precisely to disabuse oneself of the idea that the real world has been designed to promote one's own—or humanity's—happiness. Moreover, it is not merely "desire" but "*sensuous* desire" that Marx's definition (taken directly from Hegel) specifies.[52] The term "sensuous" played a surprisingly prominent role in Marx's early anti-Hegelianism (and anti–Left Hegelianism): it is most directly Feuerbach's conception of sensuousness that Marx will rethink.

There was, surprisingly, a great deal at stake for post-Enlightenment philosophy in this formulation of fetishism as the nontranscendental religion of sensuous desire. The term "fetishism" was adopted by *philosophes* such as Baron d'Holbach, Claude Helvétius, and their followers because its discourse displaced the problem of religion from a theological to a materialist problematic congenial to the emerging human sciences and to anticlerical activism alike.[53] It did so by discovering the origin of religious belief in primitive causal reasoning: a mode of thought deriving not from "reason" but from "desire and credulity."[54] Failing to distinguish the intentionless natural world known to scientific reason and motivated by practical material concerns, the savage (so it was argued) superstitiously assumed the existence of a unified causal field for personal actions and physical events, thereby positing reality as subject to animate powers whose purposes could be divined and influenced. Specifically, humanity's belief in gods and supernatural powers (i.e., humanity's unenlightenment) was theorized in terms of prescientific peoples' substitution of imaginary personifications for the unknown physical causes of future events over which people had no control and which they regarded with fear and anxiety.[55] De Brosses's own book was written to attack the universalist *figurisme* of Christian theologians and secular Neoplatonists at the Académie Royale des Inscriptions et Belles-Lettres, whose hermeneutic interpreted ancient myths and cult beliefs as allegories of New Testament events or philosophical ideas. Rejecting the adequacy of euhemerist explanations as well, de Brosses identified a savage "manner of thinking" (*façon de penser*), a "metaphor natural to man,"[56] which located divine power in terrestrial, material entities themselves, and which was purely contingent and particularistic. *Fétichisme* was the term de Brosses used for the cults and superstitions formed from this "natural propensity" toward the nonallegorical personification of material powers (which is what de Brosses means when he defines fetishism as a "direct" cult of terrestrial things *sans figure*).

Fetishism was a radically novel category: it offered an atheological explanation of the origin of religion, one that accounted equally well for theistic beliefs and nontheistic superstitions; it identified religious superstition with false causal reasoning about physical nature, making people's relation to material objects rather than to God the key question for historians of religion and mythology; and it reclassified the entire field of ancient and contemporary religious phenomena by identifying primitive fetishism throughout the historical world, from ancient Egypt (their notorious "animal gods") to archaic Greece (the oracle grove at Dodona) to contemporary Black Africa (especially the serpent cult at Ouidah) to America (manitous and such) to the Holy Bible itself (the Urim and Thummim, among many others). In short, the discourse about fetishism displaced the great object of Enlightenment criticism—religion—into a causative problematic suited to its own secular cosmology, whose "reality principle" was the absolute split between the mechanistic material realm of physical nature (the blind determinism of whose events excluded any principle of teleological causality, that is, Providence) and the end-oriented human realm of purposes and desires (whose free intentionality distinguished its events as moral action, properly determined by rational ideals rather than by the material contingency of merely natural being). Fetishism was the definitive mistake of the pre-enlightened mind: it superstitiously attributed intentional purpose and desire to material entities of the natural world, while allowing social action to be determined by the (clerically interpreted) wills of contingently personified things, which were, in truth, merely the externalized material sites fixing people's own capricious libidinal imaginings ("fancy" in the language of that day).

Yet the very distinction that constituted Enlightenment rationality was responsible for a contradiction in the way it conceived its unenlightened other: fetishism was defined as the worship of "inanimate" things even though its paradigmatic historical exemplifications were cults of animate beings, such as snakes. The special fascination that Egyptian zoolatry and African fetishism exerted on eighteenth-century intellectuals derived not just from the moral scandal of humans kneeling in abject worship before animals lower down on the "great chain of being" but from the inconceivable mystery (within Enlightenment categories) of any direct sensuous perception of animateness in material beings. This constitutive contradiction in Enlightenment thought was overcome in Kant's third critique. The first half of his *Critique of Judgment* develops a novel theory of aesthetic judgment as perception of "purposiveness" in objects.[57] This quasi-animistic subjectivity proper to aesthetic experience is identified as a legitimate faculty of the human mind (as opposed to an aberrant mode of superstitious delusion) in order to come to cognitive terms with the scandalous fact of the organism, the purposeful natural being (theorized in the second part of Kant's treatise, the critique of teleological judgment). For Kant aesthetic judgment is the "primitive" mentality become self-critical (and, thus, no longer superstitious) after having learned to distinguish between the purposive intentionality of its own practical subjectivity and the teleological systems of the objective world exemplified in biological organisms.

The phrase "sensuous desire" in post-Kantian German philosophy was thus theoretically fraught. Not only is "desire" the term for the purpose-forming subjectivity that characterizes the ethical world of humanity, but "sensuous" indicates that immediate experience of lived reality which is the primordial mode of experience (the object of aesthetic feeling) out of which we subsequently distinguish the two epistemic orders: physical nature (the object of empirical understanding) and moral action (the object of transcendental reason). "Sensuous desire" is thus the direct "aesthetic" expression-apprehension of purposes and intentions within the subjectively objective world of immediate experience.[58] Finally, "religion" was understood to refer above all to worship (or "service," *Dienst*) as the submission-abolition of the individual's arbitrary free will (*Willkür*) to some greater universal (God in Kant's ethical transcendentalism, the state in Hegel's institutional idealism). The "religion of sensuous desire" is thus the perverse submission of intellect and moral will to a sort of libidinal aesthetics; it is, by definition, the crudest form of spirituality because the sensuous object can never—as a thing in itself, untransubstantiated into the signifier or allegory of a concept or ideal—attain to any categorical universality, the only proper object of devotion or allegiance. And this is precisely the treatment of "fetishism" that Marx found in Hegel, who defined fetishism as that threshold moment of Spirit which, paradoxically, produced a distinctive world culture (that of African societies) without representing any universal principle (hence Africans were a people outside History). The reason why was precisely the one Marx pointed out to Hermes: the fetishist's "consciousness is still natural consciousness, the consciousness of sensuous desire."[59]

Not only did Marx appreciate the subversively materialist implications of this point of unthinkability in the Hegelian system, but he increasingly came to connect the paradoxical status of this nonuniversal cultural object, the fetish, with the homologously contradictory particularity of "civil society" as discussed in Hegel's *Philosophy of Right*. A close reader of Adam Smith, Hegel identified "civil society" as the social region of the self-interested economic activities of individuals, distinguishing it from the family and the state. Like fetishist cultures, civil society achieved its unity not by finding a principle of universality but by endlessly weaving itself into a "system of needs"—a libidinal economy—in which people's ability to produce the object of someone else's desire becomes the means for satisfying their own desires. The general form realizing—or reifying—this social network of desires and their objects as a market system is money; but, Hegel argues, its *universal principle* is actualized only outside itself, in the state and the civil servants who regulate the economic system for the good of the whole. Civil society is thus viewed as the collective space of particular desires and their objective forms of gratification, but there is one sort of desire that civil society can never satisfy, the desire for the infinite, for some universal actuality to which individuals, in their singular particularity, can never attain. Man (and civil society is conceived by Hegel as a realm of male individuals) can achieve this desire only outside civil society—imperfectly in the family, where man transcends himself in his ontological union with his wife and the real objectification of this transcendent unity in their child, and absolutely in religious worship and state citizenship, when a man's limited, particular will is abolished and subsumed by the universal will of God and nation. In this logic, Marx saw Hegel as simply the most sophisticated ideologue of "the cult of the government's will."

Given Hegel's argument, the modern political order of a free-market civil society supplemented and subsumed by an authoritarian national state could be criticized only by refuting his identification of the state bureaucracy as the universal class of (though not in) civil society and of state citizenship as the actualization of individuals' universal identities. The problem, then, for the materialist critique of politics was to locate a universal class and principle of identity within the realm of human particularity, the realm that theology conceived as belonging to cults of terrestrial objects and political economics conceived as belonging to the economic activities of civil society. It is from this theoretical problematic that the peculiar twinning of the primitive fetishist and the industrial proletarian found throughout Marx's writing arises. And it is from their perspective (as evoked in Marx's writing) that the bourgeois capitalist is perceived as himself a fetishist, one whose fetish, capital, is believed by its deluded cultists to embody *(super)natural causal powers of value formation,* but which is recognized by the savage, expropriated through "primitive accumulation," and by the worker, exploited through the capitalist accumulation process proper, as having no real power outside its social power to command the labor activity of real individuals.

During 1843 and the first half of 1844, Marx's thought seems to advance by means of a critical analogy between religious fetishism and civil society: Christianity (as a religion of the abstract, heavenly universal) is the modern supersession of fetishism (the religion of sensuous, earthly desires), just as the state (in Hegelian philosophy) is the universal secular institution superseding civil society (the realm of particular desires and of individuals). Marx's materialist critique sought to debunk the claim of universalist social institutions (the Christian Church and the state) to a superior ontological status by affirming the untranscendable reality of that existential mode of particular sensuous desires and concrete, embodied individuals proper to fetish worship and civil society. For Marx, then, fetishism and political economy are closer to the true world than monotheism and statism. They can thus be used to criticize the fantastic pretensions of monotheism and statism to some sort of transcendent reality; but they, in turn, become the objects of an even more fundamental critique (whose key terms are historical materialism and revolutionary communism) through which Marx sought to articulate the theory of a humane atheist morality and a radical democratic socialism.

This double critique of religion and politics received its most powerful expression in "A Contribution to the Critique of Hegel's 'Philosophy of Right'" (1844). Marx makes it clear that he sees the relation between the political critique of Hegelian constitutionalism and the religious critique of transcendental theology as more than a mere analogy. "The critique of religion is the prerequisite of every critique," he claims, since it returns our understanding from the unearthly realm of religious ideals to the immanent world of man's lived experience. "The critique of heaven is transformed into the critique of the earth."[60] More than just a homologous complement to the political critique of the state as the "inverted" universalized reflection of the particularistic economic world of civil society, the critique of religion locates the real ground of radical democratic political values: the human suffering and frustrated desires experienced by oppressed people within the concrete world of everyday life.

> Religion is the general theory of this world, its encyclopedic compendium, its logic in popular form. . . . The wretchedness of religion is at once an expression of and protest against real wretchedness. Religion is the sigh of the oppressed creature, the heart of a heartless world, and the soul of soulless conditions. . . . The critique of religion ends in the doctrine that man is the supreme being for man; thus it ends with the categorical imperative to overthrow all conditions in which man is a debased, enslaved, neglected, contemptible being.[61]

The truth of religion is found in its potently fantastic theorization of the pain and degradation of oppressed people as a form of spiritual resistance to conditions that, in radically threatening people's very humanity, reveal the specific values that constitute our identity as humans.[62] Human experience of material poverty and social oppression is here viewed as the source of a spiritually powerful moral authority that is the concrete subjective ground of a radically democratic emancipatory politics. The materialist subject of this radically human ground is twice located by Marx: in the maximally alien perspective of the primitive fetishist, a cultural other for whom material conditions are themselves spiritual values, who judges civil society from outside all civilization; and in the maximally degraded viewpoint of the proletarian, bourgeois society's internal other, forced to the physical margin of subsistence, whose value judgments express the most fundamental needs of human life.

Having (in 1844) identified the modern bearer of radically emancipatory passion as the proletariat, Marx now saw the aim of philosophy's critique of religion as the recovery of the discourse of the proletariat from its displaced, or "inverted," theological expression. During the period of *The German Ideology* (1845–1846), this project was elided in the historical materialist, social scientific polemic against ideology, false consciousness, and "critical criticism" (today called postmodernist criticism). But after he had absorbed the lessons of the political events of 1848–1850, Marx returned to the discourse about fetishism in 1857 in order to articulate not so much the disillusioned *class consciousness* of the proletariat (its members' self-conception as workers within the categories of civil society) as a communist imaginary that sees the fantastically inhuman anamorphosis of liberal political economy's vision of human life as civil society. Marx evoked the "savage" subject of religious fetishism as a (potentially theoretical) viewpoint outside capitalism capable of recognizing proletarians in their objective social identity as the economic class owning no marketable private property other than their own embodied being and "its" capacity for concrete productive activity, and therefore as the one identity within civil society in which true human being (that is, sensuous, embodied, living being) appears.

Economic Fetishism: Marx on Capital

Much that is valuable about Marx's thought has been obscured by the failure to appreciate the full novelty—and irony—in Marx's appropriation of the term "materialism." Rediscovering the centrality of the notion of the sensuous in Marx's materialism reinforces his own claims that his approach was neither mechanistic (what he calls "French materialism" in *The Holy Family*) nor economistic, neither monocausally deterministic nor dogmatically normative. It was rather a critical social materialism that emerged out of his critiques of Feuerbach's humanist anthropology and Hegel's institutional idealism: notions of natural species-being and the self-acting Concept could be criticized as idealist abstractions once Marx affirmed the primacy of sensuous desire, productive action, and embodied historicity for human being. The clearest statement of Marx's materialist-phenomenological conception of the human subject as a sensuous, active, objective, desiring being is found in the section "Critique of Hegel's Dialectic and General Philosophy" in the last of the "Economic and Philosophic Manuscripts":

To say that man is a corporeal, living, real, sensuous, objective being with natural powers means that he has real, sensuous objects as the objects of his being and of his vital expression, or that he can only express his life in real, sensuous objects. To be objective, natural and sensuous, and to have object, nature and sense outside oneself, or to be oneself object, nature, and sense for a third person is one and the same thing. . . . To be sensuous, i.e. to be real, is to be an object of sense, a sensuous object, and thus to have sensuous objects outside oneself, objects of one's sense perception. To be sensuous is to suffer (to be subjected to the actions of another). Man as an objective, sensuous being is therefore a suffering being, and because he feels his suffering, he is a passionate being. Passion is man's essential power vigorously striving to attain its object.[63]

Marx conceived human being as an essentially active, material being, one whose objects are *sensuous objects* and whose bodily life and personal self are "produced" in a single process: labor as praxis. Unless forced apart in the class divisions of exploitive societies, "self-activity and the production of material life" form a single "communist" social process.[64] After the critiques of Hegel and Feuerbach, the discourse about fetishism marks the question of the material articulation between the embodied individual of "sensuous desire" and historically specific social divisions of labor.

Marx arrived at his mature use of the discourse about fetishism—along with his mature conception of dialectical materialism—only in the 1850s, after revising his thinking about the ontic and causal status of universal representational forms. As Rancière has said, the farcical but effective masquerade of "democratic" political representations during the events of 1848–1850 fundamentally altered Marx's problematic,[65] forcing him to think beyond the problematic of "ideology" in order to appreciate the way particular representations of the universal (of the social whole) were real, causally important, nontranscendental components of the social-historical world. It was only during the writing of *Capital* in the decade from 1857 to 1867 that Marx worked out a materialist theory of the dialectical, chiasmic structure of social fetishism. As the opening chapter of *Capital* demonstrates, the method that studies social fetishism must be simultaneously phenomenological and historical, treating historically emerging universal forms as the material "power objects" of organized social systems.

In his notebooks of the late 1850s, Marx begins to speak of economic fetishism[66] in criticizing the *naturalistic* materialism underlying David Ricardo's notion of circulating capital and the vulgar economists' idea "that 'material' and half a dozen similar irrelevancies are elements of value."[67] In both these passages Marx is insisting on the *physical immateriality of value*. At first glance, it might seem paradoxical for Marx, a materialist, to be criticizing political economy's theory of value for being too materialistic. But this is the crucial starting point for Marx's mature theory of capitalist fetishism: the materiality of "value" is not physical but social. For Marx, value is a social substance that appears in a series of material forms (labor-selling people, commodified things, money). Although not physically real, the value quantity of products and money can be physically measured. This abstract, aggregate measure is average, socially necessary labor time.[68]

Part of the difficulty of *Capital's* opening chapter is that Marx's argument demonstrating that exchange value is determined by labor time is presented within the highly abstract conditions posited for the first volume of *Capital*, where he studies capitalist production apart from circulation and capital investment and, therefore, apart from real prices. For this reason, considered apart from the rest of Marx's four-volume argument, it is not especially convincing. The real virtue of this chapter, it seems to me, is to give a phenomenological model of the sort of dialectical-materialist process that, for Marx, produces capitalism, in particular, and historically arising social formations, in general. Marx presents the emergence of a universal form that is itself a material object: money-capital. When a given type of useful thing comes to function as a general-equivalent exchange object in trade activities, it comes to be recognized as embodying a new quality: that of a general form, the very medium of exchange (money). This historically emerging general form expresses, in its being as a material object, the exchange relation that produced it: it is this relation realized as a sensuous object. Money's reversibility (its ability to be the thing exchanged away or the thing exchanged for) allows the differentiation of the act of exchange into two separate acts: buying a thing with money and selling a thing for money. This initiates a real process of deferral-distantiation through differentiation (as opposed to a textual *différance*) in which the spatial and temporal separation of the moments of exchange generate the logistic (financial) instruments enabling a modern economy. This process—the monetarization of social life—culminates in the rise of central banks and the emergence of money as credit-money, an object that seems to embody its own temporal existence in its capacity to bear interest.[69] The magical moment of fetish formation in this process is the transition of the general form into a universal form, its modal shift from existence and possibility to necessity—the mysterious transubstantiation of common social practices into custom or law sanctioned by the community as a whole. In short, *Capital*'s first chapter illustrates a process of the historical production of universal forms. Arising as the real representation of material social relations, these exist as material objects; they are fetishes insofar as they have become necessary functional parts that are privileged command-control points of a working system of social reproduction. This process is not only material but dialectical: these causally effective representational forms are "universals" that incorporate (i.e., that become the practical substance—the unity—of) the particular social processes that produce them and which they thereby alter.

Because he views capitalist production as a mode in which social value is fetishistically materialized, it is crucial for Marx to make it clear that the physical materiality of things has nothing to do with their value. A quantity of social labor time is not composed of physical matter (nor is it equivalent to the physical energy expended by the worker); it is nonetheless true, he argues, that "in bourgeois production, wealth as a fetish must be crystallized in a particular substance."[70] Marx presents capital as a three-stage process accomplishing this "crystallization" (i.e., fetishization): "valorization," value creation by labor in commodity production (the subject of *Capital*, volume 1); "realization" of this value in money form during market circulation (the topic of the second volume); and "accumulation" of realized value through capital investments that set in motion further cycles of valorization, realization, and accumulation (studied in *Capital*, volume 3). The drive to extract ever more surplus labor in order to accumulate more exchange value in the fetishized form of invested capital becomes an end in itself. This is the fundamental fetishistic inversion of bourgeois production: monetarized productive capital, which had been merely the means to obtain wealth (the power to gratify concrete human desires whose origins and "logic" are external to its system), becomes identified as wealth itself. The object that had been an accidental means to achieving some desired end becomes a fixed necessity, the very embodiment of desire, and the effective, exclusive power for gratifying it. The human truth of capital is that, as a means that has become an end, it is a socially constructed, culturally real power object: it is the instrumentalized power of command over concrete humans in the form of control over their labor activity through investment decisions. Capital is a form of rule, of social government. It is this political truth that the chiasmic personification-reification structure of capitalist fetishism conceals. In Marx's mature theory, the capitalist social economy is understood as a repeating process of fetishization (i.e., of cycles of labor valorization, monetary realization, and capital accumulation). The very legal and financial categories that establish capital's social reality bring about the fetishized consciousness appropriate to it through what Marx describes as a three-level chiasmus between people and things. The most superficial level is that of personified things and reified people; this is expressed in economists' identification of the "factors of production," which they view as the real sources of value. Marx refers to this whole structure as "the Trinity Formula": land, labor, and capital (the things that appear to have the person-like power to produce value); landlord, wageworker, capitalist (the reified identities that personify the factors composing capitalist production); and, finally, rent, wages, and profits (the forms of money-capital that mediate among them). This level of fetishized objects and individuals is really an expression of the more fundamental level of fetishized relations: here Marx's labor-value critique of the circuits of exchange reveals this level of fetishism as one of reified social relations and personified material relations. People are reified in their relations insofar as their negotiations and other interactions must be expressed through the objectivity of the commodity-price system (that is, in the markets for labor, consumer goods, and capital). Moreover, as already discussed, the material relations between physical things become the social forms for capital's system of reproduction. This level of fetishized relations, in turn, expresses the chiasmic fetishization at the level of systems: the discourse of political economy confuses the scientific knowledge of the technical division of labor (whose logic is that of physical causality) with the politics of the social division of labor (whose logic is that of group entitlements). The identification of the former system with society as a whole is expressed in the Saint-Simonian slogan that socialism will replace "the government of people with the administration of things." That Marx did not stop at this technocratic social vision is demonstrated by his emphasis on class struggle. Even in a "classless" society, class analysis would still function as a critical standard for political arguments in regard to all policy options and administrative decisions whose material impact would not be uniform across the whole of society.

"Capital" is the substantive name for the unity of a socially (if unconsciously) organized material system of growth and reproduction whose effective components and visible forms are things, people, and money. The substance of capital itself is "value," that conserved quantity of social labor time which seems to move through the metamorphic phases of the capitalist economy from one form to another (from laboring people to the things they produce, from these products to the money that purchases them, from this money to the new labor and materials it buys, etc.). Commodities and capital goods, wageworkers and capitalists, money and credit, are forms or parts of a whole temporal-material system. They (we) are members of the body of capital, whose value-essence transcends and yet incarnates itself in these material beings like the divine salvational power of Christ in the faithful members and sacramental objects of his Church. Indeed, just as the mystery of the Catholic Church as the body of Christ is concentrated and expressed in the sacrament of the Eucharist, so the whole mystery of capitalist society appears at its most visible and, at the same time, at its most mysterious in the form of interest-bearing money-capital (money that "breeds" money in the form of interest). "It is in *interest-bearing capital* . . . that capital finds its most objectified form, its pure fetish form. . . . Capital—as an entity—appears here as an independent source of value; as something that creates value in the same way as land [produces] rent, and labor wages. . . . The transubstantiation, the fetishism, is complete."[71] (Capital's fetish forms, it should be stressed, are not subjective illusions: I am hardly hallucinating when I see my money increase in my savings account or when my investment in some aspect of a production cycle returns to me with a surplus.)

Marx argues that the very completion of its fetishistic system brings about the moment of capital's political truth, the moment of historical crisis when "private enterprise" is revealed as social government (and, therefore, as democratically accountable), and the political-economic reality of capitalist society suddenly appears in public culture as *fetishistic* (i.e., as an alien and perversely unnatural reality). Marx located this moment not in the extreme development of the commercialization of social appearances, where readers of Baudrillard might look for it, but in the full development of financial fetishism. The credit-debt system is the fullest institutional expression of a society's relation to itself over time; it is the realization of that social metaphysics which Marx believed to be the true transcendent "other world" existing within the immanent material world inhabited by human individuals. Marx refused the positivist temptation of a Comtian social physics by understanding political economy as a mode of social temporality and by conceiving social arrangements as a realm of historical intersubjective humanity absolutely distinct from the natural, physical world. (That is, for Marx, the truth of "metaphysics," the suprasensuous or invisible realm beyond the sensuous, visible world, is human society—our true "transcendence" is not transcendental but is immanent in the world: time is materialism's transcendent principle.)

In chapters 24 to 27 of *Capital*, volume 3, Marx discusses the evolution of interest-bearing capital (capital's "pure fetish form") into the general (global) credit system. In the consolidation of a unified credit system, capital both fulfills itself for itself and *dis-credits* itself in the eyes of society. Such a moment came early in the eighteenth century with the collapse in France of John Law's system and the bursting of similar Dutch and English speculative bubbles. Marx saw the crucial importance of the credit system during the events of 1848.[72] They are the historical basis for his remark in *Capital* that

> the credit system has a dual character immanent in it: on the one hand it develops the motive of capitalist production, enrichment by the exploitation of others' labour, into the purest and most colossal system of gambling and swindling, and restricts ever more the already small number of the exploiters of social wealth; on the other hand however it constitutes the form of transition towards the new mode of production.[73]

The social truth of capital—that it is a means of materially temporalizing those social obligations (fulfilled in the performance of types of socially valued labor) by which a population seeks to control and determine its collective future—is increasingly visible the more capital becomes concentrated in big investment funds subject to the global credit-debt system. The micropolitical fact that our real social government consists of the private, undemocratic decisions made by corporations and banks becomes visible in the macropolitics of social security funds and international debt.[74] The *global* crisis of capitalism, which Marx believed was the only way a postcapitalist *world history* would come about, reveals—through the very completion of its fetish form—the proximity of the apparently uncoercive structure of capitalist accumulation to the violent state terror of what Marx called "primitive accumulation," a perception of the dialectical unity of the voluntary and the violent that makes visible the class struggle that is the hidden political heart of capitalist economics and ideology.

CHAPTER 6

The Spirit of Civilization: Blood Sacrifice and Monetary Debt

No more the palms with ghastly trophies wave,
The boughs from weight of murder now have ease,
The daily human sacrifices cease,
For blood no longer the fetish tyrants crave.

REV. H. D. RAWNSLEY, "In Memory of Acting Consul-
General Phillips, and those who perished with him near Benin
City, January 1897" (1898)

"You, Makola! Take that herd over to the fetish" (the storehouse was in
every station called the fetish, perhaps because of the spirit of civilization
it contained)

JOSEPH CONRAD, *"An Outpost of Progress" (1896)*

Formed during the sixteenth and seventeenth centuries in cross-cultural commerce along the Atlantic coast of Africa, the discourse about African fetishes was developed into a general theory of fetishism by an eighteenth-century Frenchman who had never been closer to Africa than Naples, and it was further elaborated by a number of influential nineteenth-century European social theorists.[1] While the history of the theory of fetishism among European intellectuals is an interesting subject, in the present chapter I wish to consider the transformation of the pretheoretical Afro-European discourse about fetishes during the period of European conquest and colonization in West Africa. Guided by the thematics of the idea identified in my earlier chapters, a reflection on the history of this discourse during the nineteenth century led me, rather to my surprise, to a consideration of "blood sacrifice" (an admittedly problematic notion) and monetary debt (a notion more problematic than it might at first appear to be) as alternate logics for the material fixation of social obligations that came into conflict during the colonization of West Africa.

The pragmatic discourse about African fetishes forged in the sixteenth century had been a device to enable cross-cultural commercial transactions, and the binding promises that facilitated them, between European traders and various peoples of West and Central Africa. "Fetish" was a middleman's term, a pidgin word, an idea that expressed an immense, yet highly functional, misunderstanding. The distinctive idea of fetish objects that took shape in this context expressed the problem of incommensurable modes for the valuation of material objects. For Europeans, it expressed their impression that the false "religion" organizing African societies caused irrational distortions in Africans' economic valuations of material things. This was understood to be the result of a superstitious mentality that attributed personal intentionality and supernatural power to mere natural objects and manufactured artifacts. Moreover, Europeans forced to participate in solemn oath-taking rituals in order to formalize their relations with their African trading partners viewed such "fetish oaths" as the superstitious equivalent of the laws of contract found in civilized societies. As I discussed in [the second and third chapters of this book], already in seventeenth- and eighteenth-century accounts of "Guinea" written by northern European merchants (i.e., prior to the works of David Hume and Charles de Brosses that introduced this argument to metropolitan intellectuals), we read that the root of the fetish worshipper's superstitious mentality was his or her inability to comprehend the contingent nature of events. Unable to acknowledge the random conjunctions and nonintentional outcomes of objective events whose real causes were utterly impersonal, the African mentality was supposedly ruled by a capricious fancy resulting from an equal blindness to subjective contingency (specifically, to chance associations between a momentary desire and some object encountered by chance). Lacking the knowledge of the true causes of natural events that the Europeans felt they possessed, the primitive Africans, it was thought, attributed supernatural agency to mere material things, worshipping them as "fetish gods" whose power could bring about or prevent whatever outcomes they desired or feared. The sanction of "fetish" could function among irrational primitives as a rule of social order comparable to the rational laws of the civilized because the false causal power attributed to fetishes included the power of life and death. Thus the general European view was that African societies were ruled by a fear of death institutionalized in the otherwise nonsensical rituals of their fetish priests. I am summarizing some points made in my earlier chapters because the changes in the discourse about African fetishes that occurred during the period of European conquest and colonial administration reconfigured the idea of fetish within this thematic constellation in a manner that foregrounded another, more radical problem: that of the valuation of human life itself.

In the late nineteenth century, European powers conquered much of Black Africa in the name of civilization. While this appeal to the moral spirit of civilization was unquestionably an ideological justification for actions motivated by the politics of capitalist trade and imperialist rivalry, it also expressed a specific policy. Civilization meant the abolition of human slavery and human sacrifice and their replacement by legitimate commerce and Christianity.[2] By representing the former as the barbarous institutions at the heart of traditional African societies, the colonial discourse of "civilization" found its unifying idea in the liberal Christian respect for the value of human life. While there may be good reasons for a political historian or a social anthropologist to dismiss as "mere ideology" such causes as the right to life or the value of human life, in what follows I am going to treat the problem of the material valuation of human life as a real problem that must be resolved by the institutions of any society.

As the historical context for this theoretical reflection, I am going to consider the British colonization of the Gold and Slave Coasts (the southern parts of present-day Ghana and Nigeria). While I will begin by considering some events from the first half of the nineteenth century that led to a novel identification in British ideology of African "fetishism" with human sacrifice, my principal interest will be the conflict between very different cultural modes for valuing human life. This conflict occurred as the British began to extend and intensify their civil jurisdiction over non-Islamic populations in West Africa during the second half of the century. My index for such a comparative reflection is the manner in which the liability and the debt arising from suspiciously sudden or violent death—that is, death that appears to be a sheer contingent event—was determined by these different cultures. England had itself undergone a radical institutional transformation in this regard in the middle of the nineteenth century. In 1846 the ancient English law of accursed objects, the law of deodand, had been abolished and the new Fatal Accidents Act passed that determined the liability for such deaths in terms of wrongful negligence and the debt for such wrongful deaths in terms of the lost future wage earnings of the deceased.[3] These new legal standards were applied to British-ruled West African societies only a few decades later and clashed with some of the most fundamental institutions of West African cultures. Thus, the initial establishment of British tort law under colonial government, and indeed its lasting legacy in the postcolonial period, provides a historical context for thinking about the institutional structures of ritual blood sacrifice and capitalist monetary debt as alternate logics for valuing human life. While my comparison of these two logics will be highly tentative, I want to use these reflections to offer some even more general thoughts on debt and fetishism as concepts for comparative cultural studies.

African Fetishism and the Spirit of Civilization

Prior to the 1840s, British ideology—apart from a few apologists for the Atlantic slave trade—did not picture African fetishism, and hence West African societies, as being based on human sacrifice. While one finds many discussions of fetishism in early nineteenth-century texts, such as Henry Meredith's *An Account of the Gold Coast of Africa* (1812) or the Lander brothers' accounts of Nigeria in the 1830s, one does not find the implication that fetishism, conceived as the religion organizing all aspects of African social and political life, ultimately depended on the practice of human sacrifice.[4] This is true even of the accounts of Thomas Edward Bowdich and Joseph Dupuis concerning Ashanti, later a principal example of the supposed reliance of fetishism on human sacrifice.[5] By the early nineteenth century, the discourse about African fetishes had retained its basic ideological content for some three centuries as a result of its pragmatic function in Afro-European cross-cultural trade. As historians of Africa have explained, during the sixteenth century, "a body of Afro-European commercial custom came into existence, with patterns of exchange and cross-cultural behavior that were to be remarkably stable until the second half of the nineteenth century."[6] Fetish was a key word in the pidgin "trade language" used by African and Afro-European middlemen who mediated cross-cultural transactions. Various artifacts and sites, prescribed and proscribed behaviors, and norms for sanctioning new social relations whose meaning and logic were incomprehensible to European merchants were identified as fetish for the pragmatic purpose of furthering peaceful trade. As late as the 1850s, an acknowledgment of this functional context can be found in the work of one of the nineteenth-century governors of the Gold Coast, Brodie Cruickshank. Second to none in his contempt for African "fetishism," he nevertheless recognized that it functioned as a form of civil society (or, as he put, "an engine of civil government").[7]

> The local government on the Gold Coast must have the candour to acknowledge its obligations to Fetish, as a police agent. Without this powerful ally, it would have been found impossible to maintain that

order, which characterized the country during the last twenty years, with the physical force of the government. The extraordinary security afforded to property in the most remote districts, the great safety with which packages of gold of great value are transmitted by single messengers for hundreds of miles, and the facility with which lost or stolen property is generally recovered, have excited the astonishment of Europeans newly arrived in the country.[8]

Beginning in the 1840s, African fetishism came to be increasingly identified with the practice of human sacrifice. While the older idea of fetishism (the overvaluation and worship of even the most trivial objects chosen by the capricious fancy of the prerational mind) was retained, it was articulated with a new thematics of civilization that contrasted the European's authentic respect for the value of human life with the barbaric African practices of slavery and human sacrifice. One of the first British texts to do this was Thomas Buxton's influential book of 1839, *The African Slave Trade and Its Remedy.* For example, Buxton explains that the "fetish places" of Benin are "the depositories of the usual objects of worship. Many unfortunate slaves are sacrificed in front of these temples."[9] This new emphasis on the connection of the "fetishism" to slavery and human sacrifice (in which the sacrifice of slaves is stressed to suggest the identity of slavery and human sacrifice as ultimate violations of the value of human life) occurs increasingly in British writing during the second half of the nineteenth century as the scramble for Africa accelerated. By the early twentieth century, a familiar claim was being made when Major Arthur Glyn Leonard wrote of the Ibo of Nigeria that human sacrifice was "the substance, spirit, and practice of their religion."[10] This novel identification of African fetishism with human sacrifice was not a purely textual development confined to the writings of European ideologues. When the social position of the African and Afro-European middleman and long-established arrangements for cross-cultural trade were destroyed in the second half of the nineteenth century, the practical meaning of "fetish" in its functional context was also transformed. Ultimately, the context in which this term would come to have meaning was that of colonial law: as British officials and local merchants began to exercise and formalize their civil jurisdiction over West African populations, courts were established where, from the 1870s on, "fetish practices" of various sorts were considered as civil and criminal offenses. By the end of the century, colonial ordinances would include "putting a person in fetish" among the crimes coming under the jurisdiction of minor courts.[11] I will consider what "fetish" meant in this context of colonial law a bit later, since this sense of "fetish" was preceded by the ideological identification of fetishism with human sacrifice that was functional in the context of colonial conquest.

The shift in emphasis to human sacrifice may be traced to accounts of the death of the British governor of Sierra Leone and the Gold Coast, Sir Charles MacCarthy, in 1824. A series of bad decisions led to his death in a battle with Ashanti. His secretary, who was spared, returned home with lurid accounts of MacCarthy's decapitated corpse, of the uncannily lifelike appearance of MacCarthy's head, of having to spend nights in a hut with the severed heads of his comrades, and of being forced to attend rituals where living prisoners were sacrificed to the "fetish" as the "death-drum" pounded. Indeed, MacCarthy's skull (like those of the defeated leaders in other wars) did become a ritual object used for years in the *Odwira* ceremony, and a life mask made from MacCarthy's face was attached to the Golden Stool, the ritual object of Ashanti national sovereignty.

The public impression made by MacCarthy's death was subsequently exploited by government agents, missionaries, and spokesmen for commercial interests when Britain began its efforts to establish governmental authority on the Gold and Slave Coasts. Historians usually take the year 1830 as the beginning of the turn toward colonial activism by Britain in West Africa. On the Gold Coast, George Maclean became council president at Cape Coast Castle and began to establish an informal but real civil jurisdiction over nearby settlements. During the same year, in 1830, the world's first public railroad opened in England; in Nigeria the expedition of the Lander brothers traced the course of the Niger River, the first navigable water route into the interior of Africa to be discovered by a European power. Two years later, the first steamboat appeared on the waters of the Niger.[12] Despite the very limited resources the British government was willing to commit to adventures in West Africa, the new mobile power of gunboats for the first time permitted the extension of British commerce and military power beyond the few trade forts that had clung to the Atlantic coast for several centuries. Moreover, as colonial agents such as the Landers were mindful even in 1830, the new technology of railroads represented possible conduits of trade superior and more easily controllable even than good rivers. All that was needed was a valuable commodity from the African side, and this was found in palm oil, a good with increasing market value due to its usefulness as a lubricant in the locomotives and other machinery that proliferated with the Industrial Revolution.

The colonial efforts in West Africa begun in 1830 had taken on serious momentum by 1846. This was the year that the new problem of fatal train wrecks led to the Act to Abolish Deodands and the new Fatal Accidents

Act in England. It was also a significant year for British involvement in West Africa and for the three social forces in Britain under whose name the colonial conquest of Africa would be justified, the so-called three c's: commerce, Christianity, and civilization. In 1846 John Russell's Liberal Party succeeded the Tory government of Robert Peel, and Parliament passed the Sugar Act. This removed protectionist tariffs favoring the sugar produced by Britain's West Indian colonies and thereby dismantled what remained of the old slave-based Atlantic economic system.[13] The new commitment to "free trade" and "free labor" encouraged new commercial efforts by British merchants in West Africa to develop "legitimate trade" in palm oil. This led to aggressive efforts in the Niger Delta area by certain British merchants and those whom local Africans called "black Europeans" (traders from the colony of Sierra Leone) to displace traditional African middlemen as well as established merchants engaged in the slave trade. During the period of conquest, a successful strategy for an ambitious middleman such as Chief Dogho in the Niger Delta, who was perceptive enough to appreciate the altered power relations, was to accentuate his difference from the bloodthirsty fetishists (his trade rivals) in nearby Benin City.[14]

As for Christianity, after slavery had been legally abolished in Britain's West Indian colonies in 1833, Christian antislavery and missionary movements began to focus on Africa. In 1839 Thomas Buxton founded the Society for the Extinction of the Slave Trade and the Civilization of Africa under the nominal leadership of Prince Albert (who, in the following year, married Queen Victoria).[15] In 1842 John Beecham's Wesleyan Methodist Missionary Committee sent their principal "colored" agent on the Gold Coast, Thomas Birch Freeman, to the Niger Delta. The fruit of his efforts came in 1846 with the establishment of the first Methodist mission among the Yoruba.[16] Back in England, in support of these efforts, books on West Africa were published by Thomas Buxton in 1839 and John Beecham in 1841. Both offered sensationalized pictures of West African culture as a blood-drenched barbarism based on human sacrifice (including long and horrifying accounts of the death of Governor MacCarthy). Such extreme images of West Africa were functional as a fundraising tool. Each of the two years prior to Beecham's book, his Wesleyan Methodist Missionary Committee had run a deficit of some ten thousand pounds.[17] Missionary societies focused on the Pacific had recently done well in raising contributions by emphasizing the cannibalism of the Fiji Islands, and it was hoped that highlighting human sacrifice in West Africa would do the same. Such sensationalism was reinforced by the newspapers and magazines of this period, whose publishers found that true accounts of exotic atrocities greatly increased their sales.

As for "civilization," this meant the encouragement of "rational" European-style commerce and cash crop production, especially in palm oil, and the active suppression of the slave trade, which still thrived in several West African ports during the 1840s since slaves could be bought for ten or fifteen pounds and sold in Brazil for fifty to eighty pounds.[18] The British government had officially committed itself to fighting this activity in the Slave Trade Abolition Acts of 1842 and 1843. Moreover, at least in the public discourse of the day, the spirit of civilization meant the proactive effort to reshape African societies by abolishing human slavery and human sacrifice, for these were regarded as the ultimate violation of the liberal civilized respect for the value of human life. These efforts to transform African cultures began in the 1840s, at first through minimally interventionist efforts at treaty-making. Human sacrifice was first abolished in British controlled parts of the Gold Coast in 1844: a gunboat-enforced British treaty with Lagos first abolished human sacrifice in a Nigerian town in 1852.[19]

The other great violation of the value of human life, slavery, was a more difficult issue. Back in England, in the early 1830s, the newly elected Whig government that had been swept into power on a wave of unprecedented public activism had only reluctantly bowed to the force of public opinion by abolishing slavery in the West Indies. On the Gold Coast, Maclean had, when it suited him, interfered in African slavery not by opposing the institution itself but rather in individual cases involving "cruelty." A liberal distinction among instances of slavery according to a standard of physical mistreatment or cruelty seems also to have been operative among missionaries. Slavery was actively opposed when it seemed directly related to pagan practices of human sacrifice, as among the Ibo, or when connected to the old Afro-European Atlantic slave trade. In the absence of these, especially when traditional African slavery was seen to accommodate modern commercial relations, a different attitude could be taken, as a Basel missionary did in speaking of the Krobo of Ghana: "In Kroboland slavery is not so repugnant as in other places. Human flesh and blood is not the main currency, but palm oil and other products of the country. The main reason for the shocking slave trade is thus absent. . . . Our missionaries hardly hear about the maltreatment of a slave."[20]

It was only in 1874 that slavery was legally abolished on the Gold Coast, and even then it was in a manner that tried to guarantee that the existing labor force would remain in place.[21] The traditional institution of pawning (placing a person in the hands of another person or family as security for an unpaid debt) proved an effectively nondisruptive substitute for "slavery" that also accelerated the use of capitalist monetary debt as a medium for social relations:

> The anti-slavery ordinances of 1874–1875 apparently had no diminishing effect whatsoever on the transfer of individuals from one household to another as security for debts. On the contrary, the laws appear to have sparked a trend in the opposite direction, as well-to-do merchants, heads of farming families, and kings and chiefs turned to pawnage as a way of continuing to add domestic servants and dependents to their households as a substitute for slavery. This was a common trend in the 1880s and 1890s. . . . This upsurge in pawning was also bound up with the spread of commercial capitalism. With the increased availability of money and imported consumer goods, many families tended to spend more lavishly than before—both on material goods for their own comfort and for gifts and entertainments associated with traditional ceremonial occasions. . . . With the great value placed on land and leases beginning in the late 1870s, as a result of mechanized gold mining, and expanding later in the era of cocoa farming, there was a spate of legal disputes, which together with spiraling debts for lawyer's fees and court costs added still further to the pawning tendency.[22]

While the more extreme instances of pawning and imprisonment for debt soon also came under attack by colonial law, there is enough historical evidence at least to suggest the presence of a general tendency to replace traditional forms of debt obligation associated with socioreligious practices identified as "African fetishism" with the monetary debt relations that Karl Marx, in the third volume of *Capital,* would identify as capitalist fetishism. The conflict between these two irreconcilable forms of fetishism can be examined in political and legal conflicts over the form that debt obligations were to take. British colonialism required a modern monetary form for these not only because private British mercantile firms were monetized institutions whose reality was structured by the practices of capitalist bookkeeping and market economics but because the governmental colonies and protectorates of British West Africa were themselves monetized entities that were required to maintain themselves through their own income from local fees and taxes.[23] Attempts to do this through direct taxation of African populations caused great political resistance; but the ultimate juridical authority of British courts in resolving disputes placed power in the hands of those who could afford monetized court costs and lawyer's fees. It would seem that the colonial legal system was itself an important vehicle for restructuring social relations in the form of monetary debt.

Among the types of social obligation over which colonial governments established their jurisdiction were those arising from fatal accidents and other "suspicious deaths" (as British law would call them—that is, deaths whose suddenness or apparent unnaturalness requires some formal inquiry into their causes). The different manner in which traditional West African custom and modern British law (that is, the tort law that developed after the statutes of 1846) established the liability and debt arising from such deaths is a particularly vivid illustration of the workings of two very different cultural logics for the valuing of human life.

The next two sections of this chapter examine the issues of human sacrifice and fatal accidents—extreme instances of intentionally and unintentionally caused death—as a way to reflect on the problem of the value of human life in the light of the vicissitudes of the idea of African fetishism during the periods of colonial conquest and colonial rule.

Fetishism during the Colonial Conquest and the Problem of Human Sacrifice

During the four centuries of Afro-European commerce prior to the colonial conquest of the nineteenth century, the idea of fetish gained its meaning from the tension between African modes for the social valuation of material objects and that of European merchants. While many sorts of objects and practices were designated "fetish," the paradigmatic instance of the fetish was some movable thing to which both sacramental and economic value was attributed by parties from very different cultures involved in a possible commercial transaction. It is a premise of my project that the "fetish" in this sense existed as a social reality, not merely as a textual construct of European writers (since its meaningful existence was dependent on its functional value within a pragmatic context). Its reality was specific to a situation of routinized cross-cultural relations: in this context "fetishes" were as real as any other type of cultural object (thus my disagreement with ethnographers for whom social reality is confined to discrete cultures and to objects as named and conceived within languages proper to supposedly isolated cultures). During the period of colonial conquest, the context, meaning, and reality of fetish changed dramatically. When Afro-European relations shifted from commerce to war, the meaning of the principal material objectifications mediating these relations also changed. While bullet-repelling "medicines" and spiritually significant guns are good examples of fetishes in this context, such movable, potentially commodifiable objects were not the paradigmatic instances of "fetishes" but rather the shrines and sacred sites that became the focal points for trade monopolies and military power. The relation that was at stake in the cross-cultural reality of fetishes during the period of colonial conquest was not commerce in commodities but rather jurisdiction over populations. It was not the value and social reality of cultural objects that was at stake but the existence and political control of cultural worlds.

This is exemplified in the early effort by Governor MacCarthy to establish effective governmental authority over the towns near Cape Coast Castle in Ghana. MacCarthy's initial success in doing this placed him in conflict with the Ashanti empire, which viewed these people as its subjects. In Ghana (and many other parts of West Africa) there existed a number of established institutional forms for translocal social relations. One of these was the practice of sealing obligations between strangers (i.e., obligations not already prescribed by some preexisting kinship relation between the two parties) through the swearing of oaths at sacred sites or by invoking their names. The sanctioning power of these "fetish oaths" included "supernatural" and juridical components. A person who died without having fulfilled such a sworn obligation might be judged to have been killed by the fetish for failing to settle the debt. A person owed some unperformed obligation by another might appeal to the individual exercising the authority of the fetish to enforce the unpaid debt. As MacCarthy established his authority over the Gold Coast population, oaths began to be taken on Cape Coast Castle and in the name of "Mankata" (as MacCarthy was called). This was both a challenge to the power of Kumasi and a source of conflict when the government of Ashanti failed to receive satisfaction from MacCarthy when people over whom he claimed authority failed to fulfill some obligation to a member of Ashanti society. One of these conflicts, in which agents of the Ashantihene seized a debtor, led to the battle in which MacCarthy was killed. By transforming MacCarthy's head into a ritually empowered object belonging among the regalia of the royal lineage of Ashanti, the power and authority exercised by MacCarthy was being absorbed into that of the Ashanti sovereign.

During the period of colonial conquest, "fetishism" may best be located in the fetish shrines that were the material centers of those African political forces whose jurisdiction the British sought to supplant. Examples of these are the execution tree at Kumasi (the capital of Ashanti), the Dente oracle located on the Volta River that became the center of the Bron Confederation that arose after the fall of Ashanti to the British, the Aro shrine in Nigeria called by Europeans "the Long Ju-Ju," and, of course, the shrines of Benin City (the "City of Blood" as it came to be called) that became the ultimate illustration for Europeans of the identity of African fetishism with human sacrifice. All four of these fetish shrines were centers of local trade monopolies that blocked the expansion of British hegemony. While the Dente shrine ultimately fell within the sphere of German colonialism, the other three became targets of British military expeditions and were deliberately (physically) destroyed by the conquerors. Each was characterized by the British as a "stronghold of Fetichism,"[24] a "charnel house of fetish lore,"[25] a material locus of a "fetish power" that British soldiers and Foreign Office administrators took very seriously, despite their disbelief in "supernatural powers." The real power of fetishism, they believed, was the "absolute terror of the fetish" instilled by the practice of human sacrifice.[26] For the conquering British of that time, there was little doubt that the social regime of fetishism exploited a superstitious belief in supernatural powers among West African peoples by linking it to the real power of ritualized killing and the fear that this created in the living.

The thesis that human sacrifice in West Africa was essentially a form of state terror is not without foundation. The kingdom of Ashanti, for example, was founded in the late seventeenth century, as the Afro-European traffic in slaves and firearms began to transform West African societies. The importance of human sacrifice as a tool of imperial authority was communicated in the naming of the capital itself, Kumasi, after the tree under which criminals were executed,[27] and in the ritual decapitations associated with Bantama, the royal mausoleum.[28] The horror and dread of such sanctions were expressed in Ashanti proverbs: "Because I fear to be killed I have made my neck short"; "When you lie, you fear Kumase."[29] Such ritual occasions as the great *Odwira* ceremony, at which the leaders of subject peoples assembled in Kumasi and participated in the annual renewal of the sovereign power of the Ashantihene, along with the Golden Stool itself, were institutional innovations of the first Ashantihene, Osei Tutu, and his chief priest, Okomfo Anokye, that helped establish a royal state on a scale larger than the lineage-based social arrangements of Akan society could otherwise accommodate.

Another possible explanation of human sacrifice in precolonial West Africa—one not necessarily excluding the view of this practice as a form of state terror—emphasizes the "brutalizing" impact of the transatlantic slave trade. This is the argument of the Nigerian historian Elizabeth Isichei. For Europeans of the late nineteenth century, nowhere was the bloodthirsty depravity that was supposedly characteristic of Black African societies more evident than in the kingdom of Benin, with its mass sacrifices of war captives and infamous "crucifixion trees" that especially horrified Christian Europeans. However, Isichei argues:

> Something transformed Benin from the impressive and harmonious society described by the first European visitors in the late fifteenth and early sixteenth centuries, to the "City of Blood," its streets filled with human sacrifices, which the British conquered in the late nineteenth. It has been claimed that the slave trade cannot have caused this change, because Benin was only marginally involved in it. But perhaps Benin history is only a particularly striking illustration of the way the trade in slaves corrupted every society it touched.[30]

Even historians who disagree with this argument acknowledge that the admittedly sparse and anecdotal evidence that exists suggests an increasing frequency and scale of human sacrifice in some West African societies beginning in the late seventeenth century, when the rise of Caribbean sugar plantations kicked the Atlantic slave trade into high gear. This seems to have further accelerated as the Atlantic slave trade began to be actively suppressed in the 1830s and perhaps reached a high point during the period of the colonial conquest of West Africa by European powers at the end of the nineteenth century.

A third view, which also acknowledges the importance of the Afro-European slave trade, is offered by the historian Robin Law. Law suggests that human sacrifice is best understood as a form of "conspicuous consumption" by elites who thereby increase their prestige and status.[31] Since the rise in human sacrifices during the nineteenth century seems to coincide with the elimination of an important alternate use of slaves in trade with Europeans, Law suggests:

> The explanation is that the decline of the export of slaves caused something of a glut within West Africa, which was reflected in a general fall in the price of slaves. With such a fall in slave prices, kings and chiefs could evidently afford not only to buy more slaves, but also to kill more, without a proportionate increase in expenditure: the unit costs of human sacrifice were falling.[32]

The exchange on this subject that took place in the 1970s between Isichei and Law illustrates an intellectual difficulty that has characterized writing in the human sciences ever since these disciplines constituted themselves by distinguishing their mode of explanation from that of theology. Isichei can justify her category of "brutalization" only by explaining that her historical judgments are informed by her moral principles as a believing Christian.[33] Law criticizes Isichei's thesis by arguing that the notion of brutalization is too vague to be useful and that Isichei is actually making a moral rather than a historical argument. For Law, "the problem of human sacrifice is not, for us today, a moral question but a historical one: we should be seeking, not to condone or condemn, but to explain."[34] Instead Law proposes what could be a delightful parody of the rational choice school of social scientific argument were it not for the fact that Law seems to be serious about it. While Isichei feels she is justified in likening the ritual killings of nineteenth-century Benin to "the human sacrifices of Hiroshima,"[35] Law thinks that this conception of sacrifice undermines her authority to make historical arguments altogether. Human sacrifice, Law argues, can be defined as "the killing of people in order to secure the favor of supernatural beings."[36] Since the bombing of Hiroshima was not an act intended to secure the favor of any supernatural being (in a theological sense), it cannot be compared to the ritual killings that occurred in Benin in the 1890s.

In Law's view, sacrifice as a historical object is to be found only among people who believe in "supernatural powers" and who conceive their sacrificial acts as propitiations of such beings. But this cannot be the working definition for social scientists, since the suspension of belief in supernatural agency is fundamental to the manner in which modern science arrives at knowledge. Law's position regarding the nature of true historical knowledge is in accord with that of Meyer Fortes regarding anthropological knowledge. Fortes argues that the belief or disbelief in supernatural powers is precisely the difference between a theological and a social scientific approach to the problem of sacrifice.[37]

"Sacrifice" is thus a practice that must be defined in terms of the belief in supernatural powers by those who perform it but that can only be explained in terms of its social function by those who do not believe in supernatural powers. That is, historians and anthropologists must themselves be incapable of performing sacrificial acts, since they cannot believe in supernatural powers, while those who perform such rites must be incapable of making true explanations of what they are doing. The only solution to this dilemma is a schizophrenic one: individuals may regard themselves in a split fashion, as having a private religious identity when they are worshipping and a public, professional identity when they are making statements about history and society. This is, in fact, the case for intellectuals who write within modern liberal societies. Moreover, this split identity is institutionalized in the public discourse and laws of such societies: religious values and "supernatural" beliefs may be recognized and protected, but they must be explained and justified in terms of their secular social functions. An illustration of this is the

United States Supreme Court case of *Church of Lukumi Babalu Aye, Inc. v. City of Hialeah* (113 S. Ct. 2217 [1993]). The right of American citizens to perform acts of animal sacrifice was upheld according to the constitutional right to freedom of religious expression; the municipal law that had outlawed this practice was overturned because, from a secular perspective, the performance of animal sacrifice is the act of killing an animal and the law did not outlaw all killing of animals (such as occurs in slaughterhouses) but only those performed for a religious purpose, a clear violation of the constitutional right to private religious freedom. (Human sacrifice is illegal in the United States, despite the protection of religious freedom, only because it violates a more fundamental constitutional right, the right of people to life.)

In regard to historical and social explanation it seems to me that Robin Law's appeal to a general rational choice model of human motivation as a way to avoid the delegitimizing taint of morality erases a great deal more from historical understanding than moralizing analogies ultimately based on an author's belief in the Christian God or some other supernatural power. In attempting to aggregate his numbers (slave prices, numbers of human sacrifices performed) and thereby determine the marginal utilities that caused people to act the way they did, Law overlooks some of the specificities of singular historical events: the relatively routine practices of "human sacrifice" that some cultures performed in order to remedy the effects of sacrilegious crimes or to renew the power objects linking a sovereign to his royal ancestors are quite distinct from those rare instances of truly massive human sacrifice, such as those that occurred in Benin City in 1897 as the British military expedition was approaching.[38] The latter instances of human sacrifice were traumatic crisis responses to unparalleled events that threatened (and indeed destroyed) the social worlds of entire peoples. Such a moment has been vividly evoked in the opening pages of the Malinke writer Ahmadou Kourouma's novel *Monnew*. The novel begins with a description of a frenzy of sacrifices in Soba as the French force that will destroy their world approaches:

> Vultures came swooping in arabesques high in the sky over Soba. The sacrificial ground was covered with slaughtered cattle, sheep, and chickens, lying in pools of blood. There was too much blood, so much blood it was intoxicating.
>
> But King Djigui ordered more: "Blood! More blood! Sacrifices! More sacrifices!"
>
> His sbirros and sicarios went wild. They burst into the city and forced the people in the compounds to make sacrifices. More and

more vultures soared overhead. The sky was heavy with black cloud, the rooftops covered with a black veil.

"Blood! All kinds of blood! Sacrifices, all kinds of sacrifices!"

The sbirros knew what was lacking: human sacrifices. They went into the outlying neighborhoods, captured three albinos, dragged them into the nearby sacred grove, and slit their throats on the Senufo altars. It was a mistake. . . . The question was put to the pythonesses, geomancers, and tellers of bones and cowry shells, who repeated their verdict: everlasting endurance had not been granted.[39]

In such a crisis moment, when the existence of an entire social world is threatened, it may be that the deepest social logic of that culture receives an explicit expression. One might argue this is so not only in the fictional case of Kourouma's Soba and the historical African case of Benin but also in such cases as that of the American South during the Civil War of the 1860s. What intrigues me in regard to the fictional passage I have quoted and historical accounts of Benin in the 1890s is the emphasis on blood.

The idea of blood sacrifice has been criticized often and with good reason. Late nineteenth-century anthropologists, such as Robertson Smith, who promoted the idea as a general concept were clearly influenced by the conceptions of traditional Christian theology, which had originally distinguished itself within the cultural world of the second- and third-century Roman Empire by contrasting the sacramental practices of the Christian religion with the host of established religions whose rituals entailed the sacrifice of animals. The concepts of blood sacrifice peculiar to the Judeo-Christian tradition have proved inapplicable to many other cultural traditions that practice the sacrificial killing of living beings. However, there are now many reliable ethnographic accounts of traditional West African cultures, as well as theoretical and literary works by intellectuals belonging to these traditions, that indicate the special importance of sacramental conceptions of blood in these cultures.

In regard to the significance of blood sacrifice in West African traditions, I would suggest that it might be helpful to supplement ethnographic methods of structural analysis with what might be called a cultural phenomenological approach that combines aesthetic reflection with attention to the thematics of ordinary language. Certainly there is no substitute for knowledge of particular cultures based on "fieldwork" and the analysis of social structures guided by the concepts found in the language and key narratives of that culture. An exemplary instance of this is the careful work on the importance of blood sacrifice in Morocco by M. E. Coombs-Schilling.[40] While I would take nothing away from skillful ethnographic work, it might also be worthwhile to reflect on the vaguer, more general conceptions to be found in popular public culture and ordinary language. In the case of the cultural meaning of blood in West African traditions, while one should certainly try to investigate the relation of sacramental conceptions of blood to the structures of kinship institutions (which obviously vary from culture to culture, since some of these trace genealogical relationships in a matrilineal fashion and others in a patrilineal one), too rigorous a search for structural precision may obscure a functionally important aspect of popular culture. For instance, twentieth-century anthropologists have tended to state that the concept of kinship blood found in traditional Akan society is conceived in a purely matrilineal fashion since matrilineality characterizes the kinship structures of this culture. Claims by "informants" that blood comes from both parents, or "really" comes from the father, are therefore regarded as confusions caused by relatively recent changes in social structure that occurred during the colonial period.[41] But it is also possible to think that there exist popular, less conceptually precise conceptions of blood whose social efficacy should not be ignored. Consider the following passage from an ethnography of an Akan society of 1975:

> Rattray defines *mogya* [the Akan word for blood] as "blood or clan soul," and Abraham regards *mogya* as a type of spiritual factor. Both contend that it is the *mogya* which becomes the *onaman*, "ghost of the dead." Busia appears to view *mogya* in biological terms. My informants did not seem to regard blood as a spiritual component akin to the elements discussed above. However, blood is thought to exercise a potential effect upon character in a variety of ways: A parent who habitually behaves in a particular way, e.g., who frequently drinks or makes a habit of lying, may transmit a hereditary disposition toward such behavior to his or her child. The tendency is said to be in the blood, and attempts to eradicate it are felt to be hopeless.[42]

If there is a certain ethnographic imprecision in popular beliefs about the powers of blood—because these ideas are too vague and fluid to be clearly related to institutional structures—it may also be the case that there is such an aspect of popular culture in ritual performances involving blood sacrifice. Whatever else they are, West African practices of blood sacrifice involve the killing of a living being in a manner in which the visible shedding of blood is itself the realization and dynamization of an otherwise invisible spiritual power. Such blood is the material form of the power of life, of living existence, understood as the real substance of a society whose members include the living and the still active ancestral dead. In this sense it is the general material form of a real social substance posited and experienced by the members of these cultures. Blood is different from the other material components of sacrificial acts because its visible materiality is the general form of an invisible spiritual-social substance.

I am being Aristotelian in my use of the word "substance": a substance is the reality of the principle unifying a particular system of qualitatively different components. This conception of social substance is, I believe, the one used by Marx when he speaks of "capital." This chapter is an attempt to see what happens when one pushes the comparison between Marx's conception of capitalist fetishism and the historical idea of traditional African fetishism. Hence I am considering the comparability between blood in traditional West African cultures and money in modern capitalist cultures. Both may be conceived as the general forms of "realization" (in the Marxian sense) of a historically singular social system that is conceived and experienced as embodying a unitary substance (one a kinship substance of social reality, the other a monetary substance).

Before turning to the subject of fatal accidents as occasions for the cultural determination of the value of human life, I have a final point to make in regard to the problem of human sacrifice. It seems clear, as Robin Law has argued, that the practice of human sacrifice "expanded in scale in West Africa largely through its association with royal authority and with militarism" in the formation of such states as Ashanti and nineteenth-century Benin.[43] Such regimes were innovative responses to the new situation created by the Afro-European traffic in slaves. Yet these regimes were developed from the institutional and ideological structures of earlier West African societies, and there remains the question of the relation of the human sacrifices practiced by these so-called gunpowder empires to those found in some of the more traditional, "stateless" societies found in this region. Isichei has argued that, while human sacrifice was "the most serious of religious rituals" in West Africa prior to the impact of the Atlantic slave trade, "in their original form, these practices were not necessarily a matter of horror and dread."[44] That is, such practices were not essentially instruments of state terror. If this is so, perhaps they may be understood within a general logic of blood sacrifice that included (and indeed consisted primarily of) practices of animal sacrifice. Unnatural deaths and acts of violence were often conceived in these cultures as pollutions of the earth (the visible world of the living) by the spilled blood of members of a kinship group. If sacrificial blood may rightly be understood as the general form of spiritual power in these cultures, then it makes sense that the acts remedying wrongs that were both crimes and sacrileges involved ritual blood sacrifice (along with other forms of compensation and expiation). While the cultural significance of different sacrificial animals was determined by symbolic systems specific to particular cultures, the type and number of animals required to be sacrificed to remedy a given wrong was to some degree a quantitative value question. The more severe the violation, the greater the sacrificial value of the required remedy. In the case of the most severe violations sacrifices of the greatest value were required: the sacrifice of human beings. Since the killing of a kin member would shed blood that would itself cause further pollution, the sacrifice of an alien captive or of a slave, who did not bear the kin blood, was the only possible option. If this reasoning is correct, then Isichei is right in distinguishing the practices of human sacrifice of traditional, lineage-organized West African societies from those of royal states such as Ashanti where human sacrifice (in the form of criminal executions and rituals at royal funerals and commemorations of royal ancestors) functioned as a form of state terror that established and maintained the power of kingship. While Law's sociological view of human sacrifices as devices to enhance prestige applies to the latter, I do not see how it applies to the human sacrifices of such nonstate societies as the Ibo.

Fetishism under Colonial Law and the Problem of Fatal Accidents

There is a scene in Chinua Achebe's novel *Things Fall Apart* in which the hero, Okonkwo, is quite properly engaged in the ceremonial firing of his gun at a funeral. The gun explodes, however, and a piece of it kills the son of the deceased. "The only course open to Okonkwo," Achebe writes, "was to flee from the clan. It was a crime against the earth goddess to kill a clansman, and a man who committed it must flee from the land."[45] Achebe goes on to recount a scene of the destruction of Okonkwo's property by his neighbors in response to his accidental killing of the boy. As the author makes clear, this is not a spontaneous act of passionate revenge but rather a necessary act of sacrificial remedy:

> As soon as the day broke, a large crowd of men from Ezeudu's [the dead man whose funeral it was] quarter stormed Okonkwo's compound, dressed in garbs of war. They set fire to his houses, demolished his red walls, killed his animals, and destroyed his barn. It was the justice of the earth goddess, and they were merely her messengers. They had no hatred in their hearts against Okonkwo. His greatest

friend, Obierika, was among them. They were merely cleansing the land which Okonkwo had polluted with the blood of a clansman.[46]

The idea that an act of the destruction of property can be a remedy for a wrongful death is not alien to "the West." It is found in many early European cultures. It is, however, alien to the logic of liberal capitalist society.

As I have mentioned, legal structures for remedying accidental deaths proper to the latter type of society were established only in the mid-nineteenth century. The general theory of torts began to be articulated in England soon after the passage of the Fatal Accidents Act of 1846 and the new types of case law that it generated. This occurred during the next decade and led to the first book-length treatments of the subject, Francis Hilliard's *The Law of Torts, or Private Wrongs* (1859) and Charles G. Addison's *Wrongs and Their Remedies* (1860).[47] By the end of the century, the law of torts had become a branch of civil law equal in importance to the law of contracts.

Modern tort law was one among a number of institutional innovations that created a liberal capitalist "civil society." Much of the story of British involvement in West Africa in the nineteenth century may be summed up by saying that the politics of legitimate trade was the principal policy interest and that the British reluctantly learned that global capitalist trade cannot exist without an effective legal administration to create the sort of local civil society that permits such trade to function. The moral justification for such a colonially administered transformation of African cultures into commercial civil societies was the defense of the value of human life.

The history of the establishment in Ghana and Nigeria of a civil society suited to British capitalism is incredibly complicated. Nevertheless, some generalizations are possible. As soon as merchants aligned with British-style commerce gained significant power in an area, they or colonial government officials established petty debt courts and other judicial mechanisms for enforcing the monetary obligations entailed in this form of commerce. New judicial structures were also established in a manner that affirmed the ultimate sovereign power of Britain. When traditional institutions threatened neither modern commercial relations nor British political sovereignty, the desire was to leave them in place as a mechanism for local civil order. The ultimate formula that emerged for a dual judicial system of British and "customary" law was that customary local law would be enforced unless it was contradicted by current British law or colonial proclamation or unless it was "repugnant to natural justice, equity, and good conscience."[48]

Conflicts and disputes inevitably arose in which British procedures for doing justice in cases of suspicious deaths clashed with traditional African procedures for doing this. An early example of this occurred in 1865 at the principal British Gold Coast settlement, Cape Coast Castle. John Aggery had, with British approval, been duly elected king of the local community, but the colonial governor soon found his authority challenged by Aggery. General bad feelings soon led to a riot by the West Indies soldiers that formed the British police force in the town. One of the soldiers shot a local man, for whom a traditional "funeral" was held, as a result of which "Aggery was officially reprimanded for parading the body round the town, and right up to the castle gate, instead of dutifully suppressing the general excitement."[49] Although British officials did not recognize it as such, in carrying the body of the deceased around the town the community was following a routine procedure for determining liability in cases of suspicious deaths (although witchcraft was the usual object of suspicion):

> Until the practice was banned by the colonial government, possession was used to determine the cause of death in cases which warranted suspicion of witchcraft or sorcery. The corpse of a person who died suddenly was placed in a coffin and carried prior to burial. The carriers, possessed by the spirit of the deceased and presumably responding to his instructions, were led to the house of the guilty person and identified him by knocking the coffin against him or against his house or a tree when his name was called.[50]

By carrying the body "right up to the castle gate" in the incident of 1865, it would seem that an accusation was being made against the colonial authority, and indeed was made by Aggery in a form more comprehensible to the British governor. The soldier was tried, convicted, and sentenced to death by the colonial court, but his sentence was later commuted to hard labor for life; moreover, no civil compensation was paid by the government for the debt arising from this wrongful death. As was the pattern in cases of local leaders whom the British found troublesome, Aggery—a generally pro-British Methodist convert who had earlier suffered being "publicly flogged for refusing to return to fetish-worship" by native authorities, while also being convicted by the Cape Coast Supreme Court for "cruelty" in sentencing prisoners in his own court—was eventually seized and deported by the British.[51]

By the 1870s, "fetish practices" were a recognized category for cases coming before colonial courts on the Gold Coast and in Lagos. Many of these cases involved conflicts over jurisdictional authority. Local populations in towns tended to divide themselves into precincts where traditional associations performed necessary public works and rendered customary justice. The headquarters of these associations were identified as "fetish houses" by colonial authorities and they were suppressed as a competing court system. (The customary courts of chiefs were similarly suppressed when they came into conflict with colonial authority because they allegedly based their decisions "as much on fetish as on facts."[52]) The other sort of cases identified as "fetish practices" usually concerned traditional adjudication by means of ordeals involving the ingestion of poisonous substances, such as sasswood, by the accused.[53]

"Witchcraft" was understood by colonial courts as a separate issue, since this was a category familiar to Europeans. Britain had abolished criminal penalties for witchcraft in 1732, so that the cases involving witchcraft coming before colonial courts in Africa criminalized those who made accusations of witchcraft against another (or, in rare instances, those who claimed to be witches themselves).[54] In British law the injury done by witchcraft derived from the accusation, not the practice, and was comparable to the injury done by acts of slander; the criminal aspect of such accusations, that is, the aspect falling under the police power of the public authority, was the civil disturbances that might be caused by witchcraft accusations. Although it falls outside the parameters of this chapter, I might note that in West African traditions witchcraft tends to be conceived as the secret (usually nocturnal) eating of the (usually invisible) spiritual life substance of the human victim.

The practices that came to be criminalized as "fetishism" by colonial law in Ghana and Nigeria by the beginning of the twentieth century tended to be those customary practices that represented a logic for ordering civil society and for adjudicating disputes that could not be reconciled with the forms necessary for capitalist commerce and colonial political authority. As a committee of colonial officials and missionaries meeting in Kumasi declared in 1912, "fetish" oaths and rituals were distinguishable from merely ceremonial customary practices by the bond of social obligation they created through their enactment.[55] That is, "fetishism" under colonial law referred to a criminal method of establishing social obligations, as the phrase "putting a person in fetish" used in colonial law indicates. The irreconcilability of the "fetishism" of traditional West African societies and that of liberal capitalist societies consists of the different forms that obligatory social relations must take.

The general British model for determining liability and debt in cases of unintentional death that is still found today in Ghana and Nigeria was established by the Fatal Accidents Act of 1846. Liability or nonliability is determined according to a standard of negligence that appeals to the ordinary care and foresight an average reasonable person would take in doing something. The debt is determined by a calculation in terms of "reasonable future probabilities":

> The starting point is the amount of wages which the deceased was earning, the ascertainment of which to some extent may depend on the regularity of his employment. Then there is an estimate of how much was required or expended for his own personal and living expenses. The balance will give a datum or basic figure which will generally be turned into a lump sum by taking a certain number of years' purchase. That sum, however, has to be taxed down by having due regard to uncertainties, for instance that the widow might have again married and thus ceased to be dependent.[56]

This last point indicates one of the ways in which modern tort law intervened in traditional kinship relations. After 1846, British law awarded compensation for fatal accidents to the immediate family of the deceased. Given the complexities of kinship relations in traditional Nigerian society, the determination of who qualified for this status was sometimes difficult to make. That is, monetary compensation became tied to social identity. The usual beneficiary in these court cases was the widow of a man killed in a train or car wreck or in an industrial accident. The widow was compensated in inverse proportion to her physical attractiveness and hence marriageability (adding a modern complication to the traditional Ashanti proverb that "Personal beauty does not pay a debt").[57] As an authoritative Nigerian case explains, after the projected annual wage income of the deceased, the next important factor in determining "the annual value of dependence" is

> the possibility of remarriage in the case of a dependent widow. If she is young and attractive the court may consider her remarriage to be a strong possibility. If the widow is elderly . . . or is of unattractive appearance or disposition, or suffers from some disability, or is encumbered with a large number of young children, the court may consider her chances of remarriage to be slight.[58]

The displacement of traditional West African modes for determining the liability for a fatal accident and the debt value required to remedy such a loss of human life by modern tort law raises many issues. One of these concerns the conceptual framework that would be required to make comparisons between such very different cultural logics. This question is of interest if one believes, as I do, that neither of these modes is perfectly satisfactory and, therefore, the effort to forge a theoretical discourse for comparative cultural studies carries a certain moral and political urgency. This is my only justification for concluding with some very tentative thoughts regarding concepts that might be useful in developing a theoretical framework that does not rely on the familiar social scientific distinction between belief or nonbelief in "supernatural powers." Indeed, the original theory of fetishism proposed by Charles de Brosses in the eighteenth century was a failed attempt to do just this.

Debt, Fetishism, and Sacrifice as Concepts for Comparative Studies

In his book *Sacrifice in Africa*, the Belgian anthropologist Luc de Heusch argues that "sacrifice" is best understood in terms of debt. What he calls "the sacrificial debt" is the debt people owe for their own lives. In its most general character, de Heusch argues, sacrifice is a payment for "a debt of life."[59] The sacrificial victim or object is, in his view, always a symbolic substitute for the only true payment, that is, one's own living existence: "the most perfect sacrificial debt is that which a man must pay with his own blood in order to continue to exist."[60]

If sacrifice is best understood as the payment of a sort of existential debt, one next needs to know just what debt is. As Max Gluckman pointed out some years ago, however, in small-scale societies where people's relations to each other are actualized in a multiplicity of stable status identities, "debt is constantly applied to interpret all social relationships."[61] The anthropologist of such societies soon finds that debt is the form in which the entire system of social obligations is expressed. The most general sense of debt as any obligation owed by one person to another is too comprehensive to have much usefulness as an analytic concept. A slightly more specific meaning—one that introduces both a materialist and a temporal component—is found in the general legal concept of debt as "a fixed and certain obligation to pay money or some other valuable thing or things, either in the present of the future."[62] Adopting this notion of debt, Gluckman explains the general appeal to debt in tribal societies as an expression of the way such societies order their affairs through "the linking of specific status relationships with specific pieces of property."[63] Gluckman would thus follow Henry Maine in finding a fundamental distinction between traditional status-organized societies, whose social relations are expressed in terms of interpersonal debt, and modern societies in which the increasing importance of long-distance commerce and interactions between strangers requires that, in the absence of preexisting status relations, obligations be expressed in the form of contract. Gluckman concludes his book, however, by pointing out that the formation of an obligatory contractual relation itself requires the transfer of some material property, some "valuable consideration" as it is called in contract law, that must be understood in the same set of terms applicable to debt. While debt would thus seem to lack the specificity required of an analytic concept, what it does do, according to Gluckman, is provide a conceptual framework for comparisons between different systems of social obligation. It is thus a way to avoid what Gluckman denounces as the "cultural solipsism" to which he feels ethnographers are dangerously prone when they insist that singular cultures can be understood only in terms of their own categories.[64]

Debt is a personal obligation arising from a contingent event involving real or potential injury to another and requiring the alienation of some material value object; its institutional form is determined by and reinforces a particular culture's general system of social obligation, but what distinguishes debts among social obligations is their radically personal and historical formation. For this reason, there is something not quite right when structuralist sociology conceives debt as a homeostatic cultural device to restore a disrupted structure of social relations back to its original order (as explained by the cosmology, theology, or constitutional ideology of a particular society). This posits debt as the way an unchanging structure of social positions maintains itself against the contingent events of historical time. But if one gives theoretical priority to historical time rather than social structure, then debt may be viewed as a material objectification of novel personal obligations that may or may not be easily classified within the preexisting structure of social relations but whose cultural specificity is to be found in the manner in which the temporality of historically arising obligations receives material expression as "fixed and certain." The temporal specificity of what is meant by "fixed and certain" varies among cultures. Traditionally, among the patrilocal Tiv of Nigeria, an exchange marriage creates a definite debt relation between the groom and his new wife's male guardian; in theory, the husband now owes one of his own female wards to his wife's guardian, but the debt theoretically discharged by completing the other half of a marriage exchange is also understood to create a new permanent relation of obligation between the two men that adds a new strand of solidarity to Tiv society. Modern capitalist society requires that the form of socially important personal debts be stipulated by specific dates and years. Today, in the United States, families achieve the important identity of homeowners by achieving a level of wage income that qualifies them for a thirty-year mortgage from a lending institution; while the specific debt is to be paid off over time, the interest rates on thirty-year mortgages are explicitly linked to the interest rates on the long-term government bonds by which the state funds the permanent national debt that is essential to the ongoing solidarity of a modern society. The most important difference among cultural forms of debt, I believe, is to be found in the way social time must be expressed depending on the degree to which social relations have been monetized and thereby must be calculable according to the logic of the time value of money. This is, obviously, different from the types of social time found in noncapitalist societies.

One of the reasons that ethnography can never be the fulfillment of the anthropological project is its failure to have any satisfactory comparative method. This would require that the ethnographer have, in addition to an articulated analysis of some alien culture, an explicit analysis of his or her own society. Insofar as ethnographies are primarily produced within the world of liberal capitalist society, this means that comparative discussions must include an explicit theoretical discourse expressing the writer's understanding of such a form of social organization. Moreover, there must be a set of concepts able to describe and explain radically different cultures (including the ethnographer's own culture) and also the forms of interaction between these different cultures. In my own work I have attempted to develop two such concepts: debts, conceived as temporally specific social obligations established through materially mediated transfers of substantive value, and fetishes, conceived as the power objects that embody the general value substance of a society and that function as the material mediations for the establishment and settlement of debts. The most fundamental modes of debt and fetishism peculiar to different societies may be identified by studying the way in which societies determine the liability for death and the value of life in such "hard cases" as that of fatal accidents. For if it will ever be possible to speak the general sacramental dimension that is the foundation of any society, I suspect it will have to be done in terms of the way different cultures institutionalize that sacrificial debt of life that Luc de Heusch finds at the heart of African sacrifice.

CHAPTER 7

Death of the Deodand: Accursed Objects and the Money Value of Human Life

"Whereas the Law respecting the Forfeiture of Chattels which have moved or caused the Death of Man, and respecting Deodands, is unreasonable and inconvenient": Be it enacted by the Queen's most Excellent Majesty, by and with the Advice and Consent of the Lords Spiritual and Temporal, and Commons, in this present Parliament assembled, and by the Authority of the same, That from and after the First Day of September One thousand eight hundred and forty-six there shall be no Forfeiture of any Chattel for or in respect of the same having moved to or caused the Death of Man; and no Coroner's Jury sworn to inquire, upon the Sight of any dead Body, how the Deceased came by his Death, shall find any Forfeiture of any Chattel which may have moved to or caused the Death of the Deceased, or any Deodand whatsoever; and it shall not be necessary in any Indictment or Inquisition for Homicide to allege the Value of the Instrument which caused the Death of the Deceased, or to allege that the same has no Value.[1]

With these words the British Parliament, in the summer of 1846, passed An Act to Abolish Deodands, thereby undoing a law that had been in effect in England for over six centuries. A deodand was "an accursed thing."[2] The term itself comes from the Latin phrase *deo dandum*, which means "that which must be given to God." It is an example of the idea that evil objects are sacred, that they are charged with divine power, and that they therefore belong to God. In English law prior to 1846, any movable material object—more specifically, any piece of personal chattel property—that directly caused the death of an adult human being became deodand and, as an accursed thing, was held to be forfeit to God (whose earthly representative in such cases was the royal sovereign).

The abolition of the law of deodand was a relatively minor, but essential, part of a much more sweeping transformation in British social institutions of the 1840s that established legal structures better suited to capitalist enterprise and liberal society. But the issue it addressed was far from minor. Fatal accidents are a form of historical trauma common to any culture. For those who love and materially depend on the deceased, their disruptive force becomes a negatively lived object, an impassioned fixation, which represents a crisis not only in the violated hearts of certain individuals but also in the general structure of material social relations. Any culture must establish some procedure of compensation, expiation, or punishment to settle the debt created by unintended human deaths whose direct cause is not a morally accountable person but a nonhuman material object. This was the issue thematized in public discourse by the debate on the law of deodand. Moreover, with its abolition, British legal institutions articulated the solution of liberal capitalist society to the general problem of the relation of the value of money to the value of human life.

Since the proximate cause of the death of the deodand as a social reality was itself an inanimate material object, the locomotive, I want to begin with an event that took place sixteen years prior to the statute of abolition. From consideration of this concrete event, I am going to indulge in some inexcusably far-ranging historical reflections on accursed objects and monetary debt as material embodiments of national sovereignty. I will, however, conclude with a somewhat more scholarly account of the abolition of the deodand in 1846.

The Unfortunate Death of the Honourable William Huskisson

In September of 1830, the world's first public railroad, the Liverpool–Manchester line, made its inaugural run. The day had been carefully orchestrated not only as a business promotion, but as a national celebration. Liverpool and Manchester, the two great cities of the English cotton industry, had arranged for brass bands, speeches by local dignitaries, and a number of allegorical pageants celebrating English nationalism and industrial progress. Banners, grandstands, and archways of flowers were placed at gathering points along the route. The steam-powered cavalcade that set out from Liverpool at a stately twelve miles per hour consisted of eight locomotives, each flying a different colored flag and given striking names such as the Phoenix and the Rocket. These pulled a train of curiously upright carriages—their design was basically that of a stagecoach on railroad wheels—that were occupied by notable men of British industry and politics. There were eleven lords, four viscounts, and one marquis, the ambassadors from Austria and Russia, as well as the owners of the railroad. Among the politicians were Sir Robert Peel, the cotton magnate who, as home secretary, had just established the world's first modern police force, and William Huskisson, a popular liberal Tory from Liverpool who, inspired as a young man by the American and French Revolutions, had been present at the storming of the Bastille but had since become a progressive conservative and tireless advocate of free enterprise.

Great crowds, estimated at half a million people, had turned out that day not to see any of these men, nor even the new technological wonder, but rather to catch a glimpse of the Duke of Wellington, hero of Waterloo and more recently England's prime minister. The crowd was mostly festive, though a few red republicans showed up waving tricolored flags and carrying signs demanding the extension of voting rights to a larger segment of the population. Unfortunately, the celebration was disrupted by what the *Times* of London called a "dreadful accident" that occurred when the procession made a stop to add water to the locomotives' boilers. Among the passengers who got off to stretch their legs was William Huskisson. Huskisson had walked over to the Duke of Wellington's car—with the intention (so the newspapers said) of shaking hands with the great man in order to make up "an old quarrel"—and was standing on the tracks chatting with a group of politicians and railroad promoters. Let me quote the account of a *Times* correspondent for what happened next:

> Whilst he was standing with them, the Rocket engine, which, like the Phoenix, had to pass the Duke's car, to take up its station at the watering place, came slowly up, and as the engineer had been for some time checking his velocity, so silently that it was almost upon the group before they observed it. In the hurry of the moment all attempted to get out of the way. . . . [But Huskisson] hesitated, staggered a little as if not knowing what to do, then attempted to run forward, found it impossible to get off the road, on account of an excavation of some 14 or 15 feet in depth being on that side of it, on which he was, attempted again to get into the car, was hit by a motion of the door as he was mounting a step, and was thrown directly in the path of the Rocket, as that engine came opposite the Duke's car. He contrived to move himself a little out of its path before it came in contact with him, otherwise it must have gone directly over his head and breast. As it was, the wheel went over his left thigh, squeezing it almost to a jelly, broke the leg, it is said, in two places, laid the muscles bare from the ankle, nearly to the hip, and tore out a large piece of flesh,

as it left him. Mrs. Huskisson, who, along with several other ladies, witnessed the accident, uttered a shriek of agony, which none who heard it will ever forget.[3]

Huskisson was dragged into the Duke of Wellington's car and a tourniquet applied to his leg, but it was clear the accident was fatal. The duke and Sir Robert Peel insisted that the celebration be canceled and the train return to Liverpool. While the newspapers reported this merely as the expression of an admirably humane emotion, there was far more going on.[4] Wellington, Peel, and Huskisson led the three factions of a Tory Party that had been the ruling party in England for nearly half a century but that was now facing complete collapse. Wellington, the national hero, led the conservative Tories who wished to maintain the old political order that relied on a divinely ordained monarch, an established Anglican Church, the army, and unreformed judicial and financial institutions. Peel, the innovative and authoritarian home secretary, led those Tories who recognized the need for strong new institutions to maintain social order and fiscal efficiency. Huskisson, who had pushed through major reforms as president of the Board of Trade and then as colonial secretary, represented those Tories most deeply involved in the global economy and who believed in the principles of free trade and "liberalism" before all else. When Wellington had been called upon to form a new government in 1828, Huskisson and other critics of the duke's "illiberal" policies (they became known as Huskissonites) had bolted. The Tory coalition had been further weakened in 1829 as ultraconservatives became infuriated when Wellington had reluctantly pushed through a heavily hedged bill of Catholic emancipation. Worse yet, the winter of 1829–1830 saw a terrible economic depression set in. Many hard-pressed workers joined activist political unions. Local violence by the poor and unemployed surged. This, along with their own straitened circumstances, sent the middle classes into an apocalyptic fear of social chaos that expressed itself in a general demand for a more activist government and in a politicization of revived religious values whose focus became the demand for an immediate abolition of slavery in Britain's West Indian colonies. In June, the king had died, and a new king meant new elections in a year of crisis. The dire possibilities of such an election had been played out the following month in France, when a new election solidified an opposition backed by liberal business groups that, by the end of the month, had forced the king to abdicate. By September 15, the day of Huskisson's death, the Tory Party was facing complete disaster in next month's election. The only hope of avoiding a transfer of governmental power to an opposition Whig Party subject to

unprecedented new social forces was to get the Huskissonites back on
board. Astute politicians, Wellington and Peel saw in this bloody corpse
not only a personal tragedy but a new political fact whose ramifications
had to be divined at once. However widely disliked Huskisson may have
been in political circles for his vacillating unreliability, any treatment
of the liberal Huskissonites' fallen leader that might be perceived as
disrespectful had to be avoided. (What happened, of course, is that the
Whigs swept the election of November 1830, and the way was opened
for the Reform Act of 1832 that transformed the political constitution
of England, which the Tories had so long defended.)

However, the railroad promoters of Liverpool and Manchester were
part of the very social force that Huskisson represented, and they objected to turning a great ritual of commercial celebration into a procession of political mourning. They insisted that Wellington and Peel had a
public duty to continue, that "the success of the project, on which they
had expended so much capital, might depend on their [the procession]
being regularly finished." They warned that if the expectations of the
crowd of spectators in Manchester were not fulfilled, a riot might ensue:

> The public expected that they would have the satisfaction of seeing
> the road opened that day, and the directors were bound to fulfill their
> expectations to the best of their ability. It was quite certain that the
> news of the melancholy accident which had befallen Mr. Huskisson
> would reach Manchester, and that consideration rendered it still more
> imperative that the whole procession should move on, to correct any
> exaggerated reports of mischief which might get abroad, and to show
> the public *that the accident which happened was a mere accident, and
> had not happened through any fault of the machinery.*[5]

Wellington reluctantly agreed, and the procession continued, thereby
averting a disastrous impression regarding the newborn railroad industry from being made upon that newly powerful political entity, public
opinion. But there was one more hurdle that had to be cleared. Would
a coroner's jury declare that the locomotive involved deodand? Huskisson's body was taken back to Liverpool where it was laid on display in
the city's principal public building. In any such case of suspicious death,
the country coroner was required to impanel a jury of local citizens. The
jury was first required to view the body and form a personal impression of the death. They then heard testimony from eyewitnesses and
other concerned parties, whereupon they decided whether a criminal
homicide had taken place or merely an accidental death. If the latter,
their last act was to decide whether or not an object was at fault and, if

so, to declare the object deodand and estimate its money value, which became an amount of debt owed to the crown. In this case, as the always pro-railroad *Times* duly reported, the jury "returned a verdict of 'Accidental Death,' but affixed no deodand on the engine, from which it may be fairly inferred that they acquitted the engineers *and the machinery* of all blame."[6]

Oliver Wendell Holmes on the Problem of the Deodand

There are few ideas less rational to a modern mind than the idea of holding an inanimate object to be morally guilty for some effect it has caused. In his book of 1881, *The Common Law*, Oliver Wendell Holmes traced the basic concept of deodand back to ancient German, Roman, and Biblical laws that required the physical surrender and sacrificial destruction of any lethally noxious thing, whether it was a knife purposefully directed by the hand of a murderer or some legally inanimate object that killed a person apart from the intention of its owner. The ox that gored a neighbor to death, the wagon that ran over a stranger in the marketplace, or the slave who killed a citizen must be surrendered, although experts disagreed whether this functioned primarily as a mode of expiation for the sin tainted owner or as a way to satisfy the demand for revenge on the part of the victim's family and thereby avoid a blood feud. Holmes agreed with the latter view, since early law pursued the guilty thing itself even when its ownership had passed from the hands of its owner at the time of the death. As Holmes put it, "the liability seems to have been regarded as attached to the body doing the damage, in an almost physical sense."[7] This was in accord with Holmes's general view that "all law is directed to conditions of things manifest to the senses."[8] Hence his famous statement on the opening page of *The Common Law*: "The life of the law has not been logic; it has been experience."[9] Holmes explained his understanding of deodand, as well as his larger claim that the impulse for revenge was the origin of law, by locating its origin in an immediately lived response, specifically "the desire of retaliation against the offending thing itself," as exemplified in the angry desire one has to kick a door that has pinched one's finger.[10]

The reason why the apparently antiquarian problem of "the liability of inanimate things" was a central problem for Holmes in his effort to rethink modern liability law is illustrated by the confrontation between nineteenth-century industrial capitalism and the English law of deodand that is the subject of this chapter. Earlier in the nineteenth century, jurists had tried to frame a legal theory adequate to the new industrial world by generalizing the principles of contract law. Such a framework worked well enough for controversies that could be understood in terms of intentional agreements between voluntary parties. But the new technologies also multiplied the sorts of events in which injury occurred as an unintended consequence of mechanical operations, and the law of torts, that is, the body of laws compensating accidental wrongs occurring outside any preexisting contractual relation, had grown from a minor supplement to contract law to a separate field of equal importance. But the principles of tort law were far from certain. In *The Common Law*, Holmes attempted to establish these principles through what could be termed a historical phenomenology of material sensibilities (in opposition to the excessive formalism and Hegelianism that dominated the legal theory of his day). The task of the modern jurist was thus to discover the "anthropology contained in the history of law."[11] Influenced especially by the work of E. B. Tylor, Holmes sought to ground liability law in culturally specific standards of reasonable behavior, which in turn rested on what he called the "felt necessities" of a particular historical moment.

However, Holmes ultimately rejected this as a satisfactory solution to the nineteenth-century crisis in the understanding of civil and criminal liability.[12] The drawback of a method of cultural phenomenology as legal anthropology is its failure to take into account the conceptual effects of the multiple and often competing political institutions whose power shapes the legal discourse of a society. This is well illustrated by the concept of deodand itself. A law dictionary of 1579 inadequately defines the term thus:

> Deodande is when any man by misfortune is slaine by an horse or by a cart, or by anie other thinge that moveth, then this thing that is cause of his death, and which at the time of the misfortune mooved, shall be forfayte to the Queene, and that is called deodande, and that perteyneth to the Queenes Almener for to dyspose in almes and in deedes of charities.[13]

Although the paradigmatic event for deodand was indeed that of a material object that killed a person by its physical motion, this definition overlooks the fact that in concrete decisions about deodands, the operative distinction was the feudal, institutional one between real and personal property. Real property formed a landed estate; the division or transfer of such property fell under the normal jurisdiction of the king's courts. Movable objects that were personal chattel property, however, were transferred either through sales falling under the law merchant or through inheritance after a natural death, which was handled by ecclesiastical courts. The violence that made a chattel deodand was thus an exception to the normal division of property laws, since it placed a case involving personal property under the jurisdiction of the sovereign. It is the distinction between real and personal property that explains the oddity that a bell that fell and killed someone was not ruled deodand, despite the fact that its motion was the cause of death (because it was classified as real property, part of an estate). On the other hand, the lethal fall of a man off a stationary wagon could make the wagon deodand, despite its lack of motion (because a wagon was chattel property). Deodand is thus more accurately defined as "whatever personal chattel is the immediate occasion of the death of any reasonable creature."[14] (The latter qualification indicates that the death of an infant, who lacked reason and free will and hence the capacity for expiable sin, could not be the occasion for a judgment of deodand.)

While a historical-materialist phenomenology of the sort Holmes attempted in *The Common Law* is necessary to grasp the idea of the deodand, it seems that it must be combined with a historical analysis of the theoretical discourse forged by a society's political institutions. In the case of the English law of deodand, this means examining the political theory established to legitimate a Christian state.

The Pious Use Value of Accursed Objects and the Fiscal Body of the Christian Sovereign

The English law of deodand differed from earlier Germanic and Mediterranean laws pertaining to guilty objects since it was shaped by Christian and feudal political institutions. The deodand that was forfeit to God was not destroyed in a public sacrifice but was rather surrendered for what the Church called "pious use." That is, its material use value was transferred from the private economy of material life to what we might call the Christian economy of charity and salvation. The accursed thing or, more often, an amount of money equal to the monetary value of that thing, was surrendered by the owner to the state for use in relief of the poor and other charitable activities. Things that had caused a human death became the rightful property of the sovereign and were given over to the king's high almoner.

The deodands responsible for sudden death were classified under a legal category of sovereign property that included any catastrophic source of royal revenue. Other examples were cargo washed ashore from shipwrecks, prizes seized in war, and chance discoveries of hidden treasure or gold mines. Various events of sudden violence and fortuitous encounter (what miners used to call a "lucky strike") produced a type of

wealth that was held to belong to the sovereign if these occurred within
the sovereign's territorial jurisdiction; they fell outside the normal privileges and protections inhering in real and personal property against the
power of the state. The owner of such wealth was not the king in his
status as a mortal person, but rather the monarch in his or her identity
as the immortal body of the nation's sovereignty. As Kantorowicz mentions in his book on medieval political theology, *The King's Two Bodies*,
this was conceived not through the modern distinction between the
private sphere and the public sphere, but rather through the peculiar
medieval distinction between the king feudal and the king fiscal. The
king feudal was a particular mortal individual placed at the top of the
hierarchy of voluntarily contracted feudal relationships. The king fiscal
was the immortal king as the sovereign "crown." The latter, in Latin, was
also called the *res fisci* (literally, "the fiscal thing"). The fiscal sovereign
consisted of those materialities sacralized in the world of secular time
by mundane historical events, as opposed to those objects sanctified
through the divine salvational power that had entered the world through
Christ. The wealth that became part of the king's fisc was conceived as
a permanent, inalienable component of the sovereign, unlike the property that belonged to the king in his capacity as a mortal feudal lord,
which could be sold off at need. As the fourteenth-century legal theorist
Bracton wrote: "A thing quasi-sacred is a thing fiscal, which cannot be
given away or be sold or transferred upon another person by the Prince
or ruling king; and those things make the crown what it is, and they
regard to common utility [what moderns would call 'the public good']
such as peace and justice."[15] This Christian feudal ideology produced
what Kantorowicz calls "that seemingly weird antithesis or parallelism
of *Christus* and *fiscus*."[16] The *Christus*, the ecclesiastical body of Christ
in this world, that is, the Church with its eucharistically present Christ,
its divinely empowered priests, and its sacramental objects, was concerned with the salvation of people's immortal souls. The *fiscus*, the fiscal
body of the crown, that is, the king in his divine right as monarch, his
officers, and the quasi-sacred objects that were the sovereign's wealth,
was—in theory, at least—concerned with enacting God's law of Christian charity in the historical world of mortally embodied life. (I might
note that while the use of wealth and money for the purpose of salvation
in heaven corrupted and delegitimated the Church, most spectacularly
in the practice of selling indulgences, the use of wealth and money for
the purpose of charity on earth successfully helped legitimize both the
modern state and the charitable institutions, such as hospitals, to which
the state granted special privileges.)

In the late twelfth century, the responsibility for deodands became part of the new office of the coroner. As is implied by the name itself, which is derived from *corona*, the Latin word for crown, the coroner was the direct agent and chief accountant of the sovereign in local affairs. The coroner's duty was to safeguard the rights of the crown by impaneling juries and holding courts of inquest into such things as shipwrecks, treasure-trove, and any unexplained death that might bring revenue to the crown.[17] As I have already mentioned, in late medieval times revenue derived from deodand judgments usually took the form of the money value of the accursed object rather than the thing itself. In the terminology of English common law, this meant that the thing had become liable for an action of debt, since the term "debt" referred to a specifically monetary obligation. This also meant that if the deodand object was destroyed, the debt was canceled, since it was the thing itself, not its owner, that was the debtor. If the owner wished the continued use of the guilty object, then the money owed for its killing of a person was determined by the value of that particular object, be it a sword, an ox, a slave, or even, once such things came into existence, a locomotive.

The Incorporation of Capitalist Debt into the Sovereign Body

Before turning to the abolition of deodand, I need to mention two important changes affecting the relation between deodand judgments and monetary debt that occurred prior to the nineteenth century. One need only be noted: the institution of the coroner had undergone a democratic transformation that altered it from being a direct agent of the crown in local affairs to being a representative of the local interests that was able to use the powers of the crown. This occurred not only because local citizens made up coroner's juries, but also because the coroner himself became a locally elected official. The other, however, requires a longer discussion; the fiscal body of the state underwent a fundamental transformation by its incorporation of a capitalist system of debt.

Since the time of the emergence of Christianity as the state religion of Rome in the fourth century, the law of Christian states had been characterized by an absolute ideological opposition to commercial debt—that is, to trade credit in the form of interest-bearing loans. The lending of money for profit, no matter how small, was condemned as usury, as a violation of the fundamental Christian principle of caritas (charity). As Shael Herman notes in his book, *Medieval Usury and the Commercialization of Feudal Bonds*, the main scriptural authority for this injunction was Luke 6:35, "Lend: expect nothing in return."[18]

This position had only been reinforced with the development of European canon law in the twelfth century: Assuming money had immutable and absolute value, the Church apparently considered the idea of the time value of money as heretical as the teachings of Galileo and Copernicus. The autonomous system of canon law established by Gratian about 1142 had as one of its foundation stones an absolute ban on usury. In 1139, the Second Lateran Council deprived the unrepentant usurer of church sacraments and barred his burial in sacred ground.[19]

Lending money at interest was sacrilege because it exercised a power akin to unholy magic. Money was the tool of the great magician himself, the figure of the Antichrist, Simon Magus, when he tried to buy the miraculous power of the Holy Spirit from Saint Peter (in Acts 8:9–22). It was the need to preserve the holy power actualized in the sacrament of the Eucharist from corruption by the unholy power of money that made simony (a term derived from Simon Magus) the central issue in the Gregorian reformation of the Catholic Church.[20] Outside the Church, whose priests held a monopoly on the power of the Holy Spirit, piety in the secular world was expressed in the act of charitable giving. Charity was the most godly of acts because it came closest to God's mode of action, the gift of the natural world that God created. The realm of secular temporality was itself a gift. As Karl Pribram has written, "Time was regarded as a common property given to all men as a free gift."[21] The gift of time, with its natural fruitfulness, came under man's stewardship in the form of real property (farmland and durable goods able to produce new things because they embodied the power of nature). But consumer goods and other movable personal property lacked such productive capacity; their "intrinsic goodness" could only be consumed by the owner or given away for another to consume. Since Aristotle, money had been classed among the consumer goods. Money could only be spent or lent, and lending was properly giving since money was naturally barren. The usurer who lent money at interest was corrupting the holy gift of time in the same way that Simon Magus tried to use money to acquire the power of the Holy Spirit from Saint Peter. Charging interest was thus not merely an unnatural use of money; it was a quasi-magical act entailing spiritual pollution.

Given the inevitable need for legitimate institutional structures to accommodate the monetary credit-debt relations crucial to the development of any widespread commerce, medieval states developed a number of creative evasions of the ban on usury. One, of course, was the use of non-Christians as agents for loans. This received institutional form in

England in the curious office called the Exchequer of the Jews. Another evasion, one available to land-rich monasteries and Christian lords, was the ruse of subinfeudation; agricultural land was nominally transferred as a nontenurial lease to a lender, in his guise as vassal to the borrower, so that a loan given to a feudal debtor could masquerade as rent and the interest on the loan paid to the creditor could masquerade as direct income earned by a feudal vassal from agricultural production.[22]

By the fifteenth century, laws against interest-bearing loans had been sufficiently undermined and European commerce had reached a sufficiently critical mass so that the greatest among the financiers providing intermediation services to commercial enterprises were able to draw enough currency from the web of monetarized debt values realized in bills of exchange and other financial credit instruments to begin making very large loans to the sovereigns of Europe. Monarchs of the sixteenth century like Charles V fought their wars on credit supplied by bourgeois bankers like the Fuggers and the Medici. Moreover, they increasingly fought these wars with weapons bought on credit from commercial industrial enterprises located in free cities. The expansion or contraction of the monetary value realized by private merchants in the form of capitalized debt and trade credit became precariously dependent on the fortunes of war and the victory or defeat of the particular sovereign a money lender or materials supplier had decided to back. That is, prior to the great overseas expansion that opened a vast field for speculative investment in colonial adventures and slave plantations, great merchant capitalists wagered their surplus money on great sovereigns who waged war.

In sixteenth-century Europe, the institutional linkage between the monetary values produced by commercial credit and those arising from public debt was still rather inchoate. My favorite example of this concerns a shipload of bullion belonging to Genoese merchant bankers that was intended as a loan to the Spanish forces in the Netherlands who were fighting against the revolt of the Protestant Dutch. The dangers of the high seas forced the ship to take refuge in an English port, and Queen Elizabeth seized the treasure, which she desperately needed for her efforts to support the Dutch against the Spanish. Her seizure was legitimate according to the medieval law of sovereignty that I have already discussed, but Elizabeth, for practical political reasons, chose to treat this money as a loan, that is, as a debt owed to the bankers of Genoa who would have to be repaid. The Italian financiers accepted this shift of sides in their funding of the continental war. They could not do anything about it anyway and, after all, the money was not lost, only lent to an unexpected borrower.[23]

The crucial transformation in the fiscal body of the English sovereign occurred at the end of the following century, long after European monarchs had become thoroughly dependent on commercial credit. The great event was the founding of the Bank of England in 1694 and the creation of the first modern national debt. Unlike previous state debts, the British national debt that secured the Glorious Revolution was intended as a permanent entity that was never to be paid off. Individuals could invest in this debt by buying what we would call government bonds, from which they derived specified interest payments at specified times and which they could cash in at any time, making it a floating debt that came to be funded by all of the monied classes in the English nation. It thus became a political vehicle for building a national alliance between previously hostile agricultural and commercial economic interests, as well as an economic vehicle that provided the public money with which the new British state could build a navy whose primary political purpose was the protection and expansion of an overseas commercial empire.[24] Since the Bank of England was also the dominant source of private business loans in the nation, this institution for the first time enabled a functional unification of the body of monetary values existing in the form of private trade credit within a national economy and the body of monetary values created through public borrowing and the other fiscal activities of a sovereign state. This innovation not only transformed the nature of the fiscal sovereignty of the state, but it set the stage for the modern history of money.

Money has traditionally been defined as currency, that is, as anything generally accepted as payment for goods and services and for the settlement of debts. A particular commodity, gold (along with other precious metals) functioned as the primary world currency from the beginning of the European colonial expansion until the 1970s. This meant that the supply and hence the value of money was dependent upon the chance discovery of precious metal mines and new techniques for refining these metals, because they affected the commodity value of the currency substance.[25] But the British invention of the modern central bank made the creation and fluctuation of monetary debt values realized in the capitalist accounting practices of private business enterprises an increasingly recognizable causal factor affecting the value of money. It also made the ability of states during crises, primarily wars, to issue paper fiat money, that is money whose acceptance is coerced by the state as legal tender and whose value is secured only by the general credit of the state, a third obvious determining factor. The creation and fluctuation of monetary value in capitalist societies thus appears to be triangulated between the changing market values of commodities and commodity currencies, the private monetary debt values created by trade credit and bank loans, and the standing public debt and issues of credit-money of sovereign nation-states. That the value of money has become increasingly determined by the monetary values created in intermediated credit-debt relations, both private and public, rather than in the direct commercial exchange of commodities, is hardly news to economic historians. But economic models of the origin of monetary value do not take into account fatal accidents and other torts as an origin of novel debt liabilities and hence of new monetary values. To do so would be to acknowledge that death, the destruction of life, the very antithesis of an economically productive event, sometimes creates money.

The Abolition of Deodand: The Money Value of Human Life and Immortal Bodies without Sovereignty

During what is still usefully referred to as the Industrial Revolution, capitalist manufacturing enterprise extended its dynamic drive toward technological innovation beyond the production and supply of wars and colonial adventures. It is undeniable that many of the new objects it produced in the world of early nineteenth-century civil society were notable for their danger. Gas lighting, heavy machinery, even plate-glass windows became a new source not only of economic prosperity, but also of accidental death. Among these objects, the one with the greatest lethal potential was steam-powered transportation. In 1769 the inventor Nicolas Cugnot drove the world's first steam-powered land vehicle into a wall. (He was thrown into a French prison for being a danger on the road.) In 1801 at the trial run of the first English locomotive, the engine overturned and caught fire, while a demonstration two years later ended with a boiler explosion and four deaths. I have described the accidental death of William Huskisson on the occasion of the opening of the first public railroad in 1830.

That no deodand was declared in Huskisson's death was important at the time, since powerful forces opposed the fledgling railroad industry. In those days a corporation such as the Manchester and Liverpool Rail Road had to receive a special charter from Parliament. The fight to win this had been hard, since established interests, notably the owners of the canals with whom the railroads would compete for the domestic carrying trade, were adamantly opposed. As a publication called *The Anti-Rail-Road Journal* argued a couple of years later, the Liverpool and Manchester Rail Road, which had turned a profit in its first years only because it had received a special tax exemption, benefited a relatively small number of investors, in contrast to canals, which had a far more extensive base of investors. The establishment of railroads inevitably diminished the property value of the canals in which many of the rural middle and upper classes had invested their capital, and these latter were the principal consumers who had created a prosperous internal market in England. This forecast of dire consequences for the general economy had a certain resonance in the depressed economy of the early 1830s. The antirailroad interests warned that a new and socially destructive principle had been introduced into the politics of corporations: "It is now to be laid down as a principle on which Parliament intends to act, that encouragement is to be afforded to every scheme which shall profess to be beneficial to its proprietors contrary or to the injury occasioned to property already in existence."[26] The 1830s and 1840s do, in fact, represent the moment of the legal revolution that created modern corporations. The ancient law of corporations had concerned a special privilege granted by the state in the form of a charter to engage in and usually monopolize some socially beneficial—whether profitable or charitable—activity. The emergence of a capitalist economy required instead that incorporation be a routine procedure, a private right in civil society rather than a special privilege granted by the sovereign state. It also required that corporations be legitimized in terms of market competition rather than monopoly privilege. This entailed a theoretical contradiction between the right of property owners to enjoy a settled expectation in the stable value of the objects in which they had vested interests and the right of business owners to engage in free enterprise through market competition in which property values are always in flux and in which there are supposed to be both winners and losers (in this case, the railroad owners were the winners and the owners of canals and turnpikes the losers). This contradiction between the principles of property ownership and market competition was a fundamental problem underlying the later transformation of legal theory by such thinkers as Oliver Wendell Holmes.[27]

In this new institutional context, a parallel contradiction emerged in the sphere of public law; the state had a duty to protect the property and contracts of private individuals, but it also had a duty to act for the good of society as a whole. This often involved the confiscation of private property under the state's power of eminent domain or the diminishment of property values through state regulation, which happened to make some social groups winners and others losers. Indeed these contradictions determine the argumentative structure of legitimized politics within capitalist democracies. The logic of legitimate economic and political action that emerged in Anglo-American legal culture during the nineteenth century represented society as divided into two spheres, the public and the private. The public sphere of the sovereign state was conceived as a realm of coercive force that was justified only if it protected private rights in general and encroached on them only for reasons of the good of the whole society and not in a manner that deliberately redistributed wealth or power from one social group to another. The private sphere was conceived as a realm of voluntary association between private parties who established explicit reciprocal obligations by freely agreeing to enter into contracts. One thing Marx realized in his studies of revolution and class struggle in France at the end of the 1840s was that the discourse of political conflict between different groups in a modern society involved representing one's own group as acting in the interests of the whole society and opposing groups as acting in the interest of only their own part of society. Similarly, in legal disputes, a state's donation of land to the railroad industry, or a court's refusal to hold a railroad corporation liable for the burned wheat fields of farmers that had been ignited by a spark thrown from the wheel of a passing locomotive, could be justified by arguing that railroads and other embodiments of industrial progress benefited society as whole, whereas land owners or farmers represented only their own partial interests, and the public good outweighed these. Many of these legal controversies arose from wrongful injuries and deaths caused in unintentional accidents.

Within this new institutional and ideological context, there are two developments directly related to the emergence of a new model of the debt liability arising from accidental death. One was the civilization of such debt, in the original sense of the word "civilization": the transfer of social controversies that became justiciable cases from the criminal law of the state to the civil law of private individuals. The other was the institutional production of a new kind of (legally) immortal person: the modern limited liability corporation.

The civilization of accidental death was the issue that led to the abolition of deodand in 1846 as being "unreasonable and inconvenient." The 1840s was known in England as the decade of the "Railway Mania." By the early 1840s a disjointed network of railway lines had spread over England. This led to a proportionate increase in railroad accidents and a growing number of deodand judgments against locomotives, a very expensive capital asset. These raised economic problems for railroad corporations and theoretical problems for law courts. For instance, a fatal accident on the Eastern Counties Railway in 1840 had resulted in four deaths and a judgment of deodand on a locomotive valued at five hundred pounds; but did this mean that the company owed the crown a total of five hundred pounds or did it mean that it owed five hundred pounds for each death? One way or another deodand judgments on locomotives tended to get appealed all the way up to the queen's bench, where they were almost invariably overturned. But local juries whose towns and farms had been invaded by the new reality of mechanized transportation were continuing to use the power of deodand to do justice as they understood it. There was no other way to compensate an accidental fatal injury. In cases where a person was maimed or mutilated, he or she could sue for damages. But in the case of accidental death, the injured party having ceased to exist, no one had standing to file a civil lawsuit. It was in order to pass the Fatal Accidents Act of 1846, which would allow this, that Parliament found it necessary to abolish the law of deodand.

The debate in Parliament emphasized the irrationality of deodand as a remnant of primitive law that should have passed away long ago. Deodands, said Lord Denman, were "a remnant of a barbarous and absurd law."[28] Lord Campbell, the great law reformer of his day, stated that certain doctrines of the revered common law were "not applicable to the present state of society. One of these doctrines was, that the life of a man was so valuable that they could not put an estimate upon it in case of a death by accident."[29] That is, the irrationality of deodand was that, in holding the value of human life to be infinite and hence unmeasurable, "compensation was made, not according to the extent of the injury inflicted, but according to the value of the instrument of injury."[30] The only cautionary note raised in the debate came from a politician who mused that, although he "was no advocate for the absurdity of the law of deodand," it seemed to him that "a simple compensation to the Crown was a very ready means of getting at the compensation which was due to the injured party."[31] This was a reference to the Scottish law of deodand, under which the state remained the party conducting the lawsuit and collecting the money due, but the state would then deliver the money to the closest relative of the deceased rather than to a charitable institution. The abolition of deodand meant that it would not be the powerful state that sued railroads and other corporations for compensations but rather the relatives of the fatally injured person.[32]

There were a number of forces other than the modern industrial corporation that were working for the abolition of deodand. One of these was modern medical science, in the person of the coroner of Middlesex County, Thomas Wakely, one of the great medical reformers of the time. As editor of the journal *Lancet* and as a member of Parliament, Wakely tirelessly pressed for the reform of legal institutions in the name of modern medical science.[33] Wakely pushed the abolition of deodand in the House of Commons as part of his effort to restructure the office of the public coroner into something closer to that of a modern medical examiner. We should recall that this was an age still shocked by the scandalous activities of Burke and Hare, who robbed graves in order to provide corpses for doctors and medical researchers.[34] The transformation of the institution of the coroner into that of medical examiner was of some cultural importance, since it shifted the authority and the conceptual framework that provided the reasons explaining why a particular death occurred. Juries of ordinary citizens were basing their judgments of liability for death upon their response to the viewing of a dead body and their understanding of witnesses' narratives of what happened. Reformers like Wakely were revaluing the reasons for death within a scientific framework of purely physical causality from which moral considerations were, quite properly, removed.

The other important new social authority on death at this time that had an interest in the abolition of deodand was the insurance industry. The abolition of deodand and the passage of the Fatal Accidents Act meant that compensation for death was now a matter for civil remedies. These companies had such a remedy, a profitable one, in the form of life insurance and personal injury policies. It was the insurance industry that articulated the modern ideology explaining the proper monetary compensation for human life from a capitalist perspective. The best statement I have found of this appears in a fascinating book called *The Money Value of Man* that was published by two statisticians in collaboration with the Metropolitan Life Insurance Company. The book begins with a historical review of primitive modes for placing a money value on human life. One of these is compensation based of the value of noxious objects, as in the law of deodand. The other is, of course, human slavery. But the modern—and correct—approach, we are assured, is to view "man as a wage-earner or salaried worker."[35] Using actuarial tables of average life expectancy and the likely career trajectory and wage income of a person in a given occupation, one can calculate the amount of lifetime wage earnings lost by an individual killed in an accident before his natural time. In a capitalist society, this is obviously the correct logic for compensating a life, and we may note the class specificity it involves; people with different levels of income have differently valued lives. (The democratic wild card to this is the jury award of punitive damages, a practice the insurance industry is still ferociously fighting today.)

While medical reform and the rise of for-profit social insurance companies were important in the abolition of deodand, by far the greatest social force arose from the owners who managed and invested in corporations. The mid-1840s was the moment when the heterogeneous assemblage of rail lines built in the 1830s were gathered under the control of a few large corporations and when nearly all the liquid capital of England began to flow into railroad investment.[36] The reason for this was not only high profit rates but also financial security. While railroads were a notably dangerous enterprise for their customers, they offered unparalleled safety to their investors. This is because railroads, in contrast to older corporations, had been granted the privilege of limited liability.[37] That is, investors were liable for the debts of the business entity in which they had invested only up to the amount of money they had actually invested. (The danger of unlimited liability was once again demonstrated in the phenomenon of "debt millionaires" who invested in Lloyd's of London during its 1980s and 1990s period of excessive speculation and fraud.) In the 1840s and 1850s, the advantage of the limited liability corporation form became evident to most corporations and investors, and a series of parliamentary acts were passed that established general limited liability as an essential quality of the modern corporation.

From the anthropological perspective I am adopting here, this represents the cultural production of a new kind of transhuman person (a corporation is a person in the eyes of the law) not subject to human mortality. The material assets of a corporation are owned by this entity and continue to be should any, or all, of its human owners die. In this, modern corporations are true immortal spiritual beings, as much as any god or sovereign. However, it is precisely their private status, the absence of the divinely legitimated power and the quasi-religious public duties of sovereignty, that distinguishes them. That these immortal beings are constituted through their monetary relation to the income-producing things they own is obvious to anyone who knows how to read a double-entry balance sheet; productive assets are represented as monetary values on one side of the sheet, while the mortal ownership of these assets appears as an equal amount of monetary value on the other side. The latter are divided into what is called "owner's equity," the portion of capitalized monetary value that belongs to the corporation's owners, and liabilities, the balance of capital value that is owed as debt to outside creditors. It is debt that knits together the economic relations of different corporate entities and that becomes recognized as itself an asset in the balance sheets of banks and other financial corporations (and in the form of accounts receivable in commercial and industrial enterprises). That is, monetary debt, as constructed within this historically specific cultural system of economic accounting, is the fundamental medium of capitalist social relations.

Capitalism can fully establish itself as the structuring system of a social reality only to the extent that monetary debt in this sense becomes a practical logic and "felt necessity" in everyday social interactions. It may be that the historical limits of capitalist relations appear in those traumatic events that fall outside the economic realm of commercial exchange and contractual agreement, but whose material impact on individual human lives, in cases of accidental injury, and on whole peoples, in the form of war, nevertheless valorizes new debt relations that the modern social order must somehow realize in the form of monetary value. If there is a logic to the accumulation of such monetary values, I believe it has yet to be adequately theorized.

Acknowledgments

We are most grateful first of all to Francesco Pellizzi, the extraordinary editor of *RES: Anthropology and Aesthetics*, who shared with us the existence of chapter 4 (originally intended as Part IIIb), who facilitated the publication of this book, and who has been Pietz's champion (and ours) all this way. Francesco has a true gift for hearing an idea and returning it to you suddenly brimming with possibility, and he has the intellectual generosity to match that gift. We are privileged to work with him. Laurel Martin helped us to establish the text from Pietz's often messy files; Hayley Ackerman provided excellent editorial help at a later stage of the process, managed the image rights, and created the index. We very gratefully acknowledge their contributions. We also thank Cornell University Press for granting us the rights to use chapter 5, "Fetishism and Materialism: The Limits of Theory in Marx," which originally appeared in *Fetishism as Cultural Discourse*, edited by Emily Apter and William Pietz (1993), 119–51, © 1993 by Cornell University. James Clifford, Donna Haraway, and Katie King offered reminiscences, directions, and information regarding Pietz, which we also appreciate. Ben Kafka would like to add his particular gratitude to Elizabeth Weed, who introduced him to Pietz's work and so much more.

This book was made possible by Priya Nelson and is a reality because of her. She loved the idea of restoring this work into one volume, advocated for the book with the press, recognized its interdisciplinary value (well beyond our original sense of it), and participated in thinking through and organizing it by using contours that make sense to the breadth, rigor, and originality of Pietz's project(s). Dylan Montanari has guided the process with commitment, ability, and ingenuity, particularly as regards our responsibility to William Pietz and his family, and we are most grateful for his hard work. Profound thanks are due to Trevor Perri, who edited the manuscript with meticulous attention and a very keen and caring eye. To read this project after his interventions and corrections is to read it finalized in a way it had for so long resisted.

Stefanos Geroulanos, Dellaportata, Lixouri, Greece
Ben Kafka, Warren, CT
January 2021

Notes

Introduction

1. Wilhelm Reich, "Dialectical Materialism and Psychoanalysis," in *Sex-Pol Essays, 1929–1934*, ed. Lee Baxandall (New York: Random House, 1972), 31–32.

2. Emily Apter and William Pietz, eds., *Fetishism as Cultural Discourse* (Ithaca: Cornell University Press, 1993), 353.

3. Kobena Mercer, "Reading Racial Fetishism: The Photographs of Robert Mapplethorpe," in Apter and Pietz, eds., *Fetishism as Cultural Discourse*, 310.

4. Rosalind Morris and Daniel H. Leonard, *The Returns of Fetishism: Charles de Brosses and the Afterlives of an Idea, with a New Translation of "On the Worship of the Fetish Gods"* (Chicago: University of Chicago Press, 2017), 135.

5. Naomi Schor, "Fetishism and its Ironies," *Nineteenth-Century French Studies* 17, no. 1–2 (1988–89): 89–97.

6. See p. 165 in this volume.

7. All that Pietz had published directly on de Brosses was William Pietz, "Geography, Etymology and Tastes: Charles de Brosses and the Restoration of History," *L'Esprit Créateur* 25 (Fall 1985): 86–94, as well as a few notes in "The Problem of the Fetish, I."

8. Note, for example, the ambiguous position of the fetish in Juliet Mitchell's *Psychoanalysis and Feminism* (London: Allen Lane, 1974), 16, 85–86, 348.

9. Edward Said, *Orientalism* (London: Penguin, 1977).

10. William Pietz, "The Origin of Fetishism: A Contribution to the History of Theory" (PhD diss., University of California, Santa Cruz, 1988).

11. William Pietz, "The Origin of Fetishism," 4–5n1. Pietz interpreted this last remark as equating the hearings with Gorbachev's *glasnost*.

12. Hayden White, "The Noble Savage Theme as Fetish," in *Tropics of Discourse: Essays in Cultural Criticism* (Baltimore: Johns Hopkins University Press, 1985), 184. Originally published in Fredi Chiappelli, Michael J. B. Allen, and Robert L. Benson, eds., *First Images of America: The Impact of the New World on the Old*, vol. 1 (Los Angeles: University of California Press, 1976), 121–35.

13. James Clifford, introduction to *Writing Culture: The Poetics and Politics of Ethnography*, ed. James Clifford and George E. Marcus (Berkeley: University of California Press, 1986), 2.

14. See p. 199n81 in this volume.

15. See p. 116 in this volume.

16. Jacques Lacan, *The Ego in Freud's Theory and in the Technique of Psychoanalysis, 1954–55*, ed. Jacques Alain-Miller and trans. Sylvana Tomaselli, vol. 2 of the Seminar of Jacques Lacan (New York: Norton, 1988); Lacan, *The Psychoses, 1955–56*, ed. Jacques Alain-Miller and trans. Russell Grigg, vol. 3 of the Seminar of Jacques Lacan (London: Routledge, 1993), e.g., 32; Lacan, *Écrits* (Paris: Seuil, 1966), e.g., 24; *Écrits: The First Complete Edition in English*, trans. Bruce Fink (New York: Norton, 2006), e.g., 16; Fredric Jameson, *The Prison House of Language* (Princeton: Princeton University Press, 1975); Paul de Man, "The Resistance to Theory," *Yale French Studies* 63 (1982): 3–20; and consider also the critique of de Man by Steven Knapp and Walter Benn Michaels, "Against Theory," *Critical Inquiry* 8, no. 4. (Summer 1982): 723–42; and Michaels, *The Shape of the Signifier* (Princeton: Princeton University Press, 2004).

17. Jean Baudrillard, *For a Critique of the Political Economy of the Sign* (New York: Verso, 1981), 143. See chapter 5.

18. Juliet Mitchell and Jacqueline Rose, *Feminine Sexuality: Jacques Lacan and the école freudienne* (London: Macmillan, 1982), 96. And in a classic 1983 essay, for example, Neil Hertz derived from Freud's understanding of fetishism an argument to account for the fear of women in representations of political action and violence. Neil Hertz, "Medusa's Head: Male Hysteria under Political Pressure," *Representations* 4 (Autumn 1983): 27–54.

19. William Pietz, "The Phonograph in Africa: International Phonocentrism from Stanley to Sarnoff" in *Post-Structuralism and the Question of History*, ed. Derek Attridge, Geoff Bennington, and Robert Young (Cambridge: Cambridge University Press, 1987).

20. See p. 5 in this volume.

21. In a related series of texts concerned with the Cold War and the transformation of American capitalism in the 1980s, Pietz engaged with Orientalist and imperialist discourses as ways of othering that recursively located value back onto the West. Pietz, "The 'Post-Colonialism' of Cold War Discourse," *Social Text* 19/20 (Autumn, 1988): 55–75; "Totalitarianism and the Lessons of History: Reply to Stephanson" in *Social Text* 22 (Spring, 1989): 130–40.

22. William Pietz, "Capitalism and Perversion: Reflections on the Fetishism of Excess in the 1980s," *positions: asia critique* 3, no. 2 (Fall 1995): 545.

23. See p. 141 in this volume.

24. See p. 10 in this volume.

25. See p. 4 in this volume.

26. See p. 139 in this volume. See also Charly Coleman, "The Spirit of Speculation: John Law and Economic Theology in the Age of Lights," *French Historical Studies* 42, no. 2 (April 2019): 203–38, and *The Spirit of French Capitalism: Economic Theology in the Age of Enlightenment* (Palo Alto: Stanford University Press, 2021). On other forms of transvaluation in the early eighteenth century, see Nina L. Dubin, Meredith Martin, and Madeleine C. Viljoen, *Meltdown: Picturing the World's First Bubble Economy* (Turnhout, Belgium: Brepols-Harvey Miller Publishing, 2020).

27. See p. 10 in this volume.

28. See p. 97 in this volume.

29. For more on the rise of anthropological-style studies in the Enlightenment, see Larry Wolff and Marco Cipolloni, eds., *The Anthropology of the Enlightenment* (Palo Alto: Stanford University Press, 2007). See also Daniel H. Leonard, introduction to *The Returns of Fetishism*, ed. Morris and Leonard, 7–8.

30. For a reconsideration of the place of the *Querelle* in eighteenth-century thought, which makes clear its place in the problem of values, see Dan Edelstein, *The Enlightenment: A Genealogy* (Chicago: University of Chicago Press, 2010), chapters 2–6.

31. See p. 97 in this volume.

32. In English, see Auguste Comte, *The Positive Philosophy of Auguste Comte*, trans. Harriet Martineau, vol. 3 (London: George Bell, 1896), 7. See also chapter 5 of this volume.

33. For E. B. Tylor's citation of Comte on fetishism, see his *Primitive Culture: Researches into the Development of Mythology, Philosophy, Religion, Language, Art, and Custom*, 6th edition, vol. 1 (London: Murray, 1920), 477–78.

34. See pp. 136–37 in this volume.

35. See p. 123 in this volume.

36. Similarly, in his history of "Material Considerations," Pietz considered things "of some economic value" which held "the power to transform a subjective promise into an objective obligation." Pietz, "Material Considerations: On the Historical Forensics of Contract," *Theory, Culture & Society* 19, no. 5–6 (2002): 36.

37. See p. 159 in this volume, where Pietz writes: "one among a number of institutional innovations that created a liberal-capitalist 'civil society.'"

38. See p. 165 in this volume.

39. In conceptual history, thus, *The Problem of the Fetish* holds a fascinating place—putting the lie to the suspicion that conceptual history is at heart a conservative endeavor that keeps concepts at a distance from materiality. Pietz never allows any such distancing—any unlacing of the concept from the broader social histories, power, and multiple concrete frameworks in which it operates. Critics have focused on the affiliations of some of its practitioners or on commitments to the relative autonomy of concepts. For example, intellectual historians have grappled with the (frequent) affiliation of conceptual history with Reinhart Koselleck's or Otto Brunner's politics. See, e.g., Anson Rabinbach, "Rise and Fall of the *Sattelzeit*," in *Power and Time: Temporal Conflicts and the Making of History*, ed. Dan Edelstein, Stefanos Geroulanos, and Natasha Wheatley (Chicago: University of Chicago Press, 2020), 103–21. Koselleck's argument in his early career was an easy target for this and also for his understanding of the autonomy of concepts. So were Georges Canguilhem's relatively internalist histories of biological and medical concepts; consider his *Writings on Medicine*, trans. Stefanos Geroulanos and Todd Meyers (New York: Fordham University Press, 2012). Thus *The Problem of the Fetish* is promising in terms of intellectual history and its politics for more reasons than that it foregrounds Marx and offers and celebrates a certain reading of Marx. At stake is the way that Pietz handles the space where the problematic that leads to the fetish also contributes to the emergence of commodity capitalism.

40. See p. 11 in this volume.

41. Pietz, "Capitalism and Perversion," 558–59.

42. See p. 13 in this volume.

Chapter 1

1. MacGaffey, "Fetishism Revisited," 172.

2. Rattray, *Religion and Art in Ashanti*, 9.

3. MacGaffey, "Fetishism Revisited," 172–73. MacGaffey himself does not dismiss the term "fetish" as hopelessly corrupt and useless.

4. Leach, "Review of Gananath Obeyesekere's *Medusa's Hair*," 1459.

5. Rotenstreich, "Hypostasis and Fetishmaking."

6. Deleuze, *Difference and Repetition*, 208, translation modified.

7. I hesitate to say "modes of production." While merchant capital was not a full-blown "mode of production" (see Anderson, *Lineages of the Absolutist State*, 40–44), fifteenth-century Portuguese feudalism was already developing those absolutist political forms able to accommodate commercial forces within feudal society. Many of the African societies, especially those in Senegambia, were Islamicized, while others, such as Benin, had developed despotic tributary political structures.

8. Hegel, *The Philosophy of History*, 99.

9. Hegel, *The Philosophy of History*, 93.

10. Hegel, *The Philosophy of History*, 94, 112; translation modified on the basis of Hegel, *Vorlesungen über die Philosophie der Geschichte*, 123.

11. See chapter 5 of this volume, "Fetishism and Materialism: The Limits of Theory in Marx."

12. Mulvey, *Fetishism and Curiosity*; Steele, *Fetish: Fashion, Sex, and Power*; Krips, *Fetish: An Erotics of Culture*.

13. Pietz, "Fetish."

14. MacGaffey, "Fetishism Revisited," 172.

15. The informant was precisely that "educated African" whom Rattray denounced as a corrupt source for understanding the fetish, since he had been alienated from his own culture: "The educated African, however, has been cut off from, and is out of sympathy with, the life of his own people. . . . Concerning the past he really knows nothing, and generally cares less. Bosman, writing two hundred years ago, mentioned 'the negro who ridiculed his own country's gods.'" Rattray, *Ashanti*, 87.

16. Bosman, *A New and Accurate Description of the Coast of Guinea*, 376a.

17. Linnaeus, *A General System of Nature through the Three Grand Kingdoms of Animals, Vegetables, and Minerals*, cited in Popkin, "The Philosophical Basis of Eighteenth-Century Racism," 248.

18. See, e.g., Foucault, *Madness and Civilization*, 29.

19. Aarsleff, *From Locke to Saussure*.

20. Unger, *Knowledge and Politics*.

21. De Brosses, *Du culte des dieux fétiches*, 21; "On the Worship of Fetish Gods," 49.

22. See especially his discussions of the "Trinity Formula."

23. Binet, "Le Fétichisme dans l'amour."

24. Cadamosto, *The Voyages of Cadamosto*, 68.

25. Kant, *Observations on the Feeling of the Beautiful and Sublime*, 111.

26. For such a discussion see Godelier, "Market Economy and Fetishism, Magic and Science According to Marx's *Capital*."

27. Lévi-Strauss, *Totemism*.

28. "Every fetish appears thus as one of the two limits of symbolism. . . . The fetish on the one end, the abstract word on the other—together they determine the symbolic field: they constitute a part of the system that together they found." Pouillon, *Fétiches sans fétichisme*, 119.

29. Silla, "Langage et techniques thérapeutiques des cultes de possession des Lébou du Sénégal," 217.

30. Pietz, "The Fetish of Civilization," 76–77.

31. American Psychiatric Association, "Fetishism," in *Diagnostic and Statistical Manual of Mental Disorders*, 526–27.

32. Cushing, *Zuñi Fetishes*; Bennett, *Zuni Fetishes*; Rodee and Ostler, *The Fetish Carvers of Zuni*.

33. Jameson, *The Political Unconscious*, 95–97.

34. Marx, *Capital*, vol. 1, 169.

35. Colletti, *From Rousseau to Lenin*, 77, emphasis in original.

36. Marx, "Debates on the Law on Thefts of Wood," 225–63.

37. Leiris, "Alberto Giacometti," 209. My thanks to James Clifford for showing me this important little text.

38. Leiris, "Alberto Giacometti," 209.

39. Leiris, "Alberto Giacometti," 209.

40. Leiris, "Alberto Giacometti," 209.

41. See especially Heidegger, "The Principle of Identity."

42. Deleuze, *Difference and Repetition*, 208, translation modified.

43. Sartre, *Search for a Method*, 78 and 80.

44. Heidegger, "The Origin of the Work of Art."

45. Leiris, "Alberto Giacometti," 209.

46. Leiris, "Alberto Giacometti," 209.

47. Leiris, *L'Afrique fantôme*, 3. [Editors' note: This text has recently been translated into English as *Phantom Africa*.]

48. Perhaps it was because of his focus on routinization that Max Weber had little interest in the problem of the fetish, which he mentioned only once, in the opening pages of his *Sociology of Religion*, 2, as a kind of objective correlate of charismatic authority. Durkheim's lack of interest in the term derives from the same source as Weber's: both were concerned with the purely sociological determinants of social existence, and after 1887 the new (to Durkheim and Weber overtly subjectivist) social science of psychology had appropriated the term "fetishism."

49. Garrard, *Akan Weights and the Gold Trade*, 201–2.

50. The pioneering work on the *padrões* is Cordeiro, *Descobertas e Descobridores, Diogo Cão*.

51. Nowell, *A History of Portugal*, 53.

52. Livermore, *A New History of Portugal*, 129.

Chapter 2

1. Pliny, *Natural History*, 57 (book 12, section 75).

2. Pliny, *Natural History*, 220 (book 34, section 125).

3. Pliny, *Natural History*, 434 (book 31, section 42).

4. Cicero, *De Divinatione*, book II, chapter 11.

5. Virgil, *Aeneid*, book II.

6. Tertullianus, *De Spectaculis*, 26; *The Writings of Quintus Sept. Flor. Tertullianus*, 25–26.

7. Tertullianus, *De Spectaculis*, 10.

8. All Latin Biblical quotations are from the Vulgate: Loch, ed., *Biblia Sacra Vulgatae Editionis*.

9. Augustinus, *Locutionum in Heptateuchum libri septem*, 566, author's translation.

10. Tertullianus, *De Idololatria*, in *Opera omnia*, 34.

11. Augustinus, *Contra Faustum*, 751; *Writings in Connection with the Manichean Heresy*, 525. Arguments on this topic took on special relevance after the Council of Elvira in 305, which first made celibacy a requirement of all clergy.

12. Augustinus, *Contra Faustum*, 751.

13. Augustinus, *Contra Fortunatum Manichaeum*, 117, author's translation. The Migne edition finds the use of *factitiam* unusual enough to suggest *facturam* instead in a note.

14. Augustinus, *Contra Fortunatum Manichaeum*, 117.

15. Aquinas, *Summa Theologica*, part I, question 75, article 6.

16. Cicero, *De Senectute, De Amiticitia, De Divinatione*, book II, section 28.

17. Quoted in an excellent discussion of Christian ideas about superstition: Séjourné, "Superstition," 2765.

18. Augustinus, *On Christian Doctrine*, 545; *De Doctrina Christiana*, 50.

19. A modern Catholic catechism makes the same distinction in regard to these that Augustine made in distinguishing *facticii* from "voluntary" eunuchs: "Active participation indicates that sacramentals are not some kind of fetishes that work magically by just being had or worn or said. It requires voluntary effort based on faith in order to achieve the purpose for which they were instituted." Hardon, *The Catholic Catechism*, 553.

20. Augustinus, *On Christian Doctrine*, 54.

21. On this point and on medieval witchcraft law in general, see Hansen, *Quellen und Untersuchungen zur Geschichte des Hexenwahns und der Hexenfolgung im Mittelalter* and Lea, *Materials toward a History of Witchcraft*.

22. "Pagan" was another term owing its Christian meaning to Tertullian, who adapted it from its meaning of "peasant, citizen, civilian" (in Tacitus) to mean anyone who was not a member (a "soldier") of the Christian church militant. The term "heretic" was properly applied only to baptized Christians who denied some aspect of official church doctrine. Although early Christian jurisprudence distinguished between maleficium and heresy in theory, in practice a precedent was set for associating them. It was Theodosius who first established an Inquisition to prosecute crimes of heresy; the first case tried by the Inquisition concerned the Priscillianists, an ascetic Christian sect influenced by Egyptian gnosticism who won many followers in Spain and southern France in the fourth, fifth, and sixth centuries. charges of magical practices were among the slew of accusations brought forward in the process of crushing the movement. While the doctrinal deviation of heresy did not necessarily entail acts of superstitious sacrilege (*maleficia*), neither did it necessarily exclude them.

23. Pharr, *The Theodosian Code and Novels, and the Sirmondian Constitutions*, 237; Haenel, *Codices Gregorianus Hermogenianius Theodosianus*, 866.

24. Members of the college of official Roman diviners who interpreted the flight of birds through the various celestial *templi* and the signs in the manner a chicken ate grain. Augurs did not actually predict the future; rather they determined the approval or disapproval of the gods in regard to some proposed action.

25. Competitors of the augurs from Etruria who interpreted signs in the internal organs of animals, and in unusual occurrences such as monstrous births or storms.

26. The general term for pagan priests.

27. Both were practices involving inspired verbal prophecy.

28. "Astrologers," conceived as persons whose knowledge of the workings of the universe was based on the "science of numbers."

29. Pharr, *The Theodosian Code*, book IX, tit. 16, sec. 3.

30. Deuteronomy 18:10, Micah 5:12, Nahum 3:4, and, most importantly, Exodus 22:18.

31. *Liber Iudicum, aut Codex Wisigothorum*, book II, tit. IV, sec. 1, in *Los códigos españoles concordados y anotados*, vol. 1, 12.

32. *Fuero Juzgo*, book II, tit. IV, in *Los códigos españoles*, 117.

33. Ligatures are amulets. For a discussion of the sexual ligature known as the *aiguillette*, see Le Roy Ladurie, "The Aiguilette," 84–96. For a discussion of traditional Portuguese amulets, see Pires *Amuletos Alemtejanos*. In this text I use the masculine form *venefici* for personal plural constructions, but the feminine *venefica* for the singular. I do this because the legal texts I am studying tend to use the masculine *veneficus* when speaking of practitioners of *veneficium* in general, while the feminine gender tends to be used when a concrete individual was being posited (i.e., the traditional stereotype of the venefica as an old woman).

34. Navarro, ed., *Forum Turolij*, vol. 2, 209.

35. Du Cagne, *Glossarium Mediae et infimae latinitatis*, vol. 3, 393b.

36. Du Cagne, *Glossarium Mediae et infimae latinitatis*, vol. 3, 393.

37. *Codigo de las Siete Partidas*, part VII, tit. xxiii, in *Los códigos españoles*, 427.

38. Translated in Oliviera Marques, *Daily Life in Portugal in the Late Middle Ages*, 227. The Portuguese text is quoted in Herculano de Carvalho e Araújo, *Crenças Populares Portuguesas*, 158.

39. Quoted in Herculano de Carvalho e Araújo, *Crenças Populares Portuguesas*, 166.

40. Oliveira Marques, *Daily Life in Portugal in the Late Middle Ages*, 227.

41. Oliveira Marques, *Daily Life in Portugal in the Late Middle Ages*, 30.

42. Lea, *A History of the Inquisition of Spain* (1906), 17.

43. Such was done by Foucault in his chapter on "The Prose of the World" in *The Order of Things*.

44. Lea, *A History of the Inquisition of Spain*, vol. 3, 88.

45. Quoted in Trimingham, *A History of Islam in West Africa*, 1–2.

46. Markham, ed. and trans., *Book of Knowledge*, 33.

47. For the relation of the Islamic empires of the sub-Saharan savannah to the peoples along the coast of Upper Guinea see Levtzion, *Ancient Ghana and Mali*, and Rodney, *A History of the Upper Guinea Coast, 1545 to 1800*.

48. Translated in Blake, *Europeans in West Africa*, vol. 1, 79; for the Portuguese, see De Pina, *Chronica d'El Rei Dom João II*, 52.

49. Pacheco Pereira, *Esmeraldo de situ orbis*, 97; for the Portuguese, see Pacheco Pereira, *Esmeraldo de situ orbis*, 95.

50. Tinoco, "An Account of the People who Live between Cabo Dos Mastos and Magrabomba on the Guinea Coast," 345.

51. "A report on the Kingdome of Congo, a Region of Africa" (1591), was written by Philippo Pigafetta, in Italian, based on the recollected experiences of a Portuguese sailor. The exact wording of the original oral Portuguese "text" is thus inaccessible. The 1624 version of this incident, translated by François Bontinck from a Portuguese document into French as *Histoire du Royaume du Congo*, has it that "Le roi fit proclamer l'abandon de toutes les pratiques fétichistes et la destruction des maisons où l'on s'y adonnait." (The king ordered the abandonment of all fetishes and the destruction of the houses devoted to them.) But that later "il s'adonna de nouveau aux coutumes paiennes et aux pratiques superstitieuses et fétichistes" (he devoted himself again to pagan customs and to superstitious and fetishist practices) (106, 113). Prominent among the divinely powerful objects of the Kongo peoples were humanoid statues fitting the traditional European image of an "idol" (although their hollow stomachs wherein ritually combined ingredients were placed did not conform to the European notion of the idol). The image of the "Congo idol" became a commonplace in popular literature and discourse, to the extent that Melville describes the bent-kneed cult statue of the South Sea Islander Queequeg as

"his Congo idol" (in *Moby Dick*, 4). In any event, the principal loci for the development of the complex idea of the *fetisso* out of the Portuguese term *feitiço* were the Gold and Slave coasts, where Akan- and Ewe-speaking populations were the dominant presence.

52. Pigafetta, "A Report on the Kingdome of Congo," 492.

53. Tinoco, "An Account of the People who Live between Cabo Dos Mastos and Magrabomba," 149.

54. Tinoco, "An Account of the People who Live between Cabo Dos Mastos and Magrabomba," 239.

55. Marees, "A Description and Historicall Declaration of the Golden Kingdome of Guinea," 280–81. For the original Dutch text, see Marees, *Beschryvinghe ende historische verhael van het Gout Koninckrijck van Gunea*. Subsequent citations are to the English text first, then the Dutch text in brackets.

56. Marees, "A Description and Historicall Declaration of the Golden Kingdome of Guinea," 217 [39].

57. Bosman, *A New and Accurate Description of the Coast of Guinea*, 154.

58. Astley, *A New General Collection of Voyages and Travels*, 3, 25.

59. Riemersma, *Religious Factors in Early Dutch Capitalism*, 55–57.

60. Quoted in Riemersma, *Religious Factors in Early Dutch Capitalism*, 27.

61. Cadamosto, *The Voyages of Cadamosto*, 76; for the Italian, see Ca' da Mosto, *Delle Navigazioni di Messer Alvise Da Ca' Da Mosto*, 198.

62. Cadamosto, *The Voyages of Cadamosto*, 68.

63. Barlow, *A Brief Summe of Geographie*.

64. Marees, "A Description and Historicall Declaration of the Golden Kingdome of Guinea," 293 [72].

65. Smith, *A New Voyage to Guinea*, 26.

66. Cadamosto, *The Voyages of Cadamosto*, 51. Ramusio, *Il viaggio di Giovan Leone e le navigazioni*, 190.

67. Smith, *A New Voyage to Guinea*, 15.

68. Atkins, *A Voyage to Guinea, Brasil, and the West Indies, in His Majesty's Ships the Swallow and Weymouth*, 84.

69. Lok, "The Second Voyage to Guinea," 154.

70. An exception is the Arab writer Al-Dimashqui who wrote in the early fourteenth century and was clearly under the influence of Aristotle: "Their [West Africans'] brains have little moisture and therefore their intelligence is dim, their thoughts not sustained, and their minds dull so that opposites, such as reliability and treachery, good faith and deceit are not found in them. No divinely revealed laws [*nawamis* from the Greek *nomos*] have come to them, nor has any prophet been sent among them, for they are incapable of unifying opposites, whereas the concept of lawfulness is precisely commanding and forbidding, desiring and abstaining." Translated in Levtzion and Hopkins, eds., *Corpus of Early Arabic Sources for West African History*, 148.

71. Loyer, *Relation du voyage du Royaume d'Issyny*, 213.

72. See the English translation attributed to "Monsieur Duquesne": Le Maire, *A New Voyage to the East-Indies in the Years 1690 and 1691*, 78. Like many of the concepts and figures contributing to the idea of the fetish, the notion of primitives who worship the first thing they see in the morning was a commonplace of accounts of exotic lands long before the Portuguese voyages of discovery.

73. Barbot, *A Description of the Coasts of North and South Guinea*, 310.

74. Bosman, *A New and Accurate Description of the Coast of Guinea*, 367a.

75. Marees, "A Description and Historicall Declaration of the Golden Kingdome of Guinea," 316.

76. Marees, "A Description and Historicall Declaration of the Golden Kingdome of Guinea," 257 [20].

77. Towerson, *The First Voyage Made by Master William Towerson*, 191.

78. Marees, "A Description and Historicall Declaration of the Golden Kingdome of Guinea," 319.

79. Quoted in Wolfson, *Pageant of Ghana*, 76.

80. Snelgrave, *A New Account of Guinea, and the Slave-Trade*, 22.

81. See, for instance, Bosman, *A New and Accurate Description of the Coast of Guinea*, 134.

82. Marees, "A Description and Historicall Declaration of the Golden Kingdome of Guinea," 260 [24].

83. Marees, "A Description and Historicall Declaration of the Golden Kingdome of Guinea," 293.

84. Villault, *Relation des costes d'Afrique, appellées Guinée*, 281.

85. Loyer, *Relation du voyage du Royaume d'Issyny*, 216.

86. Loyer, *Relation du voyage du Royaume d'Issyny*, 212–13.

87. Loyer, *Relation du voyage du Royaume d'Issyny*, 215.

88. Barbot, *A Description of the Coasts of North and South Guinea*, 316.

89. Barbot, *A Description of the Coasts of North and South Guinea*, 318.

90. Atkins, *A Voyage to Guinea*, 80.

91. Astley, *A New General Collection of Voyages and Travels*, 3:25.

92. Astley, *A New General Collection of Voyages and Travels*, 4:666.

Chapter 3

1. Variously spelled "Whydah," "Whidah," "Whidaw," "Ouidah," "Juida," "Juda," and, by Bosman, "Fida." This was the principal port for slaves from Dahomey. In Bosman's day it was an independent Ewe-ruled state; not many years after his departure it was conquered by Dahomey.

2. This is the date given by Pierre Vilar in *A History of Gold and Money*, 253–62, in his chapter on "The 18th-Century Conjuncture." For the story of the "guinea," see Porteus, *Coins in History*, 212–14, 219, 233.

3. Curtin et al., *African History*, 224.

4. Le Blanc, *Les voyages fameux du Sieur Vincent Le Blanc marseillois*, 33.

5. Villault, *Relation des costes d'Afrique, appellées Guinée*, 55–56.

6. Smith, *A New Voyage to Guinea*, 26–27.

7. See the section on "*Feitiço* in Portuguese Guinea" in chapter 2.

8. Villault, *Relation des costes d'Afrique, appellées Guinée*, 261.

9. Villault, *Relation des costes d'Afrique, appellées Guinée*, 82–83.

10. Atkins, *A Voyage to Guinea*, 79. See also Villault, *Relation des costes d'Afrique, appellées Guinée*, 224–25.

11. Marees, "A Description and Historicall Declaration of the Golden Kingdome of Guinea," 336.

12. Bosman, *A New and Accurate Description of the Coast of Guinea*, 119.

13. Astley, *A New General Collection of Voyages and Travels*, 2:411.

14. Atkins, *A Voyage to Guinea*, 183–84.

15. Bosman, *A New and Accurate Description of the Coast of Guinea*, 82.

16. Bosman, *A New and Accurate Description of the Coast of Guinea*, 154.

17. Bosman, *A New and Accurate Description of the Coast of Guinea*, 77.

18. Bosman, *A New and Accurate Description of the Coast of Guinea*, 78.

19. Atkins, *A Voyage to Guinea*, 88.

20. Atkins, *A Voyage to Guinea*, 61.

21. Loyer, *Relation du voyage du Royaume d'Issyny*, 171.

22. Loyer, *Relation du voyage du Royaume d'Issyny*, 175.

23. Bosman, *A New and Accurate Description of the Coast of Guinea*, 121.

24. Loyer, *Relation du voyage du Royaume d'Issyny*, 213, cited in the previous chapter.

25. Barbot, *A Description of the Coasts of North and South Guinea*, 310.

26. Astley, *A New General Collection of Voyages and Travels*, 3:27.

27. For an example of this common interpretive explanation see Hegel, *The Philosophy of History*, 99.

28. Barbot, *A Description of the Coasts of North and South Guinea*, 312.

29. Villault, *Relation des costes d'Afrique, appellées Guinée*, 225–26.

30. Astley, *A New General Collection of Voyages and Travels*, 3:27.

31. Gueudeville, *Le Nouveau théâtre de monde, ou la géographie royale*, 21.

32. Atkins, *A Voyage to Guinea*, 94.

33. See chapter 2.

34. Atkins, *A Voyage to Guinea*, 100–101.

35. Barbot, *A Description of the Coasts of North and South Guinea*, 25.

36. Bosman, *A New and Accurate Description of the Coast of Guinea*, 221–22.

37. Bowditch, *Mission from Cape Coast Castle to Ashantee*, 103, 115–16.

38. Astley, *A New General Collection of Voyages and Travels*, 1:617.

39. Lander, *Records of Captain Clapperton's Last Expedition to Africa*, x–xi.

40. See passages previously quoted on this theme from Cadamosto, *The Voyages of Cadamosto*, 51, and Smith, *A New Voyage to Guinea*, 15.

41. Loyer, *Relation du voyage du Royaume d'Issyny*, 167–68.

42. Marees, "A Description and Historicall Declaration of the Golden Kingdome of Guinea," 293.

43. Astley, *A New General Collection of Voyages and Travels*, 2:301–2.

44. Holbach, "Mumbo-Jumbo," in *Essays on the "Encyclopédie" of Diderot and D'Alembert*.

45. Loyer, *Relation du voyage du Royaume d'Issyny*, 175.

46. Loyer, *Relation du voyage du Royaume d'Issyny*, 176.

47. Marees, "A Description and Historicall Declaration of the Golden Kingdome of Guinea," 316.

48. Loyer, *Relation du voyage du Royaume d'Issyny*, 216.

49. Bosman, *A New and Accurate Description of the Coast of Guinea*, 148.

50. Smith, *A New Voyage to Guinea*, 81.

51. Bowditch, *Mission from Cape Coast Castle to Ashantee*, 262.

52. Bowditch, *Mission from Cape Coast Castle to Ashantee*, 79.

53. Bowditch, *Mission from Cape Coast Castle to Ashantee*, 120.

54. Bowditch, *Mission from Cape Coast Castle to Ashantee*, 257.

55. Bowditch, *Mission from Cape Coast Castle to Ashantee*, 150.

56. Lander and Lander, *Journal of an Expedition to Explore the Course and Termination of the Niger*, 43. Similar obstructions are recounted on pages 114 and 155.

57. Lander and Lander, *Journal of an Expedition to Explore the Course and Termination of the Niger*, 132.

58. Meredith, *An Account of the Gold Coast of Africa*, 33.

59. Meredith, *An Account of the Gold Coast of Africa*, 35n.

60. Marees, "A Description and Historicall Declaration of the Golden Kingdome of Guinea," 319.

61. Astley, *A New General Collection of Voyages and Travels*, 4:669.

62. Atkins, *A Voyage to Guinea*, 87.

63. Bosman, *A New and Accurate Description of the Coast of Guinea*, 39.

64. Barbot, *A Description of the Coasts of North and South Guinea*, 309.

65. Dupuis, *Journal of a Residence in Ashantee*, 107n.

66. Dantzig, "Willem Bosman's 'New and Accurate Description of the Coast of Guinea,'" 105.

67. See Feinberg, "An Eighteenth-Century Case of Plagiarism," 45–50.

68. Astley, *A New General Collection of Voyages and Travels*, 1:viii.

69. Harrison, *The Library of Isaac Newton*, 107; Harrison and Laslett, *The Library of John Locke*, 90; Keynes, *The Library of Edward Gibbon*, 75; Smith, *Lectures on Jurisprudence*.

70. See Bayle, *Oeuvres Diverses*, 970–72. This is discussed by Frank Manuel in *The Eighteenth Century Confronts the Gods*, which is by far the best work on eighteenth-century thinking about non-monotheist religion—one to which I am much indebted.

71. Bosman, *A New and Accurate Description of the Coast of Guinea*, 367a.

72. Bosman, *A New and Accurate Description of the Coast of Guinea*, 132.

73. Astley, *A New General Collection of Voyages and Travels*, 3:25.

74. Balthasar Bekker, *The World Bewitched* (1695), 69–74. Bekker's discussion of *fetissos* is noted by Manuel, *The Eighteenth Century Confronts the Gods*, 193.

75. Bosman, *A New and Accurate Description of the Coast of Guinea*, 227.

76. Bosman, *A New and Accurate Description of the Coast of Guinea*, 157.

77. Bosman, *A New and Accurate Description of the Coast of Guinea*, 146–47, as amended by Dantzig, "English Bosman and Dutch Bosman," 247–48.

78. While I had not read Robert Darnton's *The Great Cat Massacre* when I originally wrote this chapter, I am encouraged in my effort here by his insightful investigation of another animal-massacre story of the Enlightenment.

79. Labat, *Voyage du Chevalier des Marchais*, 2:175–76; Astley, *A New General Collection of Voyages and Travels*, 3:30–31; Prévost, *Histoire générale des voyages*, 14:376; Anonymous, "A Description of the Manners, Religion, Customs, etc. of the Inhabitants of Whidah on the Slave Coast," 295; Holbach, "Serpent-Fétiche," 108–9; de Brosses, *Du culte des dieux fétiches*, 32–35; de Brosses, "On the Worship of Fetish Gods," 52.

80. Bosman, *A New and Accurate Description of the Coast of Guinea*, 381–82.

81. For a method of interpreting the ideology of texts in terms of semiotic structures and character systems see Jameson, *The Political Unconscious*. My basic understanding of ideology is that it involves the formation of a discourse that imposes a simple semiotic (Greimasian) structure on a complex historical situation representing a problem which resists solution in reality. The ideological structure makes the problem appear as existing in essence on the level of ideas and consciousness rather than reality and action. This structure of ideas completes itself as ideology in the form of a dramatic scenario, whose typical characters embody conceptual components of the ideologized problem. Such ideological personas are then perceived as existing in reality.

82. Bosman, *A New and Accurate Description of the Coast of Guinea*, 152.

83. Astley, *A New General Collection of Voyages and Travels*, 3:36.

84. Astley, *A New General Collection of Voyages and Travels*, 3:32.

85. Labat, *Voyage du Chevalier des Marchais en Guinée, Isles Voisines, et à Cayenne*, 179.
86. Barbot, *A Description of the Coasts of North and South Guinea*, 308.
87. Holbach, "Mumbo-Jumbo" (originally volume 10 of the *Encyclopédie*, 860–61).
88. Kant, *Observations on the Feeling of the Beautiful and Sublime*, 113.
89. Sade, *Philosophy in the Bedroom*, 256 and 244.
90. Sade, *Philosophy in the Bedroom*, 357.
91. Sade, *Juliette*, 792.
92. De Brosses, *Du culte des dieux fétiches*, 42; "On the Worship of Fetish Gods," 55.
93. Labat, *Voyage du Chevalier des Marchais*, 178–79. He notes that the priests are also merchants who engage in trade with the Europeans, "but their clearest and greatest revenue consists in the industry by which they abuse the credulity and simplicity of the people" (189).
94. Labat, *Voyage du Chevalier des Marchais*, 167.
95. Atkins, *A Voyage to Guinea*, 114.
96. Labat, *Voyage du Chevalier des Marchais*, 182.
97. Astley, *A New General Collection of Voyages and Travels*, 3:36.
98. Snelgrave, *A New Account of Guinea, and the Slave-Trade*, 3.
99. Snelgrave, *A New Account of Guinea, and the Slave-Trade*, 11.
100. [Editors' note: In the version of this essay in *RES*, Pietz notes the following, and we restore it here for the ways it makes explicit a certain politics of his argument regarding the eighteenth century.] Having read my discussion of this text, Francesco Pellizzi remarks that this anecdote implies a distinction between particular interests (those of the king, priests, and so on) and what is in the interest of society as a whole. The opposition between individuals' self-interests and the public interest was, indeed, an issue emerging in writing of the early eighteenth century. It eventually received a definitive theoretical articulation in Rousseau's distinction between the "will of all" and the "general will" that appeared in his *The Social Contract* of 1762.
101. As discussed above and in the previous chapter.
102. Quoted in Popkin, "The Philosophical Basis of Eighteenth-Century Racism," 248.

Chapter 4

1. De Brosses receives only the briefest mention in Duchet, *Anthropologie et histoire au siècle des lumières*; Evans-Pritchard, *A History of Anthropological Thought*; Malefijt, *Images of Man*; Mühlmann, *Geschichte der Anthropologie*; Penniman, *A Hundred Years of Anthropology*; Slotkin, *Readings in Early Anthropology*; and none at all in Harris, *The Rise of Anthropological Theory*.
2. By the awkward term "problem-idea" I refer to a theoretically significant notion in an established historical discourse which, in its very resistance to clear conceptual definition, maps out the deep structure of a problematic fundamental to the order of knowledge authorized by that discourse.
3. Manuel, *The Eighteenth Century Confronts the Gods*, 188.
4. Tourneux, ed., *Correspondance littéraire, philosophique et critique*, 231.
5. Manuel, *The Eighteenth Century Confronts the Gods*, 15.
6. Hume, *A Treatise of Human Nature*, 43.
7. Hume, *The Natural History of Religion*, 24.
8. Hume, *The Natural History of Religion*, 29–30.
9. De Brosses, *Du culte des dieux fétiches*, 215–20; "On the Worship of Fetish Gods," 110–11.

10. De Brosses, *Du culte des dieux fétiches*, 26; "On the Worship of Fetish Gods," 50.

11. "But I can't ignore the story of the fetishism customary in Juidah, a small kingdom on the coast of Guinea, which will serve as an example for everything the occurs similarly in the rest of Africa; especially by the description of the cult rendered to the striped serpent, one of the most celebrated divinities of the blacks." De Brosses, *Du culte des dieux fétiches*, 25–26; "On the Worship of Fetish Gods," 50. I have already analyzed the ideological structure of anecdotes about the Ouidan serpent fetish.

12. Astley, *A New General Collection of Voyages and Travels*, 3:25.

13. Astley, *A New General Collection of Voyages and Travels*, 4:666.

14. De Brosses, *Du culte des dieux fétiches*, 223, 218; "On the Worship of Fetish Gods," 112, 111.

15. De Brosses, *Du culte des dieux fétiches*, 182; "On the Worship of Fetish Gods," 100.

16. Barbot, *A Description of the Coasts of North and South Guinea*, 311.

17. Pietz, "Geography, Etymology, and Taste," 86–94.

18. De Brosses, *Lettres du Président de Brosses à Ch.-C. Loppin de Gemeaux*, 301–2.

19. De Brosses, *Du culte des dieux fétiches*, 285; "On the Worship of Fetish Gods," 132.

20. Clifford, "On Ethnographic Authority."

21. De Brosses, *Du culte des dieux fétiches*, 16–17; "On the Worship of Fetish Gods," 47.

22. De Brosses, *Du culte des dieux fétiches*, 61; "On the Worship of Fetish Gods," 60.

23. De Brosses, *Du culte des dieux fétiches*, 5; "On the Worship of Fetish Gods," 44.

24. De Brosses, *Du culte des dieux fétiches*, 7; "On the Worship of Fetish Gods," 44.

25. De Brosses, *Du culte des dieux fétiches*, 8; "On the Worship of Fetish Gods," 45.

26. De Brosses, *Du culte des dieux fétiches*, 11; "On the Worship of Fetish Gods," 45.

27. De Brosses, *Du culte des dieux fétiches*, 10; "On the Worship of Fetish Gods," 45.

28. De Brosses, *Du culte des dieux fétiches*, 26; "On the Worship of Fetish Gods," 50.

29. De Brosses, *Du culte des dieux fétiches*, 11; "On the Worship of Fetish Gods," 46. A late eighteenth-century slaver like Archibald Dalzel is concerned primarily with denigrating Africans in order to show they deserve the enslavement, due to their natural slavishness or their extreme depravity. He is not interested in theoretical explanations of fetishism but rather acknowledges the complexity of the notion of fetishes as proof of the stupidity of Africans: "With respect to Dahomean religion, it will hardly be expected that we should be able to say much. Like that of many other countries, it consists of a jumble of superstitious nonsense, of which it is impossible to convey any satisfactory idea to the reader. The Portuguese word, *feitiço*, or, as the English pronounce it, fetish, signifying witchcraft, has been adopted by most of the maritime natives of Africa, as well as by the Europeans who trade thither. This word at present is very comprehensive in its signification, meaning either the several objects of worship, whether ideal or corporeal, the act of worship itself, or the various amulets, charms, and superstitious mummery of the priests, or fetish-men, who abound in this country." Dalzel, *The History of Dahomey*, vi. See also "Bel and the Dragon" in Charles, ed., *The Apocrypha and Pseudepigrapha of the Old Testament*, 652–64.

30. "The politics of interpretation . . . arises in those interpretive practices that are ostensibly most remote from overtly political concerns, practices carried out under the aegis of a purely disinterested search for the truth or inquiry into the natures of things that appear to have no political relevance at all. This politics has to do with the kind of authority the interpreter claims vis-à-vis the established political authorities of the society of which he is a member, on the one side, and vis-à-vis other interpreters in his own field of study or investigation, on the other, as the basis of whatever rights he conceives

himself to possess and whatever duties he feels himself obligated to discharge in his status as a professional seeker of truth." White, *The Content of the Form*, 58.

31. Hobbes, *Leviathan*, 28.

32. Hobbes, *Leviathan*, 28–29.

33. Hobbes, *Leviathan*, 28–29.

34. Diderot, "Letter to President de Brosses," 1064.

35. Voltaire, *Candide*, 60–61; for the French see Pomeau, ed., *Les Oeuvres complètes de Voltaire*, 48:184–85.

36. Voltaire, *Candide*, 16; Pomeau, ed., *Les Oeuvres complètes de Voltaire*, 48:119–20.

37. There has been increased interest in the incident of Candide's encounter with the fetish worshipper since 1958, when Ira O. Wade discovered an early version of the tale that lacked this particular episode. It is believed the episode must have been written by Voltaire in the fall of 1758, after the original version was complete. One source for it has been located in a denunciation of the sugar industry and its taintedness with the blood of slaves in the book by Helvétius which in those months was causing such an uproar in France (see Pomeau, ed., *Les Oeuvres complètes de Voltaire*, 48:46). I would like to point out another source for the passage: in the fall of 1758 Voltaire was involved in a negotiation by correspondence to rent the estate of Tournay from Charles de Brosses. Voltaire was surely aware of de Brosses's *Du culte des dieux fétiches*, which had caused a scandal of smaller proportions than that of Helvétius the previous year. Indeed there is a letter of September 1758, from de Brosses to Voltaire, in which de Brosses mentions his "treatise on the antiquity of the cult of the fetishes in the Orient." Foisset, ed., *Voltaire et le président de Brosses*, 24.

Chapter 5

For various references, ideas, and encouragement related to this chapter, I am grateful to Francesco Pellizzi, Bruce Robbins, Andrew Ross, Gayatri Spivak, Katie King, and Michael Taussig. For any number of decisive theoretical conversations, I thank Vivian Sobchack, Robert Meister, and Norman O. Brown. [Editors' note: This chapter was first published as "Fetishism and Materialism: The Limits of Theory in Marx," in *Fetishism as Cultural Discourse*, eds. Emily Apter and William Pietz (Ithaca: Cornell University Press: 119–51).]

1. Saussure, *Course in General Linguistics*, 79–81, 110–22. The idea is that any finite continuous sensible field—the continuum of heard phonic sound or of some quantifiable monetary substance—which may be arbitrarily divided within itself (e.g., the differentiation of voiced sound into phonemes, of gold into coins of a certain normative weight) can have an infinite capacity to represent objects of a different order of being, for example, a word for a "thing," a dollar for a commodity. An idealist theory, Saussure's example of a "value" is a chess knight, whose essence is the complex of paradigmatic and syntagmatic rules for its recognition and use within the game; the materiality of the piece itself is irrelevant: a pebble, a coin, any random token could have the value "knight" if it occupies the position and is moved correctly within the game.

2. Lévi-Strauss, "The Structural Study of Myth," 227.

3. For the image of the hall of mirrors, see Lévi-Strauss, "The Structural Study of Myth," 214; and *The Savage Mind*, 263.

4. Barthes, *Mythologies*, 9.

5. Barthes, *Mythologies*, 145–46.

6. Rancière, "How to Use 'Lire *Le Capital*,'" 382.

7. This latter has been theorized by Vivian Sobchack in *The Address of the Eye*.

8. Baudrillard, *For a Critique of the Political Economy of the Sign*, 143.

9. Jameson, *Postmodernism, or The Cultural Logic of Late Capitalism*, 395.

10. Baudrillard, *For a Critique of the Political Economy of the Sign*, 144.

11. Baudrillard, *The Mirror of Production*, 22–23. Also Baudrillard, *For a Critique*, 63–87.

12. Baudrillard, *For a Critique*, 92. See also Julia Kristeva's treatment of fetishism as "an objectification of the pure signifier" in "From One Identity to Another," in *Desire in Language*, 139. All emphases in quotations cited in this chapter are those of the original authors.

13. For Kant's mature conception of fetishism, see *Religion within the Limits of Reason Alone*, 165–68.

14. In contrast to Kant, Hegel emphasized the importance of random association and contingency in fetishism, which he viewed as the first spiritual expression of human subjectivity per se, in the form of arbitrary caprice and particular desire, projected and objectified as power in some (any) material object—"the first stone they come across," as Hegel puts it in his discussion of fetish worship in his *Phenomenology of Mind*, 42. The fetish's "objectivity is nothing other than the fancy of the individual projecting itself into space" (Hegel writes: "Diese Gegenständlichkeit nichts anderes ist als die zur Selbstanschauung sich bringende individuelle Willkür." This is more literally translated as: "This objectivity is nothing other than the individual arbitrary will bringing itself into self-intuiting appearance"). *The Philosophy of History*, 94.

15. For the Derridean notion of the fetish, the main text is *Glas*: "The fetish's consistency, resistance, remnance, is in proportion to its undecidable bond to contraries. Thus the fetish—in general—begins to exist only insofar as it begins to bind itself to contraries. . . . The economy of the fetish is more powerful than that of the truth—decidable—of the thing itself or than a deciding discourse of castration (*pro aut contra*). The fetish is not opposable. It oscillates like the dapper of a truth that rings awry [*cloche*]." "The fetish no longer has any decidable status. *Glas* of phallogocentrism" (227, 226). For Derrida's essentially Hegelian conception of matter as "radical heterogeneity" and his belief that such a view is actually an advance over Marxian "dialectical materialism," see *Positions*, 64–66, 94.

16. Althusser, "Ideology and Ideological State Apparatuses," 162.

17. Althusser, "Ideology and Ideological State Apparatuses," 170–71.

18. Althusser, "Contradiction and Overdetermination," in *For Marx*, 108.

19. Althusser, "Contradiction and Overdetermination," 114.

20. Laclau, *New Reflections on the Revolution of Our Time*, 5–17.

21. Laclau, *New Reflections on the Revolution of Our Time*, 79; Žižek, "Beyond Discourse-Analysis," an appendix to *New Reflections on the Revolution of Our Time* by Laclau, 252.

22. Žižek, *The Sublime Object of Ideology*, 5.

23. Žižek, *The Sublime Object of Ideology*, 5–6.

24. Žižek, *The Sublime Object of Ideology*, 7.

25. For influential readings of Marx along these lines, which exemplify the postmodernist's magisterial incomprehension of what Marx was actually talking about, see White, "Marx: The Philosophical Defense of History in the Metonymical Mode," in *Metahistory*, 281–330; and Mitchell, "The Rhetoric of Iconoclasm."

26. Balibar, "The Vacillation of Ideology," in *Marxism and the Interpretation of Culture*, 168.

27. I am more in agreement with Jacques Rancière when he insists, against Balibar, that "fetishism is not at all a theory of ideology." in "How to Use 'Lire Le Capital,'" 382. Perhaps because Rancière's contribution to the Althusserian ur-text, *Reading Capital*, was dropped from the second French edition of that work (as a result of his break with Althusser over the events of 1968) and was not included in the English translation, the fact that the principal Althusserian text on fetish theory was by Rancière has been largely ignored by anglophone theorists. The main section of Rancière's essay was eventually translated as "The Concept of 'Critique' and the 'Critique of Political Economy' (from the *1844 Manuscript* to *Capital*)," 352–76, followed by his own self-criticism, "How to Use 'Lire Le Capital,'" 377–84. For British responses of this time defending against any possible revival of interest in the problem of fetishism, see Brewster, "Fetishism in *Capital* and *Reading Capital*" (1976), 344–51; Carver, "Marx's Commodity Fetishism," 39–63; Geras, "Essence and Appearance," 69–85; Rose, "Fetishism and Ideology," 27–54.

28. For this conception of Marxian method, see Meister, *Political Identity: Thinking through Marx*, a book to which I am greatly indebted.

29. Meister, *Political Identity*, 243–44.

30. Marx, *Das Kapital: Kritik der politische Ökonomie*, vol. 1 (1969), 50. *Capital*, vol. 1, 163, translation modified.

31. Marx, *Capital*, 3:969.

32. Marx, *Grundrisse*, 891.

33. Meiners, *Allgemeine kritische Geschichte der Religionen*; Reinhard, *Abriß einer Geschichte der Entstehung und Ausbildung der religiösen Ideen*; Dulaure, *The Gods of Generation*; Dupuis, *The Origin of All Religious Worship*.

34. It is taken for granted by most nineteenth-century writers on religion, from Saint-Simonian advocates of the New Christianity (see the 1829 lecture of Saint-Amand Bazard, *Développement religieux de l'homme*, 121–48) to atheistic anarchists such as Michael Bakunin (in *God and the State*, 511).

35. A review of a German critical history of religion refers to fetishism as "the worship of tools." Taylor, Review of D. Heynig, *Theorie der sämtlichen Religionsarten*, 646.

36. Coleridge, *The Friend*, 518. Matthew Arnold's later criticism of "the Nonconformist fetish" (in *Culture and Anarchy*, 168–70) was more Kantian in its identification of fetishes with "mechanical" rules and maxims.

37. Comte, "First Theological Phase: Fetishism," in *The Positive Philosophy of Auguste Comte*, 545–61; and "Positive Theory of the Age of Fetichism, or General Account of the Spontaneous Regime of Humanity," in *System of Positive Polity*, 65–130. For a contemporary English exposition of the Comtian view, see Lewes, "Ages of Fetishism and Polytheism," in *Comte's Philosophy of Science*, 273–87.

38. Tylor, "The Religion of Savages," 84; McLennan, "The Worship of Plants and Animals, Part I: Totems and Totemism," 422–24. John Stuart Mill was already conceiving fetishism as animist superstition in an essay, "Utility of Religion," written in the 1850s, in *Collected Works of John Stuart Mill*, vol. 10. See also his notion of fetishism in essays of the 1860s, "Theism," in *Collected Works*, 10:442–43; and "Sir William Hamilton's Theory of Causation," in *Collected Works*, 9:300. For Herbert Spencer, see "The Origin of Animal Worship" and "Idol-Worship and Fetich-Worship." For the German social-scientific idea of fetishism, see Bastian, "Die Fetische," 11–23; and Schultze, *Fetishism*.

39. Ellis, *The Land of Fetish*; Glave, "Fetishism in Congo Land," 825–36; Kingsley, "The Fetish View of the Human Soul," 138–51; Nassau, "The Philosophy of Fetishism," 257–70, and *Fetishism in West Africa*; Milligan, "The Dark Side of the Dark Continent," 890–903.

More serious were Nina-Rodrigues, *L'animisme fétichiste des nègres de Bahia*; and in an extension of the term that stuck, Cushing, *Zuñi Fetishes*.

40. See the debate between Max Müller and Andrew Lang: Müller, "Is Fetishism a Primitive Form of Religion?" 54–131; Lang, "Fetishism and the Infinite," 212–42, and "Mr. Max Muller and Fetishism," 453–69.

41. D'Alviella, "Origines de l'idolatrie," 1–25; Chantepie de la Saussaye, *Manual of the Science of Religion*; Tiele, *Elements of the Science of Religion*, vol. 1; Jevons, *An Introduction to the History of Religion*.

42. Wilhelm Wundt has much to say about fetishism in *Elements of Folk Psychology*, especially on pages 220–29, and it is in denouncing Wundt that Mauss rejects the term completely. See Mauss, "L'art et le mythe d'après M. Wundt," in *Oeuvres*, vol. 2, 216–17 and 244–45, where he writes: "The notion of the fetish ought, we think, to disappear definitively from science and be replaced by that of mana. . . . Moreover, when one writes the history of the science of religions and of ethnography, one will be astonished at the unmerited and fortuitous role that a notion of the type of that of the fetish has played in theoretical and descriptive works. It corresponds to nothing but an immense misunderstanding between two civilizations, the African and the European." For this period, also see the attempt to sort things out by Haddon, *Magic and Fetishism*. Remarkably late is the long discussion of fetishism by William Graham Sumner and Albert Galloway Keller, in *The Science of Society*, 979–1058.

43. Marx, "The Leading Article in No. 179 of the *Kölnische Zeitung*," in Marx and Engels, *Collected Works* 1:189.

44. For his excerpts see Marx, "Exzerpte zur Geschichte der Kunst und der Religion," in *Marx-Engels Gesamtausgabe*, 2:1, 320–34, 342–67. Marx used the German translation of de Brosses by Pistorius, *Ueber den Dienst der Fetischengotter*. Marx also made excerpts at this time from Meiners's *Allgemeine kritische Geschichte der Religionen* but did not focus on Meiners's discussions of fetishism; he does make a number of notes on Meiners's discussion of priapism, but for late eighteenth- and early nineteenth-century historians of ancient religion including Robert Payne Knight, J. A. Dulaure, and Meiners, phallicism and fetishism were distinct phenomena.

45. Marx, "Exzerpte," 322.

46. In this passage, Marx is presenting the Hegelian criticism of Kant's discussion titled "The Impossibility of an Ontological Proof of the Existence of God," in *Critique of Pure Reason*, 500–507. As is so often the case when reading Marx, it is important to notice that here he is representing in discursive form a critique (Hegel's critique of Kant) that is not his own, which he intends the reader to regard as itself an object for critical analysis.

47. "Difference between the Democritean and Epicurean Philosophy of Nature," in Marx and Engels, *Collected Works*, 1:103–4.

48. Quoted in Marx, "The Leading Article," 188. Hermes's point echoes Hegel: "In a general sense, religion and the foundation of the State are one and the same; they are in their real essence identical." *Lectures on the Philosophy of Religion*, 247. Marx on the other hand, by 1842 was already moving beyond even a left Hegelian critique of the relation of religion and the state, holding "that religion should be criticized in the framework of criticism of political conditions rather than that political conditions should be criticized in the framework of religion." Letter to Arnold Ruge, 30 November 1842, Marx and Engels, *Collected Works*, 1:395. In his polemic against "the Cologne Hermes," Marx reminds his readers that the Hermes of Greek mythology was the servant of the gods; Marx likens his opposing stance to that of Prometheus, who, wishing to empower humanity, "hates

all the gods." Making the politics of his critique of religion explicit later in his article on Hermes, Marx explains that in contemporary Germany serving "the gods" means serving the state: "For where under Protestantism, there is no supreme head of the church, the rule of religion is nothing but the religion of rule, the cult of the government's will." Marx, "The Leading Article," 199.

49. Marx, "The Leading Article," 189.

50. This was originally to be part of a collaborative book with Bruno Bauer attacking Hegel's theory of religion, but Marx subsequently broke with Bauer. In a letter to Arnold Ruge, 20 March 1842, Marx mentions that his "article 'On Christian Art,' which has now been transformed into 'On Religion and Art, with Special Reference to Christian Art,' must be entirely redone." Marx and Engels, *Collected Works*, 1:385. A month later Marx wrote to Ruge that "the article on religious art . . . has steadily grown into almost book dimensions, and I have been drawn into all kinds of investigations which will still take a rather long time" (1:387). In March, however, with the dismissal of Bauer from his lectureship, Marx had abandoned his own hopes of an academic career and accepted the position as editor of the *Rheinische Zeitung*, and the book on art and religion was never finished. Nevertheless, much of Marx's thought on this subject can be found scattered in his writings of the 1840s.

51. Marx, "The Leading Article," 189.

52. See the section of Hegel's *Lectures on the Philosophy of Religion* concerning "natural, immediate religion," whose most primitive expression, in accordance with a colonialist imaginary about which neither Hegel nor Marx became significantly self-critical, was African religion. Hegel writes: "In this primal natural religion, consciousness is still natural consciousness, the consciousness of sensuous desire" ("In dieser ersten, natürlichen Religion ist das Bewußtsein noch natürliches und sinnlich begehrendes Bewußtseins"— more literally, "In this first, natural religion, consciousness is still a natural and sensuously desiring consciousness") (264). Within this primordial form of religion, according to Hegel, fetishism emerges as the negation of the moment of "magic" through the first capricious expressions of human subjectivity itself.

53. See Holbach's entry "Serpent-Fétiche" in volume 15 (1765) of the *Encyclopédie*, and his other articles mentioning the fetishes of African religion ("Maramba," "Mumbo-Jumbo," and "Ovissa") in *Essays on the "Encyclopédie" of Diderot and D'Alembert*, 159–75; and Helvétius's fetish-worship anecdote in his controversial (and much-read) work of 1758, *De l'esprit*, 300–301. The familiarity of the figure of the African fetish worshiper in eighteenth- and nineteenth-century European cultural discourse (as opposed to the way it was theorized by intellectuals) was a result of the booming transatlantic slave trade of the time. The ideological function of attributing the slave state of the African to his inherent mental slavishness (bowing down in obeisance before mere blocks of wood) rather than to the plantation commodity-production system of European businessmen, is obvious enough to the twentieth-century reader.

54. De Brosses, "Mémoire sur l'oracle de Dodone," 89.

55. The original Enlightenment formulation of this argument was David Hume, *The Natural History of Religion*, published in 1757 and more or less transcribed by de Brosses into the last section of his work on fetishism.

56. De Brosses, *Du culte des dieux fétiches*, 215–16; "On the Worship of Fetish Gods," 110.

57. Comte's theory of the ineluctable, heuristically valuable mode of "fetishistic" pseudocausal thought closely resembles Kant's treatment of the purposive feelings

proper to aesthetic experience, both in its conception and in its role within their general philosophies.

58. The method for examining this world of sensuous desire is phenomenological description rather than logical analysis. For a succinct explication of the phenomenological dialectics of the "subjectively objective world" of sensuous, embodied experience, see Sobchack, "The Active Eye."

59. In Hegel's view, the fetish never attains the form of religion proper since "religion is the relation of Spirit to Spirit, the knowledge by Spirit of Spirit in its truth [i.e., as the universal], and not in its immediacy or naturalness." *Lectures on the Philosophy of Religion*, 1:263. It occupies a similarly liminal position in relation to art: "The immediate reverence for natural objects—nature worship and fetish worship—is . . . not yet art." *Aesthetics: Lectures on Fine Art*, 315–16. For Hegel, the fetishist operates at the brink of the actualization of absolute spirit, never transcending the particularity of the immediate sensuous world to enter the actuality of Ideas.

60. In Marx, *Critique of Hegel's "Philosophy of Right,"* 131–32.

61. Marx, *Critique of Hegel's "Philosophy of Right,"* 137.

62. This view has received its most profound theological expression in Latin American liberation theology. See Gutiérrez, *The Power of the Poor in History*.

63. In Marx, *Early Writings*, 390. This passage was brought to my attention in the appendix "The Hegelian System" in Meister's *Political Identity*, 351–57.

64. Marx and Engels, *The German Ideology*, 96.

65. Rancière, "How to Use 'Lire *Le Capital,*'" 380–81.

66. Long before, Marx had applied the idea of fetishism to economic relations. In the fall of 1842 (three months after his article against Hermes), Marx concluded an article on trials of peasant "thefts" of firewood by citing the anecdote about the Cuban fetish worshipers. What had been a mere rhetorical gesture in that article was elaborated into a more serious theorization of the fetishism of the modern economic order when, toward the end of 1843, he began his serious studies of political economics. (It is not surprising that Marx approached political economy, the theory of civil society articulated in terms of its own categories, as the secular theology of a modern fetishism). See the third of the "Economic and Philosophic Manuscripts" (written between April and August 1844) in *Early Writings*, 341–42.

67. Marx, *Contribution to the Critique of Political Economy*, 48. For the criticism of Ricardo, see Marx, *Grundrisse*, 687.

68. A definite quantity of socially necessary labor time has gone into the making of each type of product; thus each product "contains" a determinate quantity of labor value. At the end of a given production cycle, the totality of products thus represents a definite quantity of labor hours. This aggregate value-quantity is reflected in the total money supply at the end of the cycle, so that each dollar also represents a determinate amount of labor value. Exploitation can be measured by the difference between the labor value of the money wage paid to a given labor group and the total labor value of their product. The distribution of surplus value to different sectors of capital can be measured by the difference between the labor value of a given sector's aggregate product and the labor value of the money price actually realized in the sale of that product. This is a simplified exposition of the discussion "Class and Exploitation," in Meister, *Political Identity*, 277–312.

69. It is with the development of a banking system that it becomes obvious that the substance of money is time or, more precisely, the temporalization of social power. In

his aptly titled *Secrets of the Temple* (59–65), William Greider lucidly explains how banks create money simply by contracting new credit-debt relations—in effect lending the same money several times in a miraculous multiplication that is possible because deposits are withdrawn, loans are paid off, and interest comes due over varying periods of time.

70. Marx, *Contribution to the Critique of Political Economy*, 155.

71. Marx, *Theories of Surplus Value*, part 3, 494, 498.

72. See the opening chapter of *The Class Struggles in France, 1848–1850*, 49, where Marx writes: "The revolt of the proletariat is the abolition of bourgeois credit, for it signifies the abolition of bourgeois production and its social order. Public and private credit are the thermometers by which the intensity of a revolution can be measured. *They fall, the more the passion and potency of the revolution rises.*"

73. Marx, *Capital*, 3:572.

74. See Alain Lipietz, *The Enchanted World: Inflation, Credit, and the World Crisis.*

Chapter 6

[Editors' note: Originally published in *RES: Anthropology and Aesthetics* 28 (Autumn, 1995): 23–38. As originally published, the essay begins with a reference to chapters 1–3 of this volume ("Some years ago, I published a series of articles in *RES* that examined the origin of the idea of fetish.") Then Pietz comments, in the first footnote: "A very rough version of the present essay was presented at the Ethnohistory Workshop of the University of Pennsylvania on 20 October 1994. I am deeply grateful for the supportive criticism and advice I received from Nancy Farris, Webb Keane, Achille Mbembe, Lee Cassanelli, Molly Roth, and the other participants. I also wish to thank Felix Asiedu for generously giving me a copy of his superb essay 'Ritualized Executions and Concepts of Sacrifice in XIXth-Century Asante.' As ever, I am indebted to the thought and friend-ship of Francesco Pellizzi. The poem by Rev. H. D. Rawnsley that I have taken as one of my epigraphs is quoted from Robert Home, *City of Blood Revisited* (1982), 102. The other epigraph is from Joseph Conrad's 'An Outpost of Progress' (1898), 466."]

1. I have considered certain aspects of this development in my "Fetishism and Ma-terialism: The Limits of Theory in Marx," chapter 5 of this volume; also in my "Fetish."

2. "Legitimate commerce" was a phrase commonly used by British writers after the abolition of the slave trade. That is, "legitimate" meant both legal under existing statutes and moral, in contrast to the immoral and now illegal traffic in human beings.

3. I have examined this historical moment in a companion chapter to this one, "Death of the Deodand: Accursed Objects and the Money Value of Human Life," chapter 7 of this volume.

4. Lander, *Records of Captain Clapperton's Last Expedition to Africa*; Lander and Lander, *Journal of an Expedition to Explore the Course and Termination of the Niger.*

5. Bowditch, *Mission from Cape Coast Castle to Ashantee*; Joseph Dupuis, *Journal of a Residence in Ashantee.*

6. Curtin et al., *African History*, 244.

7. Cruickshank, *Eighteen Years on the Gold Coast of Africa*, vol. 2, 157.

8. Cruickshank, *Eighteen Years on the Gold Coast of Africa*, vol. 2, 160.

9. Buxton, *The African Slave Trade and Its Remedy*, 231.

10. Leonard, *The Lower Niger and Its Tribes*, 441.

11. Elias, *The Nigerian Legal System*, 98.

12. Curtin, *The Image of Africa*, 303.

13. Schuyler, *The Fall of the Old Colonial System*, 151–57.

14. The importance of Chief Dhogo's role in the relations between Britain and Benin is discussed in Home, *City of Blood Revisited*.

15. Blackburn, *The Overthrow of Colonial Slavery*, 467.

16. Newbury, *The Western Slave Coast and Its Rulers*, 44–45.

17. Metcalfe, "Introduction," in John Beecham, *Ashantee and the Gold Coast*, iv.

18. Newbury, *The Western Slave Coast and Its Rulers*, 38.

19. Law, "Human Sacrifice in Pre-Colonial West Africa," 78; Elias, *The Nigerian Legal System*, 49.

20. From "Der Kroboneger," in *Der evangelische Heidenboten* (1888), quoted and translated in Wilson, "The 'Bloodless Conquest' in Southeastern Ghana," 295.

21. By the 1870s, British institutions and ideology had been restructured to accommodate the principles of both liberal democracy and racial empire. While the expanded franchise of Reform Act of 1832 has first expressed itself in acts to abolish colonial slavery, the much expanded male franchise of the Reform Act of 1867 was established in the wake of the elimination of democratic self-rule for the colony of Jamaica and the rise of an ideological consensus on the unfitness of uncivilized Black Africans for self-government. For the latter moment, see Hall, "Rethinking Imperial Histories."

22. Dumett and Johnson, "Britain and the Suppression of Slavery in the Gold Coast Colony, Asante, and the Northern Territories," in *The End of Slavery in Africa*, ed. Miers and Roberts, 94.

23. Indeed, the first Protectorate in Nigeria was established by means of a loan from London that local colonial authorities were forced to pay off in the course of establishing the new governmental apparatus.

24. "We have just destroyed another stronghold of Fetishism in West Africa," announced the Christian journal *The Living Age* (April 3, 1897), 62, upon hearing of the sack of Benin City. The characterization of these shrines as centers of "fetishism"—viewed as the source of all that was barbarous and corrupt in West African societies—was so common that there seems little reason to introduce a long series of quotations in this regard.

25. Cardi, "Ju-Ju Laws and Customs of the Niger Delta," 52.

26. Niger Coast Protectorate, *Annual Report for the Year 1896–1897*, 14. This was the general view of late nineteenth-century British government agents; see Home, *City of Blood Revisited*, 8, 32–33.

27. "*Kumase*. Deriv. *Kum*, to kill, and *ase*, under. Lit. 'under the kill tree,' from a tree in the center of the town under which human sacrifices and executions took place." Rattray, *Ashanti Proverbs*, 156.

28. Rattray, *Religion and Art in Ashanti*, 130–35.

29. Rattray, *Ashanti Proverbs*, 148, 155.

30. Isichei, *The Ibo People and the Europeans*, 47.

31. Law articulates what might be called the rational choice version of the conspicuous consumption argument. I consider what might be called the irrational expenditure version developed by Georges Bataille in my essay "Capitalism and Perversion."

32. Law, "Human Sacrifice in Pre-Colonial West Africa," 77–78.

33. Isichei, "The Quest for Social Reform in the Context of Traditional Religion," 463.

34. Law, "Human Sacrifice in Pre-Colonial West Africa," 56.

35. Isichei, "The Quest for Social Reform in the Context of Traditional Religion," 470.

36. Law, "Human Sacrifice in Pre-Colonial West Africa," 58.

37. Fortes, *Religion, Morality, and the Person*, 287–301.

38. Oddly, while Law's method ignores crisis events when explaining the causes of historical decisions, Law acknowledges the traumatic effects of historical events. Human sacrifice, Law argues, was abandoned only through "the sort of psychological shock provided in Asante by the catastrophic defeat by the British in 1874." See Law, "Human Sacrifice in Pre-Colonial West Africa," 86.

39. Kourouma, *Monnew*, 3–4.

40. Coombs-Schilling, *Sacred Performances*.

41. Fortes, "Kinship and Marriage among the Ashanti," 264; cited in Minkus, "The Philosophy of the Akwapim Akan of Southern Ghana," 240.

42. Minkus, "The Philosophy of the Akwapim Akan of Southern Ghana," 241. The references in this quotation are to Rattray, *Religion and Art in Ashanti*, 318; Abraham, *The Mind of Africa*, 61; Busia, "The Ashanti of the Gold Coast," 199.

43. Law, "Human Sacrifice in Pre-Colonial West Africa," 86.

44. Isichei, *The Ibo People and the Europeans*, 57.

45. Achebe, *Things Fall Apart*, 124.

46. Achebe, *Things Fall Apart*, 125.

47. Friedman, *A History of American Law*, 409.

48. This was the formulation that had developed by the end of the nineteenth century; see Elias, *The Nigerian Legal System*, 13. Variations may be found going back to 1856, when a Gold Coast Council Order gave the colonial Supreme Court that then existed the power to hear cases from settlements and "protected territories" without consulting local native authorities: "the Court was adjured to pay equitable regard to local customs, where these were not repugnant to Christianity or to natural justice"; David Kimble, *A Political History of Ghana*, 198.

49. Kimble, *A Political History of Ghana*, 211.

50. Minkus, *The Philosophy of the Akwapim Akan of Southern Ghana*, 192.

51. Kimble, *A Political History of Ghana*, 201n8, 214, and 219.

52. Kimble, *A Political History of Ghana*, 464.

53. Newbury, *The Western Slave Coast and Its Rulers*, 84.

54. Chanock, *Law, Custom and Social Order*, 85–102.

55. Kimble, *A Political History of Ghana*, 156.

56. *Davies v. Powell Duffryn Associated Colleries Ltd.* A.C. 601 (1942), 617; cited in Gilbert Kodilinye, *Nigerian Law of Torts*, 268.

57. Rattray, *Ashanti Proverbs*, 184.

58. *Owolo v. Olise* F.N.L.R. 179 (1967), 187; cited in Kodilinye, *Nigerian Law of Torts*, 268.

59. Heusch, *Sacrifice in Africa*, 215.

60. Heusch, *Sacrifice in Africa*, 202.

61. Gluckman, *The Ideas in Barotse Jurisprudence*, 239.

62. Black, *Black's Law Dictionary*, 363.

63. Gluckman, *The Ideas in Barotse Jurisprudence*, 251.

64. Gluckman, *The Ideas in Barotse Jurisprudence*, 263.

Chapter 7

Thanks to Michael Taussig for inviting me to give the talk from which this chapter is drawn as part of the Columbia University Department of Anthropology's "Angel of History" lecture series. Cordial apologies to Shael Herman, who so generously sent me the manuscript of a work of scrupulous scholarship that I have used so cavalierly. Thanks also to Tomoko Masuzawa for her interest in this chapter and for inviting me to give the talk at the University of North Carolina "Fetishism" conference that began my interest in developing a materialist critique of the work of Georges Bataille, which has been continued in this chapter. [Editors' note: By "continued," Pietz is also referencing his essay "Capitalism and Perversion: Reflections on the Fetishism of Excess in the 1980s," *positions: asia critique* 3, no. 2 (1995): 537–65.]

1. Anon., *The Statutes of the United Kingdom of Great Britain and Ireland*, vol. 18, 233.

2. Holmes, *The Common Law*, 35.

3. *Times*, September 17, 1830.

4. My characterization of this political moment relies on Jonathan Parry, *The Rise and Fall of Liberal Government in Victorian Britain*.

5. *Times*, September 17, 1830, emphasis added.

6. *Times*, September 18, 1830, emphasis added.

7. Holmes, *The Common Law*, 11.

8. Holmes, *The Common Law*, 49.

9. Holmes, *The Common Law*, 1.

10. Holmes, *The Common Law*, 34, 11.

11. Holmes, *The Common Law*, 37.

12. The reasons why Holmes abandoned custom as the standard for reasonableness in liability law are discussed by Horwitz, "The Place of Justice Holmes in American Legal Thought," 31–71.

13. Rastell, *An Exposition of Certaine Difficult and Obscure Words and Termes of the Lawes of this Realme*, 62.

14. Jacob, *Jacob's Law Dictionary*, vol. 2, 245.

15. Bracton, *De legibus et consuetudinibus Angliae*, fol. 14; translated by Kantorowicz in *The King's Two Bodies*, 173.

16. Kantorowicz, *The King's Two Bodies*, 173.

17. Holdsworth, *A History of English Law*, 82–85.

18. Herman, *Medieval Usury and the Commercialization of Feudal Bonds*, 14.

19. Herman, *Medieval Usury and the Commercialization of Feudal Bonds*, 24.

20. Morris, *The Papal Monarchy*, 101.

21. Pribram, *A History of Economic Reasoning*, 18.

22. Elaborate notions of leasing have seen a great revival since 1995, when Citibank and other Western banks, in conjunction with financial institutions in Malaysia and the Gulf states, began to invent the accounting methods of "Islamic banking." Like medieval Christian law, Islamic sharia law bans the charging of interest.

23. This little-noted aspect of the famous "ship money affair" is mentioned in Neale, *Queen Elizabeth I*, 176, 183–84.

24. For an excellent discussion of this, see Brewer, *The Sinews of Power*.

25. I am referring to theories of money then current; the idea that prices were in truth more influenced by population growth was not part of orthodox economic theory prior to the nineteenth century. For a brilliant survey of price movements and their determinants, see Fischer, *The Great Wave*.

26. Cort, *The Anti-Rail-Road Journal*, 52.

27. The argument of this paragraph and the one that follows relies heavily on Robert Meister's still unpublished study of American constitutional law. [Editors' note: It is not clear what work Pietz refers to here.]

28. *Hansard's Parliamentary Debates*, 3rd ser., vol. 87 (1846), col. 974. (Sixth session of the fifteenth parliament of the United Kingdom, House of Lords, May 7, 1846).

29. *Hansard's Parliamentary Debates*, 3rd ser., vol. 87, col. 968 (April 24, 1846).

30. *Hansard's Parliamentary Debates*, 3rd ser., vol. 87, col. 625 (August 11, 1846)

31. S. Wortley in *Hansard's Parliamentary Debates*, 3rd ser., vol. 87, col. 625 (August 11, 1846).

32. The debates also offer one harbinger of the coming class differential in monetary compensations for accidental death when Lord Campbell starts joking with the Lord Chancellor: "There is one objection to these Bills which I have heard. It has been said, 'Suppose the Lord Chancellor were to meet with an untimely end by a railway accident, which we all pray may never occur, how would the Jury estimate the loss to his family? What would be considered as the value of the tenure of his office? (The LORD CHANCEL-LOR: Hear, hear!) What would be considered a fair compensation to be awarded to his family for their loss?'" *Hansard's Parliamentary Debates*, 3rd ser., vol. 87, col. 173 (May 7, 1846).

33. For the important social contributions of Wakely, see Sprigge, *The Life and Times of Thomas Wakely*.

34. The role of British medical science in revising the institutions and ideology dealing with death in the decades prior to the 1840s, culminating in the Anatomy Act of 1832, has been discussed by Ruth Richardson in *Death, Dissection and the Destitute*.

35. Dublin and Lotka, *The Money Value of Man*, 3.

36. Ward-Perkins, "The Commercial Crisis of 1847," in Carus-Wilson, ed., *Essays in Economic History*, 3:264. Baxter states that the capital speculatively invested in railroads at this time was "more than half as large as the national debt" so that railroads became "virtually mortgaged to the debenture and preference capitalist." "Railway Extension and its Results," in Carus-Wilson, ed., *Essays in Economic History*, 3:37.

37. "Railways had no old traditions to hamper their freedom. . . . It was the railways that won the acceptance of general limited liability." Shannon, "The Coming of General Limited Liability," in *Essays in Economic History* (1966), 1:375–76.

Bibliography

Aarsleff, Hans. *From Locke to Saussure*. Minneapolis: University of Minnesota Press, 1982.

Abraham, W. E. *The Mind of Africa*. Chicago: University of Chicago Press, 1966.

Achebe, Chinua. *Things Fall Apart*. New York: Doubleday, 1959.

Adams, John. *Sketches Taken during Ten Voyages to Africa between the Years 1786 and 1800*. London: Hurst, Robinson and Company, 1800.

Althusser, Louis. *For Marx*. Translated by Ben Brewster. London: Verso, 1977.

———. "Ideology and Ideological State Apparatuses." In *Lenin and Philosophy, and Other Essays*, translated by Ben Brewster. New York: Monthly Review Press, 1971.

American Psychiatric Association. "Fetishism." In *Diagnostic and Statistical Manual of Mental Disorders*, 4th ed., 526–27. Washington, DC: American Psychiatric Association, 1994.

Anderson, Perry. *Lineages of the Absolutist State*. London: New Left Books, 1974.

Anonymous. "A Description of the Manners, Religion, Customs, etc. of the Inhabitants of Whidah on the Slave Coast." *The British Magazine, or Monthly Repository for Gentlemen and Ladies* 2 (June 1761): 295.

———. *Los códigos españoles concordados y anotados*. Madrid: Imprenta de la Publicidad, á cargo de M. Rivadeneyra, 1848–49.

———. *The Statutes of the United Kingdom of Great Britain and Ireland*, vol. 18, acts 9–10 Victoria (1846), c. 62. London: Eyre and Spottiswoode, 1847.

Aquinas, Thomas. *Summa Theologica*. Translated by the Fathers of the English Dominican Province. London: Burns, Oates & Washbourne, 1920.

Arnold, Matthew. *Culture and Anarchy*. 1869; Cambridge: Cambridge University Press, 1971.

Astley, Thomas. *A New General Collection of Voyages and Travels*. London, 1743–1747.

Atkins, John. *A Voyage to Guinea, Brasil, and the West Indies; in His Majesty's Ships, the Swallow and Weymouth*. London, 1737.

Augustine of Hippo (Aurelius Augustinus). *Contra Faustum*. In *Corpus scriptorum ecclesiasticorum latinorum*, vol. 25, parts I–II, edited by Iosephus Zycha. Lipsiae: Freytag, 1894.

———. *Contra Fortunatum Manichaeum*. In *Patrologia Cursus Completus*, vol. 42, edited by J.-P. Migne. Paris, 1886.

———. *De Doctrina Christiana*. In *Patrologia Cursus Completus*, vol. 34, edited by J.-P. Migne. Paris, 1861.

———. *Locutionum in Heptateuchum libri septem*. In *Corpus scriptorum ecclesiasticorum latinorum*, vol. 28, part I, edited by Iosephus Zycha. Lipsiae: Freytag, 1894.

———. *On Christian Doctrine*. Translated by J. F. Shaw. In *Nicene and Post-Nicene Fathers of the Christian Church*, vol. 2, edited by Philip Schaff. Buffalo: Christian Literature Co., 1887.

———. *Writings in Connection with the Manichean Heresy*. Translated by Rev. Richard Stothert. Edinburgh: Clark, 1872.

Azurara, Gomes Eannes de. *The Chronicle of the Discovery and Conquest of Guinea*. Translated by Charles Raymond Beazley and Edgar Prestage. London: Hakluyt Society, 1896.

Bak, Robert C. "Distortions of the Concept of Fetishism." *The Psychoanalytic Study of the Child* 29 (1974): 191–214.

Bakunin, Michael. *God and the State*. 1870–72; New York: Dover, 1970.

Balibar, Etienne. "The Vacillation of Ideology." Translated by Andrew Ross and Constance Penley. In *Marxism and the Interpretation of Culture*, edited by Cary Nelson and Lawrence Grossberg. Urbana: University of Illinois Press, 1988.

Barbot, Jean. *A Description of the Coasts of North and South Guinea*. London: A. & J. Churchill, 1732.

Barlow, Roger. *A Brief Summe of Geographie*. Edited by E. G. P. Taylor, London: Hakluyt Society, 1929.

Barros, Joao de. *Da Asia de Joao de Barros*. Lisbon, 1778.

Barthes, Roland. *Mythologies*. Translated by Annette Lavers. New York: Hill and Wang, 1972.

Bastian, Adolf. "Die Fetische." In *Der Mensch in der Geschichte*, vol. 2, 11–23. Leipzig: Wigand, 1860.

Baudrillard, Jean. *For a Critique of the Political Economy of the Sign*. Translated by Charles Levin. St. Louis: Telos Press, 1981.

———. *The Mirror of Production*. Translated by Mark Poster. St. Louis: Telos Press, 1975.

Bayle, Pierre. *Oeuvres Diverses*, vol. 3. Hildesheim: Georg Olm, 1966.

Bazard, Saint-Amand. *Développement religieux de l'homme: Fétichisme, polythéisme, monothéisme Juif et Chrétien*. In *Oeuvres de Saint-Simon et d'Enfantin*, vol. 41. 1829; Aalen: Otto Zeller, 1964.

Bekker, Balthasar. *The World Bewitched*. 1691; London: R. Baldwin, 1695.

Belucci, G. *Il feticismo primitivo in Italia*. Perugia: Unione tipografica cooperativa, 1907.

Bennett, Hal Zina. *Zuni Fetishes: Using Native American Objects for Meditation, Reflection, and Insight*. San Francisco: HarperSanFrancisco, 1993.

Binet, Alfred. "Le Fétichisme dans l'amour." *Revue philosophique* 24 (1887): 142–67, 252–74.

Black, Henry Campbell. *Black's Law Dictionary*, rev. 5th ed. St. Paul: West, 1979.

Blackburn, Robin. *The Overthrow of Colonial Slavery, 1776–1848*. New York: Verso, 1988.

Blake, John William, ed. *Europeans in West Africa, 1450–1560*. 2 vols. London: Hakluyt Society, 1942.

Bontinck, François, trans. *Histoire du Royaume du Congo (c. 1624). Traduction annotée du Ms. 8080 de la Bibliothèque nationale de Lisbonne*. Louvain: Nauwelaerts, 1972.

———. "La Première ambassade congolaise à Rome (1514)." *Études d'Histoire Africaine* 1 (1970): 37–73.

Boroja, Julio Caro. *The World of the Witches*. Chicago: University of Chicago Press, 1964.

Bosman, Willem. *A New and Accurate Description of the Coast of Guinea*. 1705; London: Cass, 1967.

Bowditch, Thomas Edward. *Mission from Cape Coast Castle to Ashantee*. 1819; London: Cass, 1966.

Bracton, Henry of. *De legibus et consuetudinibus Angliae*. 4 vols. Edited by G. E. Woodbine. New Haven: Yale University Press, 1915–42.

Brewer, John. *The Sinews of Power: War, Money, and the English State, 1688–1783*. Cambridge: Harvard University Press, 1990.

Brewster, Ben. "Fetishism in *Capital* and *Reading Capital*." *Economy and Society* 5 (1976): 344–51.

Brosses, Charles de. *Du culte des dieux fétiches, ou Parallèle de l'ancienne Religion de l'Égypte avec la Religion actuelle de Nigritie*. Geneva: Cramer, 1760.

———. *Histoire des navigations aux terres Australes*. Paris: Durand, 1756.

———. *Lettres du Président de Brosses à Ch.-C. Loppin de Gemeaux*. Edited by Yvonne Bezard. Paris: Firmin Didot, 1929.

———. *Mémoire de la formation mécanique des langues et des principes physiques de l'étymologie*. Paris: Vincent, 1765.

———. "Mémoire sur l'oracle de Dodone." In *Mémoires de littérature de l'Académie royale des inscriptions et belles-lettres* 35, 1770.

———. *On the Worship of Fetish Gods*. Translated by Daniel H. Leonard. In Rosalind C. Morris and Daniel H. Leonard, *The Returns of Fetishism: Charles de Brosses and the Afterlives of an Idea*. Chicago: University of Chicago Press, 2017.

Buchner, Max. "Fetichism of the Bantu Negroes." *Popular Science Monthly* 25 (1884): 767–72.

Budge, E. A. Wallis. *From Fetish to God in Ancient Egypt*. 1988; New York: Dover, 1934.

Busia, K. A. "The Ashanti of the Gold Coast." In *African Worlds*, edited by Daryll Forde, 190–209. London: Oxford University Press, 1954.

Buxton, Thomas Fowell. *The African Slave Trade and Its Remedy*. 1967; London: Cass, 1839.

Cadamosto, Alvise. *The Voyages of Cadamosto, and Other Documents on Western Africa in the Second Half of the Fifteenth Century*, edited and translated by G. R. Crone. 1507; London: Hakluyt Society, 1937.

——— [Ca' da Mosto, Alvise da]. *Delle Navigazioni di Messer Alvise Da Ca' Da Mosto, gentiluomo veneziano*. In Giovambattista Ramusio, *Il viaggio di Giovan Leone e le navigazioni*, vol. 1. Venice: L. Plet, 1837.

Cardi, C. N., comte de. "Ju-Ju Laws and Customs of the Niger Delta." *Journal of the Anthropological Institute of Great Britain and Ireland* 29, no. 1–2 (1899): 51–64.

Carus-Wilson, E. M., ed. *Essays in Economic History*. 3 volumes. New York: St. Martin's, 1966.

Carver, Terrell. "Marx's Commodity Fetishism." *Inquiry* 18 (1975): 39–63.

Castilhon, Jean-Louis. *Zingha, Reine d'Angola: Historie Africaine*. Paris: Lacombe, 1769.

Chanock, Martin. *Law, Custom and Social Order: The Colonial Experience in Malawi and Zambia*. Cambridge: Cambridge University Press, 1985.

Chantepie de la Saussaye, P. D. *Manual of the Science of Religion*. Translated by Beatrice S. Colyer-Fergusson. London: Longmans, Green, 1891.

Charles, R. H., ed. *The Apocrypha and Pseudepigrapha of the Old Testament*, vol. 1. Oxford: Clarendon Press, 1913.

Chatélain, Heli. "African Fetishism." *Journal of American Folklore* 7 (1894): 303–6.

Cicero. *De Divinatione*, in *De Senectute, De Amiticitia, De Divinatione*. Translated by William Armistead Falconer. Cambridge: Harvard University Press, 1953.

Clifford, James. "On Ethnographic Authority." *Representations* 12 (1983): 118–46.

Coleridge, Samuel Taylor. *The Friend*, part I, in *The Collected Works of Samuel Taylor Coleridge* (4:1). 1809; Princeton: Princeton University Press, 1969.

Colletti, Lucio. *From Rousseau to Lenin: Studies in Ideology and Society*. Translated by John Merrington and Judith White. London: NLB, 1972.

Comte, Auguste. *Auguste Comte and Positivism: The Essential Writings*. Edited by Gertrude Lenzer. New York: Harper and Row, 1975.

———. *Cours de philosophie positive*, 3rd ed. Vol. 5. 1840; Paris: Baillière, 1869.

———. *Introduction to Positive Philosophy*. Revised translation by Frederick Ferre. 1840; Indianapolis: Bobbs-Merrill, 1970.

———. *The Positive Philosophy of Auguste Comte*. Translated by Harriet Martineau. New York: Eckler, 1840.

———. *System of Positive Polity, or Treatise on Sociology, Instituting the Religion of Humanity*. Translated by J. H. Bridges et al. 1853; London: Longmans, Green, and Co, 1875–77.

Conrad, Joseph. "An Outpost of Progress." In *The Portable Conrad*, edited by Morton Dauwen Zabel, 459–89. New York: Viking, 1898.

Coombs-Schilling, M. E. *Sacred Performances: Islam, Sexuality, and Sacrifice*. New York: Columbia University Press, 1989.

Cordeiro, Luciano. *Descobertas e Descobridores, Diogo Cão*. Lisbon, 1892.

Cort, Richard. *The Anti-Rail-Road Journal; or, Rail-Road Impositions Detected, contains an answer to the Edinburgh Review and Mechanic's Magazine*. London: W. Lake, 1835.

Crooke, W. "Review of Census of India, 1901." *Folk-Lore* 15 (1904): 222–24.

Cruickshank, Brodie. *Eighteen Years on the Gold Coast of Africa*, vol. 2. 1853; London: Cass, 1960.

Curtin, Philip. *The Image of Africa: British Ideas and Action, 1780–1850*. Madison: University of Wisconsin Press, 1964.

Curtin, Philip, Steven Feierman, Leonard Thompson, and Jan Vansina. *African History*. London: Longman, 1978.

Cushing, Frank H. *Zuñi Fetishes*. Bureau of American Ethnology, Second Annual Report (1883). Las Vegas: K. C. Publications, 1974.

D'Almada, André Álvares. *Tratado Breve dos Rios de Guine do Cabo-Verde*. 1594; Porto: 1841.

D'Alviella, Goblet. "Origines de l'idolatrie." In *Revue de l'histoire des religions*, vol. 12, edited by Jean Reville, 1–25. Paris: Leroux, 1885.

Dalzel, Archibald. *The History of Dahomey: An Inland Kingdom in Africa*. 1793; London: Cass, 1967.

Dantzig, Albert van. "English Bosman and Dutch Bosman: A Comparison of Texts." *History in Africa* 2 (1975): 185–216.

———. "English Bosman and Dutch Bosman: A Comparison of Texts: III." *History in Africa* 4 (1977): 247–73.

———. "Willem Bosman's 'New and Accurate Description of the Coast of Guinea': How Accurate Is It?" *History in Africa* 1 (1974): 101–8.

Darnton, Robert. *The Great Cat Massacre and Other Episodes in French Cultural History*. New York: Basic Books, 1984.

Defert, Daniel. "The Collection of the World: Accounts of Voyages from the Sixteenth to the Eighteenth Centuries." *Dialectical Anthropology* 7 (1982): 11–20.

Deleuze, Gilles. *Difference and Repetition*. Translated by Paul Patton. New York: Columbia University Press, 1994.

De Pina, Ruy. *Chronica d'El Rei Dom João II*. In *Monumenta Missionaria Africana: Africa*

Occidental, vol. 1 (1471–1531), edited by Padre Antonio Brasio. Lisbon: Agencia Geral do Ultramar, 1952.

Derrida, Jacques. *Glas*. Translated by John P. Leavey Jr. and Richard Rand. 1974; Lincoln: University of Nebraska Press, 1986.

———. *Positions*. Translated by Alan Bass. Chicago: University of Chicago Press, 1981.

Diderot, Denis. "Letter to President de Brosses." *Oeuvres complètes*, vol. 13. 1757; Paris: Le Club Français du Livre, 1972.

Donelha, André. *Descrição da Serra Leoa e dos Rios de Guiné do Cabo Verde, 1625 / An Account of Sierra Leone and the Rivers of Guinea of Cape Verde 1625*. Edited and translated by P. E. H. Hair. Lisbon: Junta de Investigações Cientificas do Ultramar, 1977.

Dublin, Louis I., and Alfred J. Lotka. *The Money Value of Man*, rev. ed. New York: The Ronald Press, 1946.

Du Cange, Charles du Fresne. *Glossarium Mediae et infimae latinitatis*, vol. 3. Paris: Librairie des sciences et des arts, 1938.

Duchet, Michèle. *Anthropologie et histoire au siècle des lumières: Buffon, Voltaire, Rousseau, Helvétius, Diderot*. Paris: Maspero, 1971.

Dulaure, Jacques Antoine. *Des cultes qui ont précédé et amené l'idolâtrie ou l'adoration des figures humaines*. Paris: Fournier Frères, 1805.

———. *The Gods of Generation: A History of Phallic Cults among Ancients and Moderns*. 1805; New York: Panurge Press, 1933.

Dupuis, Charles François. *Origine de tous les cultes, ou religion universelle*. Paris: Babeuf, 1822.

———. *The Origin of All Religious Worship*. 1794; New Orleans, 1872.

Dupuis, Joseph. *Journal of a Residence in Ashantee*. 1824; London: Cass, 1966.

Durkheim, Emile. "De la définition des phénomènes religieux." *L'Année sociologique* 2 (1899): 1–28.

———. *The Elementary Forms of Religious Life*. Translated by Joseph Ward Swain. 1912; New York: Free Press, 1965.

———. Review of Schultze's *Psychologie der Naturvolker*. In *L'Année sociologique* 4 (1900): 137–38.

Elias, T. Olawale. *The Nigerian Legal System*. London: Routledge & Kegan Paul, 1954.

Ellis, A. B. *The Land of Fetish*. London: Chapman and Hall, 1883.

Evans-Pritchard, Edward. *A History of Anthropological Thought*. New York: Basic Books, 1981.

Fage, J. D. "Slaves and Society in Western Africa, c. 1445–c. 1700." *Journal of African History* 21 (1980): 289–310.

Feinberg, H. M. "An Eighteenth-Century Case of Plagiarism: William Smith's *A New Voyage to Guinea*." *History in Africa* 6 (1979): 45–50.

Fernandes, Valentim. *Description de la Côte Occidentale d'Afrique (Sénégal au Cap de Monte, Archipels, 1506–1510)*. Translated by Th. Monod, A. Teixeira da Mota, and R. Mauny. Bissau: Centro de Estudos da Guine Portuguesa, 1951.

Fernbach, Amanda. *Fantasies of Fetishism: From Decadence to Post-Human*. New Brunswick: Rutgers University Press, 2002.

Fischer, David Hackett. *The Great Wave: Price Revolutions and the Rhythm of History*. New York: Oxford University Press, 1996.

Foisset, Th., ed. *Voltaire et le président de Brosses: Correspondance inédite*. Paris: Didier, 1858.

Fortes, Meyer. "Kinship and Marriage among the Ashanti." In *African Systems of Kinship and Marriage*. Edited by A. R. Radcliffe-Brown and Daryll Forde. London: Oxford University Press, 1950.

——. *Religion, Morality, and the Person: Essays on Tallensi Religion.* Edited by Jack Goody. Cambridge: Cambridge University Press, 1987.

Foucault. Michel. *Madness and Civilization: A History of Insanity in the Age of Reason.* Translated by Richard Howard. New York: Random House, 1965.

——. *The Order of Things: An Archaeology of the Human Sciences.* New York: Random House, 1970.

Friedman, Lawrence M. *A History of American Law.* New York: Simon & Schuster, 1973.

Garrard, Timothy F. *Akan Weights and the Gold Trade.* London: Longman, 1980.

Geras, Norman. "Essence and Appearance: Aspects of Fetishism in Marx's *Capital.*" *New Left Review* 65 (1971): 69–85.

Ginzburg, Carlo. *The Night Battles: Witchcraft and Agrarian Cults in the Sixteenth and Seventeenth Centuries.* Translated by John and Anne Tedeschi. Baltimore: Johns Hopkins University Press, 1983.

Glave, E. J. "Fetishism in Congo Land." *Century Magazine* 41 (1891): 825–36.

Gluckman, Max. *The Ideas in Barotse Jurisprudence.* New Haven: Yale University Press, 1965.

Godelier, Maurice. "Market Economy and Fetishism, Magic and Science According to Marx's *Capital*" and "Fetishism, Religion, and Marx's General Theories Concerning Ideology." In *Perspectives in Marxist Anthropology*, translated by Robert Brain, 152–85. Cambridge: Cambridge University Press, 1977.

Greider, William. *Secrets of the Temple.* New York: Simon and Schuster, 1987.

Gueudeville, Nicholas. *Le Nouveau théâtre de monde, ou la géographie royale.* Leide: Pierre Vander Aa, 1713.

Gutierrez, Gustavo. *The Power of the Poor in History.* Translated by Robert R. Barr. Maryknoll. New York: Orbis Books, 1984.

Haddon, Alfred C. *Magic and Fetishism.* London: Constable, 1906.

Haenel, Gustavus, ed. *Codices Gregorianus Hermogenianius Theodosianus.* Bonn: Adolphum Marcum, 1842.

Hair, P. E. H. "Barbot, Dapper, Davity: A Critique of Sources on Sierra Leone and Cape Mount." *History in Africa* 1 (1974): 25–54.

——. "Some Minor Sources for Guinea, 1519–1559: Enciso and Alfonce/Fonteneau." *History in Africa* 3 (1976): 19–46.

Hall, Catherine. "Rethinking Imperial Histories: The Reform Act of 1867." *New Left Review* 208 (1994): 3–29.

Hansard's Parliamentary Debates: Forming a Continuation of "The Parliamentary History of England from the Earliest Period to the Year 1803." 3rd series, vol. 87 (1846). New York: Kraus Reprint Co., 1971.

Hansen, Joseph. *Quellen und Untersuchungen zur Geschichte des Hexenwahns und der Hexenfolgung im Mittelalter.* Bonn: Georgi, 1901.

Hardon, John A., SJ. *The Catholic Catechism.* Garden City, NY: Doubleday, 1975.

Harris, Marvin. *The Rise of Anthropological Theory: A History of Theories of Culture.* New York: Crowell, 1968.

Harrison, John. *The Library of Isaac Newton.* Cambridge: Cambridge University Press, 1978.

Harrison, John, and Peter Laslett. *The Library of John Locke.* Oxford: Oxford University Press, 1965.

Hazoume, Paul. "Consécration à un fétiche (Dahomey)." *Anthropos* 32 (1937): 283–87.

Hegel, G. W. F. *Aesthetics: Lectures on Fine Art*, vol. 1. Translated by T. M. Knox. Oxford: Clarendon Press, 1975.

———. *Lectures on the Philosophy of Religion*, vol. 1. Translated by Rev. E. B. Speirs and J. Burdon Sanderson. New York: Humanities Press, 1974.

———. *Phenomenology of Mind*. Translated by A. V. Miller. 1805; Oxford: Clarendon Press, 1971.

———. *The Philosophy of History*. Translated by J. Sibree. New York: Dover, 1956.

———. *Vorlesungen über die Philosophie der Geschichte*. Vol. 12 of *Werke in zwanzig Bänden*, edited by E. Moldenhauer and K. M. Michel. Frankfurt am Main: Suhrkamp, 1970.

Heidegger, Martin. "The Origin of the Work of Art." In *Poetry, Language, Thought*, translated by Albert Hofstadter, 17–87. New York: Harper and Row, 1971.

———. "The Principle of Identity." In *Identity and Difference*, translated by Joan Stambaugh, 23–41. New York: Harper and Row, 1969.

Helvétius, Claude. *De l'esprit*, in *Oeuvres d'Helvétius*, vol. 1. Paris: Briand, 1758.

Henige, David. "Companies Are Always Ungrateful: James Phipps of Cape Coast, a Victim of the African Trade." *African Economic History* 9 (1980): 27–47.

Hepworth, Walter. "Fetichism." In *Encyclopedia Britannica*, 9th ed., vol. 9, 118–19. New York: Scribner's, 1879.

Herculano de Carvalho e Araújo, Alexandre. *Crenças Populares Portuguesas*. In *Opusculos*, 3rd ed., vol. 9. Lisbon: Bastos, 1908.

Herman, Shael. *Medieval Usury and the Commercialization of Feudal Bonds*. Berlin: Dunker and Humblot, 1993.

Heusch, Luc de. *Sacrifice in Africa: A Structuralist Approach*. Bloomington: Indiana University Press, 1985.

Hillier, J. "Part of Two Letters from J. Hillier, dated Cape Corse, Jan. 3, 1687/8 and Apr. 25. 1688. Wrote to the Reverend Dr. Bathurst, President of Trinity Colledge, Oxon; giving an account of the customs of the inhabitants, the air, & c. of the place, together with an account of the weather there from Nov. 24. 1686. to the same day 1687." *Philosophical Transactions of the Royal Society*, vol. 19, no. 232 (1697): 687–707.

Hobbes, Thomas. *Leviathan; or The Matter, Forme and Power of a Commonwealth, Ecclesiasticall and Civil*. 1651/1668; New York: Collier, 1962.

Holbach, Baron d'. "Maramba," "Mumbo-Jumbo," and "Ovissa." In *Essays on the "Encyclopédie" of Diderot and D'Alembert*, edited by John Lough. London: Oxford University Press, 1968.

———. "Serpent-Fétiche." In *Encyclopédie*, vol. 15 (1765): 108–9.

Holdsworth, William S. *A History of English Law*, vol. 1. London: Methuen, 1903.

Holmes, Oliver Wendell, Jr. *The Common Law*. Boston: Little, Brown, 1881.

Home, Robert. *City of Blood Revisited: A New Look at the Benin Expedition of 1897*. London: Rex Collings, 1982.

Hornung, Erik. *Conceptions of God in Ancient Egypt: The One and the Many*. Translated by John Baines. Ithaca: Cornell University Press, 1971.

Horwitz, Morton J. "The Place of Justice Holmes in American Legal Thought." In *The Legacy of Oliver Wendell Holmes, Jr.*, edited by Robert W. Gordon. Stanford: Stanford University Press, 1992.

Hume, David. *The Natural History of Religion*. 1757; Stanford: Stanford University Press, 1957.

———. *A Treatise of Human Nature*. 1770; Baltimore: Penguin, 1969.

Iacono, Alfonso M. *Le fétichisme: Histoire d'un concept*. Paris: Presses Universitaires de France, 1992.

Isichei, Elizabeth. *The Ibo People and the Europeans: The Genesis of a Relationship to 1906.* New York: St. Martin's, 1983.

———. "The Quest for Social Reform in the Context of Traditional Religion: A Neglected Theme of West African History." *African Affairs* 77, no. 309 (1978): 463–78.

Jacob, Giles. *Jacob's Law Dictionary,* vol. 2. New York: Riley, 1811.

Jameson, Fredric. *The Political Unconscious: Narrative as a Socially Symbolic Act.* Ithaca: Cornell University Press, 1981.

———. *Postmodernism, or The Cultural Logic of Late Capitalism.* Durham: Duke University Press, 1991.

Jevons, Frank Byron. *An Introduction to the History of Religion,* 3rd ed. 1890; London: Methuen, 1896.

Jones, Adam. "William Smith the Plagiarist: A Rejoinder." *History in Africa* 7 (1980): 327–28.

Kant, Immanuel. *Anthropology from a Pragmatic Point of View.* Translated by Mary J. Gregor. 1797; The Hague: Martinus Nijhoff, 1974.

———. *Critique of Judgment.* Translated by J. H. Bernard. 1790; New York: Hafner, 1951.

———. *Critique of Pure Reason.* Translated by Norman Kemp Smith. 1781; New York: St. Martin's Press, 1965.

———. *Observations on the Feeling of the Beautiful and Sublime.* Translated by John T. Goldthwait. 1764; Berkeley: University of California Press, 1960.

———. *Religion within the Limits of Reason Alone.* Translated by Theodore M. Greene and Hoyt H. Hudson. 1793; New York: Harper and Row, 1960.

Kantorowicz, Ernst H. *The King's Two Bodies: A Study in Medieval Political Theology.* Princeton: Princeton University Press, 1957.

Keynes, Geoffrey. *The Library of Edward Gibbon,* 2nd ed. London: St. Paul's Bibliographies, 1980.

Kimble, David. *A Political History of Ghana: The Rise of Gold Coast Nationalism, 1850–1928.* Oxford: Clarendon Press, 1963.

Kingsley, Mary H. "The Fetish View of the Human Soul." *Folk-Lore* 8 (1897): 138–51.

Kirk, Ruth F. *Zuni Fetishism.* 1943; Albuquerque: Avanyu Publishing, 1988.

Knight, Richard Payne. *Discourse on the Worship of Priapus: A History of Phallic Worship.* 1786; Amsterdam: Fredonia Books, 2001.

Kodilinye, Gilbert. *Nigerian Law of Torts.* London: Sweet & Maxwell, 1982.

Kourouma, Ahmadou. *Monnew: A Novel.* Translated by Nidra Poller. San Francisco: Mercury House, 1993.

Krafft-Ebing, Richard von. *Psychopathia Sexualis.* Translated by F. J. Rebman. New York: Medical Art Agency, 1920.

Kramer, Henry [Heinrich], and James [Jacob] Sprenger. *Malleus Maleficarum.* Bungay, Suffolk, England: John Rodker, 1928.

Krips, Hentry. *Fetish: An Erotics of Culture.* Ithaca: Cornell University Press, 1999.

Kristeva, Julia. *Desire in Language: A Semiotic Approach to Literature and Art.* Translated by Thomas Gora, Alice Jardine, and Leon S. Roudiez. New York: Columbia University Press, 1980.

Kunzle, David. *Fashion and Fetishism: A Social History of the Corset, Tight-Lacing, and Other Forms of Body Sculpture in The West.* Totowa, NJ: Rowman and Littlefield, 1982.

Labat, Jean-Baptiste. *Voyage du Chevalier des Marchais en Guinée, Isles Voisines, et à Cayenne, fait en 1725, 1726 et 1727.* Paris, 1730.

Laclau, Ernesto. *New Reflections on the Revolution of Our Time.* London: Verso, 1990.

Lander, Richard. *Records of Captain Clapperton's Last Expedition to Africa,* vol. 1. 1830; London: Cass, 1967.

Lander, Richard, and John Lander. *Journal of an Expedition to Explore the Course and Termination of the Niger,* vol. 1. London: Murray, 1832.

Lang, Andrew. "Fetishism and the Infinite." In *Custom and Myth,* 212–42. London: Longmans, Green, 1893.

———. "Mr. Max Müller and Fetishism." *Mind* 16 (1879): 453–69.

Latour, Bruno. *Petite réflexion sur le culte moderne des dieux fétiches.* Paris: Synthélabo Groupe, 1996.

Law, Robin. "Human Sacrifice in Pre-Colonial West Africa." *African Affairs* 84, no. 334 (1985): 53–87.

Lea, Henry Charles. *A History of the Inquisition of Spain,* 4 vols. London: Macmillan, 1906.

———. *Materials toward a History of Witchcraft,* 3 vols. New York: Yoseloff, 1957.

Leach, Edmund. "Review of Gananath Obeyesekere's *Medusa's Hair.*" *London Times Literary Supplement,* December 18, 1981: 1459.

Le Blanc, Vincent. *Les voyages fameux du Sieur Vincent Le Blanc marseillois.* Paris: Glovsier, 1648.

Leiris, Michel. "Alberto Giacometti." *Documents,* vol. 1, no. 4 (1929): 209–10.

———. *L'Afrique fantôme.* 1934; Paris: Gallimard, 1981.

———. *Phantom Africa.* Translated by Brent Hayes Edward. New York: Seagull Books, 2017.

Le Maire, Jean Jacques, and Abraham Duquesne. *A New Voyage to the East-Indies in the Years 1690 and 1691: Being a Full Description of the Isles of Maldives, Cicos, Andamants, and the Isle of Ascension.* London: Daniel Dring, 1696.

Leonard, Arthur Glyn. *The Lower Niger and Its Tribes.* 1906; London: Cass, 1968.

Le Roy Ladurie, Emmanuel. "The Aiguilette: Castration by Magic." In *The Mind and Method of the Historian,* translated by Sian Reynolds and Ben Reynolds, 84–96. Chicago: University of Chicago Press, 1978.

Lévi-Strauss, Claude. *The Savage Mind.* Chicago: University of Chicago Press, 1966.

———. "The Structural Study of Myth." In *Structural Anthropology,* translated by Claire Jacobson and Brooke Grundfest Schoepf. Garden City: Doubleday, 1967.

———. *Totemism.* Translated by Rodney Needham. Boston: Beacon, 1963.

Levtzion, Nehemiah. *Ancient Ghana and Mali.* New York: Africana, 1980.

Levtzion, Nehemiah, and J. F. P. Hopkins. *Corpus of Early Arabic Sources for West African History.* Translated by J. F. P. Hopkins. Cambridge: Cambridge University Press, 1981.

Lewes, G. H. "Ages of Fetishism and Polytheism." In *Comte's Philosophy of Science,* 273–87. 1853; London: Bell, 1897.

Linnaeus, Carolus. *A General System of Nature through the Three Grand Kingdoms of Animals, Vegetables, and Minerals.* 1735; London, 1806.

Lipietz, Alain. *The Enchanted World: Inflation, Credit, and the World Crisis.* Translated by Ian Patterson. London: Verso, 1985.

Livermore, Harold V. *A New History of Portugal.* Cambridge: Cambridge University Press, 1967.

———. *A New History of Portugal,* 2nd ed. Cambridge: Cambridge University Press, 1976.

Loch, Valentius, ed. *Biblia Sacra Vulgatae Editionis.* Ratisbonae: Manz, 1895.

Lok, John. "The Second Voyage to Guinea set out by Sir George Barne, Sir John Yorke,

Thomas Lok, Anthonie Hickman and Edward Catlein, in the yeare 1554." In *The Principal Navigations, Voyages, Traffiques and Discoveries of the English Navie*, vol. 6, edited by Richard Hakluyt. Glasgow: MacLehose, 1904.

Loyer, Père Godefroy. *Relation du voyage du Royaume d'Issyny*. Paris, 1714.

MacGaffey, Wyatt. "Fetishism Revisited: Kongo Nkisi in Sociological Perspective." *Africa* 47, no. 2 (1977): 172–84.

Malefijt, Annemarie de Waal. *Images of Man*. New York: Knopf, 1974.

Manuel, Frank. *The Eighteenth Century Confronts the Gods*. Cambridge: Harvard University Press, 1959.

Marees, Pieter de. *Beschryvinghe ende historische verhael van het Gout Koninckrijck van Gunea*. 1602; 's-Gravenhage: Nijhoff, 1912.

———. "A Description and Historicall Declaration of the Golden Kingdome of Guinea." In Samuel Purchas, *Hakluytus Posthumus, or Purchas His Pilgrimes*, vol. 6. 1602; Glasgow: MacLehose, 1905.

Marett, R. R. "Fetishism." *Encyclopedia of the Social Sciences*, vol. 5. Edited by Edwin R. A. Seligman. New York: Macmillan, 1931.

Mark, Peter. "Fetishers, 'Marybuckes' and the Christian Norm: European Images of Senegambians and their Religions, 1550–1760." *African Studies Review* 23, no. 2 (1980): 91–99.

Markham, Clements, ed. and trans. *Book of Knowledge*. London: Hakluyt Society, 1912.

Marx, Karl. *Capital*, vol. 1. Translated by Ben Fowkes, New York: Random House, 1977.

———. *Capital*, vol. 3. Translated by David Fernbach. New York: Random House, 1981.

———. "The Class Struggles in France, 1848–1850." In *Surveys from Exile*, edited by David Fernbach. New York: Random House, 1974.

———. *Contribution to the Critique of Political Economy*. Edited by Maurice Dobb and translated by S. W. Ryazanskaya. New York: International, 1970.

———. *Critique of Hegel's "Philosophy of Right."* Translated by Annette Jolin and Joseph O'Malley. Cambridge: Cambridge University Press, 1977.

———. *Das Kapital: Kritik der politische Ökonomie*, vol. 1, *Der Produktionsprozess des Kapitals*. Frankfurt am Main: Ullstein, 1969.

———. "Debates on the Law on Thefts of Wood." In Karl Marx and Friedrich Engels, *Collected Works*, vol. 1, 225–63. New York: International, 1975.

———. *Early Writings*. Translated by Rodney Livingstone and Gregor Benton. New York: Vintage, 1975.

———. *Grundrisse: Foundations of the Critique of Political Economy*. Translated by Martin Nicolaus. New York: Random House, 1973.

———. *Theories of Surplus Value*, part 3. Translated by Jack Cohen and S. W. Ryazanskaya. Moscow: Progress, 1971.

Marx, Karl, and Friedrich Engels. *Collected Works*, vol. 1. New York: International, 1975.

———. *The German Ideology*, 3rd rev. ed. Moscow: Progress, 1976.

———. *Marx-Engels Gesamtausgabe*. 2:1. Berlin: Dietz, 1976.

Mauss, Marcel. *Oeuvres*, 3 vols. Edited by Victor Karady. Paris: Éditions de Minuit, 1968.

McCallum, E. L. *Object Lessons: How to Do Things with Fetishism*. Albany: State University of New York Press, 1999.

McLennan, John F. "The Worship of Animals and Plants." *Fortnightly Review* n.s. 4 (October 1869): 407–27; (November 1969): 562–82; 38, 7 (February 1870): 194–216.

Meiners, Christoph. *Allgemeine kritische Geschichte der Religionen*. Hannover: Helwing, 1806–7.

Meister, Robert. *Political Identity: Thinking through Marx*. London: Blackwell, 1991.

Melville, Herman. *Moby Dick*. 1851; Berkeley: University of California Press, 1979.

Meredith, Henry. *An Account of the Gold Coast of Africa*. 1812; London: Cass, 1967.

Merleau-Ponty, Maurice. *The Visible and the Invisible*. Translated by Alfonso Lingis. 1964; Evanston, IL: Northwestern University Press, 1968.

Metcalfe, G. E. "Introduction." In John Beecham, *Ashantee and the Gold Coast*. 1841; London: Dawsons, 1968.

Miers, Suzanne, and Richard Roberts, eds. *The End of Slavery in Africa*. Madison: University of Wisconsin Press, 1988.

Mill, John Stuart. *Collected Works of John Stuart Mill*. Toronto: University of Toronto Press, 1963.

Milligan, Rev. Robert H. "The Dark Side of the Dark Continent: The Mental and Moral Degradation of Fetishism." *The Missionary Review of the World* 40 (1917): 891–903.

Minkus, Helaine K. "The Philosophy of the Akwapim Akan of Southern Ghana." PhD diss., Northwestern University, 1975.

Mitchell, W. J. T. "The Rhetoric of Iconoclasm: Marxism, Ideology, and Fetishism." In *Iconology: Image, Text, Ideology*, 151–208. Chicago: University of Chicago Press, 1986.

Moore, Francis. "Travels into the Inland Parts of Africa." In *A New Collection of Voyages, Discoveries and Travels*, vol. 4. Edited by John Knox. 1735; London: Knox, 1767.

Morris, Colin. *The Papal Monarchy: The Western Church from 1050 to 1250*. Oxford: Clarendon Press, 1989.

Mühlmann, Wilhelm E. *Geschichte der Anthropologie*. Frankfurt am Main: Athenaeum, 1968.

Müller, Friedrich Max. "Is Fetishism a Primitive Form of Religion?" In *Lectures on the Origin and Growth of Religion*, 54–131. London: Longmans, Green, 1882.

Mulvey, Laura. *Fetishism and Curiosity: Cinema and the Mind's Eye*. Bloomington: Indiana University Press, 1996.

Nassau, Rev. Robert H. *Fetishism in West Africa*. London: Duckworth, 1905.

———. "The Philosophy of Fetishism." *Journal of the Royal African Society* 17 (1903–4): 257–70.

Navarro, Francisco Aznar, ed. *Forum Turolij*, vol. 2. Zaragoza: M. Escar, 1905.

Neale, J. E. *Queen Elizabeth I: A Biography*. Garden City, NY: Doubleday, 1957.

Newbury, C. W. *The Western Slave Coast and Its Rulers*. Oxford: Clarendon Press, 1961.

Niermeyer, J. F. *Mediae Latinitatis Lexicon Minus*. Leiden: Brill, 1976.

Niger Coast Protectorate. *Annual Report for the Year 1896–1897*. London: Her Majesty's Stationery Office, 1899.

Nina-Rodrigues, Dr. *L'animisme fétichiste des nègres de Bahia*. Bahia, Brazil: Resi, 1900.

Nipperdey, H. "Fetich-Faith in Western Africa." *Popular Science Magazine* 31 (1887): 801–4.

Nowell, Charles E. *A History of Portugal*. New York: Van Nostrand, 1952.

Ogilby, John. *Africa*. London: Tho. Johnson, 1670.

Oliveira Marques, A. H. de. *Daily Life in Portugal in the Late Middle Ages*. Translated by S. S. Wyatt. Madison, Milwaukee, and London: University of Wisconsin Press, 1971.

———. *History of Portugal*. Volume 1, *From Lusitania to Empire*. New York: Columbia University Press, 1972.

Pacheco Pereira, Duarte. *Esmeraldo de situ orbis*. Translated by George H. T. Kimble. London: Hakluyt Society, 1937.

———. *Esmeraldo de situ orbis*, critical edition with notes by Augusto Epiphanio da Silva Dias. Lisbon: Sociedad de Geographia de Lisboa, 1905.

Parry, Jonathan. *The Rise and Fall of Liberal Government in Victorian Britain*. New Haven: Yale University Press, 1993.

Pels, Peter, and Oscar Salemink. "Introduction: Five Theses on Anthropology as Colonial Practice." *History and Anthropology* 8 (1994): 1–34.

Penniman, T. K. *A Hundred Years of Anthropology*. London: Duckworth, 1935.

Pharr, Clyde, ed. and trans. *The Theodosian Code and Novels, and the Sirmondian Constitutions*. Princeton: Princeton University Press, 1952.

Pietz, William. "Capitalism and Perversion: Reflections on the Fetishism of Excess in the 1980s." *positions: asia critique* 3, no. 2 (1995): 537–65.

———. "Death of the Deodand: Fatal Accidents and the Money Value of Human Life." *RES: Anthropology and Aesthetics* 31 (1997): 97–198. Reproduced here as chapter 7.

———. "Fetish." In *Critical Terms for Art History*, 2nd ed., edited by Richard Shiff and Benjamin Nelson, 306–17. Chicago: University of Chicago Press, 2003.

———. "Fetishism and Materialism: The Limits of Theory in Marx." In *Fetishism as Cultural Discourse*, edited by Emily Apter and William Pietz, 119–51. Ithaca: Cornell University Press, 1993. Reproduced here as chapter 5.

———. "The Fetish of Civilization: Sacrificial Blood and Monetary Debt." In *Colonial Subjects*, edited by Peter Pels and Oscar Salemink, 53–81. Ann Arbor: University of Michigan Press, 1999.

———. "Geography, Etymology, and Taste: Charles de Brosses and the Restoration of History." *L'Esprit Créateur* 25, no. 3 (1985): 86–94.

———. "How to Grow Oranges in Norway." In *Border Fetishisms*, edited by Patricia Spyer, 245–52. New York: Routledge, 1998.

———. "Material Considerations: The Historical Forensics of Contract." *Theory, Culture & Society* 19, no. 5–6 (2002): 35–60.

———. "Person." In *Critical Terms in Buddhist Studies*, edited by Donald Lopez. Chicago: University of Chicago Press, 2005.

———. "The Phonograph in Africa: International Phonocentrism from Stanley to Sarnoff." In *Post-Structuralism and the Question of History*, edited by Derek Attridge, 263–85. Cambridge: Cambridge University Press, 1987.

———. "The Problem of the Fetish, I." *RES: Anthropology and Aesthetics* 9 (1985): 5–17. Reproduced here as chapter 1.

———. "The Problem of the Fetish, II: The Origin of the Fetish." *RES: Anthropology and Aesthetics* 13 (1987): 23–46. Reproduced here as chapter 2.

———. "The Problem of the Fetish, IIIa: Bosman's Guinea and Mercantile Ideology." *RES: Anthropology and Aesthetics* 15 (1989): 105–24. Reproduced here as chapter 3.

———. "The Sin of Saul." In *Iconoclash: Beyond the Image Wars in Science, Religion and Art*, edited by Bruno Latour and Peter Weibel, 63–65. Cambridge: MIT Press, 2002.

Pigafetta, Philippo. "A Report of the Kingdome of Congo, a Region of Africa, and of the Surrounding Countries." In *Hakluytus Posthumus, or Purchas His Pilgrimes*, vol. 6. Edited by Samuel Purchas. 1591; Glasgow: James MacLehose and Sons, 1906.

Pires, A. Thomas. *Amuletos Alemtejanos in his Estudios e Notas Elvenses*, vol. 5. Elvas: Torres de Canvalho, 1904.

Pliny. *Natural History*, vol. 4. Translated by H. Rackham. Cambridge: Harvard University Press, 1938.

Pomeau, René, ed. *Les Oeuvres complètes de Voltaire*, vol. 48. Oxford: Voltaire Foundation, 1980.

Popkin, Richard H. "The Philosophical Basis of Eighteenth-Century Racism." *Studies in Eighteenth-Century Culture: Racism in the Eighteenth Century* 3 (1973): 245–62.

Porteus, John. *Coins in History.* New York: Putnam, 1969.

Pouillon, Jean. *Fétiches sans fétichisme.* Paris: Maspero, 1975.

Prévost, Abbé. *Histoire générale des voyages.* 18 vols. Paris, 1747–68.

Pribram, Karl. *A History of Economic Reasoning.* Baltimore: Johns Hopkins University Press, 1983.

Ramusio, Giovambattista. *Il viaggio di Giovan Leone e le navigazioni di Alvise da Ca da Mosto, di Pietro di Cintra, di Annone, di un piloto portoghese e di Vasco di Gama; quali si leggono nella raccolta di Giovambattista Ramusio,* Vol. 1. 1550; Venice: L. Plet, 1837.

Rancière, Jacques. "The Concept of 'Critique' and the 'Critique of Political Economy' (from the *1844 Manuscript* to *Capital*)." Translated by Ben Brewster. *Economy and Society* 5 (1976): 352–76.

———. "How to Use 'Lire *Le Capital*.'" Translated by Tanya Asad. *Economy and Society* 5 (1976): 377–84.

Rastell, John. *An Exposition of Certaine Difficult and Obscure Words and Termes of the Lawes of this Realme.* 1618; Amsterdam: Da Capo Press, 1969.

Ratton, Charles. *Fetish Gold.* Philadelphia: University Museum and the Anko Foundation, 1975.

Rattray, R. S. *Ashanti.* Oxford: Clarendon Press, 1923.

———. *Ashanti Law and Constitution.* Oxford: Clarendon Press, 1929.

———. *Ashanti Proverbs (The Primitive Ethics of a Savage People).* 1914; Oxford: Clarendon Press, 1969.

———. *Religion and Art in Ashanti.* Oxford: Clarendon Press, 1927.

Reinhard, Philipp Christian. *Abriß einer Geschichte der Entstehung und Ausbildung der religiösen Ideen.* Jena: Akademische Buchhandlung, 1794.

Resende, Garcia de. *Crónica del Rey Dom João II.* 1553; Coimbra: Atlântida, 1798.

Richardson, Ruth. *Death, Dissection and the Destitute.* London: Penguin, 1988.

Riemersma, Jelle C. *Religious Factors in Early Dutch Capitalism, 1550–1650.* The Hague: Mouton, 1967.

Rodee, Marian, and James Ostler. *The Fetish Carvers of Zuni.* Albuquerque and Zuni, NM: The Maxwell Museum of Anthropology and the Pueblo of Zuni Arts and Crafts, 1990.

Rodney, Walter. *A History of the Upper Guinea Coast, 1545 to 1800.* New York: Monthly Review Press, 1980.

Romanes, George J. "Fetichism in Animals." *Nature* 17, no. 426 (1877): 168–69.

Rose, Nikolas. "Fetishism and Ideology." *Ideology and Consciousness* 2 (1977): 27–54.

Rotenstreich, Nathan. "Hypostasis and Fetishmaking: Kant's Concepts and their Transformations." *Kant-Studien* 1 (1980): 60–77.

Roussier, Paul, ed. *L'Etablissement d'Issiny 1687–1702: Voyages de Ducasse, Tibierge el D'Amon à la Côte de Guinée.* Paris: Librairie Larose, 1935.

Ruiters, Dierick. "Flambeau de la Navigation" (1623). Translated by G. Thilmans and J. P. Rossie. In *Bulletin de l'Institut fondamental d'Afrique Noire,* Series B: Sciences Humaines, 31, no. 1 (1969): 106–19.

Sade, Marquis de. *Juliette.* Translated by Austryn Wainhouse. 1797–1801; New York: Grove Press, 1968.

———. *Philosophy in the Bedroom.* Translated by Richard Seaver and Austryn Wainhouse. 1795; New York: Grove Press, 1965.

Sartre, Jean-Paul. *Search for a Method*. Translated by Hazel E. Barnes. 1957; New York: Random House, 1968.

Saussure, Ferdinand de. *Course in General Linguistics*. Translated by Wade Baskin. 1916; New York: McGraw-Hill, 1966.

Schultze, Fritz. *Fetishism: A Contribution to the Anthropology of Religion*. Translated by Joseph Fitzgerald. 1871; New York: Humboldt, 1885.

Schuyler, Robert Livingston. *The Fall of the Old Colonial System: A Study in British Free Trade, 1770–1870*. New York: Oxford University Press, 1945.

Schwabe, J. J. *Allgemeine Historie der Reisen*. 14 vols. Leipzig, 1747–74.

Séjourné, P. "Superstition." In *Dictionnaire de Théologie Catholique*, vol. 14, edited by A. Vacant and E. Mangenot. Paris: Letorzey, 1941.

Serrão, Joaquim Veríssimo. *Historia Portugal*. Vol. 2. Rev. 3rd ed. Lisbon: Editorial Verbo, 1980.

Silla, Ousmane. "Langage et techniques thérapeutiques des cultes de possession des Lébou du Sénégal." *Bulletin de l'Institut fondamental d'Afrique noire*, Series B: Sciences Humaines, 31, no. 1 (1969): 215–38.

Slotkin, J. S. *Readings in Early Anthropology*. New York: Wenner-Gren Foundation, 1965.

Smith, Adam. *Lectures on Jurisprudence*. 1763; Oxford: Oxford University Press, 1978.

Smith, William. *A New Voyage to Guinea*. London: Nourse, 1744.

Snelgrave, William. *A New Account of Some Parts of Guinea, and the Slave-Trade*. London: Knapton, 1734.

Sobchack, Vivian. "The Active Eye: A Phenomenology of Cinematic Vision." *Quarterly Review of Film and Video* 12, no. 3 (1990): 21–36.

———. *The Address of the Eye: A Phenomenology of Film Experience*. Princeton: Princeton University Press, 1992.

Spencer, Herbert. "Idol-Worship and Fetich-Worship." *Popular Science Monthly* 8 (1875): 158–64.

———. "The Origin of Animal Worship." *Fortnightly Review* (1870), reprinted in *Essays Scientific, Political, and Speculative*, 308–30. New York: Appleton, 1904.

Sprigge, S. Squire. *The Life and Times of Thomas Wakely*. 1899; New York: Krieger, 1974.

Steele, Valerie. *Fetish: Fashion, Sex, and Power*. New York: Oxford University Press, 1996.

Sumner, William Graham, and Albert Galloway Keller. *The Science of Society*, vol. 2. New Haven: Yale University Press, 1927.

Taylor, W. Review of D. Heynig, *Theorie der sämtlichen Religionsarten*, in *Monthly Magazine, or British Register* 11 (1801): 646.

Tertullianus, Quintus Septimius Florens. *Opera omnia*, vol. 1., 8–32. Lipsiae: Weigel, 1854.

———. *The Writings of Quintus Sept. Flor. Tertullianus*, vol. 1. Edited by Rev. Alexander Roberts and James Donaldson. Edinburgh: Clark, 1869.

Thomas, Keith. *Religion and the Decline of Magic*. New York: Scribner's, 1971.

Tiele, C. P. *Elements of the Science of Religion*, vol. 1. New York: Scribner's, 1897.

Tinoco, Antônio Velho. "An Account of the People who Live between Cabo Dos Mastos and Magrabomba on the Guinea Coast" (1574). In André Donelha, *Descrição da Serra Leoa e dos Rios de Guiné do Cabo Verde, 1625 / An Account of Sierra Leone and the Rivers of Guinea of Cape Verde 1625*. Edited and translated by P. E. H. Hair. Lisbon: Junta de Investigações Científicas do Ultramar, 1977.

Tobla-Chadesson, Michèle. *Le fétiche africain: Chronique d'un malentendu*. Paris: L'Harmattan, 2000.

Tourneux, Maurice, ed. *Correspondance littéraire, philosophique et critique par Grimm, Diderot, Raynal, Meister, etc.*, vol. 9. Paris: Garnier, 1878.

Towerson, William. "The first voyage made by Master William Towerson Marchant of London, to the coast of Guinea, with two ships, in the yeare 1555." In Richard Hakluyt, *The Principal Navigations, Voyages, Traffiques and Discoveries of the English Navie*, vol. 6. Glasgow: MacLehose, 1904.

Trimingham, John Spencer. *A History of Islam in West Africa*. London: Oxford University Press, 1970.

Tylor, E. B. "Ordeals and Oaths." *Popular Science Monthly* 9 (1876): 307–22.

———. *Primitive Culture*. 2 vols. 1871; New York: Holt, 1889.

———. "The Religion of Savages." *Fortnightly Review* 4 (1866): 71–86.

Unger, Roberto Mangabeira. *Knowledge and Politics*. New York: Free Press, 1975.

Vilar, Pierre. *A History of Gold and Money, 1450–1920*. Translated by Judith White. Atlantic Highlands: Humanities Press, 1976.

Villault, Nicolas. *Relation des costes d'Afrique, appellées Guinée*. Paris: Thierry, 1669.

Voltaire. *Candide, Zadig and Selected Stories*. Translated by Donald M. Frame. 1759; New York: New American Library, 1961.

Wade, Ira O. *Voltaire and Candide: A Study in the Fusion of History, Art, and Philosophy*. Princeton: Princeton University Press, 1959.

Weber, Max. *The Sociology of Religion*. Translated by Ephraim Fischoff. 1922; Boston: Beacon Press, 1956.

Weston, Peter J. "Some Images of the Primitive Before 1800." *History of European Ideas* 1, no. 3 (1981): 215–36.

White, Hayden. *The Content of the Form: Narrative Discourse and Historical Representation*. Baltimore: Johns Hopkins University Press, 1987.

———. *Metahistory: The Historical Imagination in Nineteenth-Century Europe*. Baltimore: Johns Hopkins University Press, 1973.

Wilson, Louis E. "The 'Bloodless Conquest' in Southeastern Ghana: The Huza and Territorial Expansion of the Krobo in the 19th Century." *International Journal of African Historical Studies* 23, no. 2 (1990): 269–97.

Wolfson, Freda. *Pageant of Ghana*. London: Oxford University Press, 1958.

Wundt, Wilhelm. *Elements of Folk Psychology: Outlines of a Psychological History of the Development of Mankind*. Translated by Edward Leroy Schaub. 1912; New York: Macmillan, 1916.

Žižek, Slavoj. *The Sublime Object of Ideology*. London: Verso, 198

Index

www.ingramcontent.com/pod-product-compliance
Lightning Source LLC
Chambersburg PA
CBHW032124020426
42334CB00016B/1058